I0109488

THE DIANE ELSON READER

"Diane Elson has been and is one of the most important voices in demonstrating male bias in economic thinking and policy making. This collection brings together some of her most important, and provocative, essays, and will be warmly welcomed."

A. Haroon Akram-Lodhi, Professor Emeritus of Economics,
Global Justice and Development, Trent University, Canada

"Diane Elson, one of the most insightful economists of our time, has been a pioneer of the feminist economics critique of standard economic models, which ignore social relations of power, in particular gender, in the economy. Her work on feminist macroeconomics and economic development, which is covered in this volume, shows why economic policies based on models that ignore these power relations, have had such poor outcomes."

Imraan Valodia, Director, Southern Centre for Inequality Studies,
University of the Witwatersrand

"This foundational work on feminist political economy and development highlights the centrality of gender inequalities in today's world and how to address these in sustainable, equitable and caring ways. It is a must-read for all who wish to understand the gendered nature of macroeconomics and its effects."

Shirin M. Rai, FBA, author of *Depletion: The Human Costs of Caring*

"Diane Elson's book is a masterclass in feminist economics, illuminating the path to a more equitable future. Her groundbreaking research has transformed our understanding of gender and macroeconomics, inspiring a new generation of scholars and policymakers."

Lekha S. Chakraborty, Professor and Chair,
National Institute of Public Finance and Policy, New Delhi

"With clarity, deep knowledge, and an even deeper commitment to gender equality, Diane Elson offers an invaluable rethinking of development and macroeconomic theory and policy. This collection constitutes an important historical document of her contributions as a visionary feminist economist."

Maria S. Floro, Professor Emerita of Economics,
American University, Washington, DC

"As one of the leading lights of feminist economics, Diane Elson's work has reframed the economics discipline, challenging its gender-blind assumptions and laying the intellectual groundwork for a generation of scholars and practitioners. This book brings together a lifetime of her extraordinary scholarship, from the foundational concepts she pioneered to the gender-aware and policy-relevant economic frameworks that continue to shape the field. This is not just a book to read – it's a book to think with."

Sheba Tejani, Senior Lecturer in International Development, King's College London

"Diane Elson is a personal hero, as her work opened up avenues for exploration for so many of us. Her writing helped me understand the 'structural adjustment' that I was studying and living through, and her analysis of the gendered cost of crises continues to influence my own approach."

Valeria Esquivel, International Labour Organization

THE DIANE ELSON READER

Gender, Development and Macroeconomic Policy

DIANE ELSON

agenda
publishing

© Diane Elson 2025

This work is licensed under a Creative Commons Attribution-NonCommercial-NoDerivatives v4.0 International Licence (CC BY-NC-ND 4.0). Permission for reproduction is granted by the author and publisher free of charge for non-commercial purposes. To view a copy of the licence visit https://creativecommons.org/licenses/by-nc-nd/4.0/.

First published in 2025 by Agenda Publishing

Agenda Publishing Limited
PO Box 185
Newcastle upon Tyne
NE20 2DH
www.agendapub.com

ISBN 978-1-78821-855-9

British Library Cataloguing-in-Publication Data
A catalogue record for this book is available from the British Library

Typeset by Newgen Publishing UK
Printed and bound in the UK by 4edge

EU GPSR authorised representative:
Logos Europe, 9 rue Nicolas Poussin, 17000 La Rochelle, France
contact@logoseurope.eu

CONTENTS

PREFACE

This book reflects more than 45 years of research on gender, development and macroeconomic policy, details of which can be found on the companion website www.drdianeelson.com.

It contains a new introductory essay and a selection of previously published papers, covering the following topics: concepts of gender and of development; male bias in development and in macroeconomic policy; the gendered economy at macro, meso and micro levels; the circular flow resources and the depletion of human capabilities; production; social reproduction and economic growth; the dominance of finance over production and social reproduction; gender responsive budgeting; gender equality, inclusive growth, green and caring economies; gender equality and economic crisis; and the impact of feminist macroeconomics on research and policy. The empirical data cited in each chapter reflects the time of original publication: an interesting exercise for students reading the book would be to update the relevant data. The passage of time has not invalidated the analysis and conclusions even though the IMF recently declared that gender-equality was a macro-critical issue. The underlying structural biases in economic development have persisted.

Because it is an open access book that is freely available online its contents are constrained by willingness of publishers to grant permission for republication in this format. I am grateful to all the publishers that gave permission for book chapters to be included and note with regret that in all but one case publishers would not give permission for inclusion of journal articles.

All the papers included are single-authored but draw on ideas shaped by collaborations with Ruth Pearson, Nilufer Çağatay, Caren Grown, Maria Floro, Rhonda Sharp, Isa Bakker, Brigitte Young, Marzia Fontana, Jasmine Gideon, Radhika Balakrishnan and James Heintz. I thank them all for stimulating discussions and helpful comments over the years.

I thank the Wellspring Philanthropic Foundation for funding the project on building capacity in feminist economics of which this book is a part; and especially Gaby Oré Aguilar for her encouragement to share my research as widely as possible.

I am grateful to the WiSE Centre for Economic Justice at Glasgow Caledonian University for hosting the project, and in particular to Sara Cantillon (former Director of WiSE) and Alison Lockhart (Senior Officer Research Administrator) for their support.

Putting the book together would have been impossible without the excellent assistance of Carolina Herrera Cano, PhD candidate at WiSE and Alison Howson at Agenda Publishing. Many thanks to them both.

As backlash against women's rights intensifies in many places, it is more than ever necessary to keep alive the idea that economic analysis can be challenged and transformed so that fostering equalities (gender, class, race, ethnicity, location) becomes a central objective. This book is offered as a contribution to that struggle.

1

INTRODUCTION: 30 YEARS OF THINKING ON GENDER, DEVELOPMENT AND MACROECONOMIC POLICY

In this introduction I reflect on the foundations of my thinking on gender, development and macroeconomic policy; highlight some of the ways in which what may appear to be gender-neutral policies and processes have hidden biases; present ways of visualising economies as gendered structures and precarious processes, which always run the risk of depleting as well as sustaining human capabilities; argue that mainstream economic growth models obscure the dislocations between production and social reproduction; discuss how production and social reproduction have become dominated by finance, limiting possibilities for gender responsive budgeting, and shaping the impact of and response to economic crises; examine ideas of inclusive growth and green and caring economies; and discuss how far feminist thinking on macroeconomics has had an impact on macroeconomics research and policy discussions.

Gender

My research is rooted in an understanding of gender as a structure of economic, social and political power that puts women and girls at a disadvantage compared to men and boys, power that is inscribed in the ownership and control of resources, the division of labour, laws, social norms, ideologies and everyday practices. It is intertwined with the structures of power of class and race, so that gender disadvantage is differentiated by class and race. It is also intertwined with structures of imperialism, colonialism and their legacies, so that gender relations differ across countries. The lives of women and girls are shaped in multiple ways by these structures of power, so that 'women' and 'girls' are not homogenous groups. Biological differences play an important role, but they are not destiny. As Simone de Beauvoir, the French existentialist philosopher and fierce supporter of anti-colonial struggles, wrote in her pioneering book, *The Second Sex* (published in French in 1949): "One is not born, but rather becomes, a woman" (Beauvoir de 2009: 293), referring to processes of socialisation that reward conformity with and internalisation of gendered social norms and punish resistance to these norms. Nevertheless, a woman still has a degree of agency: De Beauvoir's analysis illuminates the ongoing tension between freedom and constraint in women's lives.

In material terms, some women are better off than many men, though misogyny can oppress even rich and powerful women. In examining development and macroeconomic policy, it is useful to consider the standpoint of the most disadvantaged women, who are oppressed and subordinated in multiple intersecting ways, but who nevertheless find ways of exercising some agency.

There is space for agency because gender as a structure of power is not solid, timeless and unmoving. It is a set of contradictory processes that while subordinating women, do change over time and can be challenged. In analysing the gendered character of export-oriented industrialisation in the 1970s, Ruth Pearson and I distinguish three tendencies: a tendency to *intensify* existing forms of gender subordination; a tendency to *decompose* existing forms of gender subordination and a tendency to *recompose* new forms of gender subordination (Elson & Pearson 1981: 157). The outcome of this dialectic can be shaped by the emergence of collective organizations of women and by feminist analysis that is alive to women's experiences and challenges ideas that development processes like industrialisation and growth are gender-neutral (see Chapter 9).

Development

Stemming from my interpretation of Marx (Elson 1979) I understand development as process of economic and social transformation in which changes in work are fundamental: increasing intensity and productivity of labour; increasing commodification of labour; new forms of exploitation of labour. It is a process which is contradictory and crisis-ridden; and in which there is a basis for public actions of various kinds to change outcomes. This dialectical approach to understanding development avoids both the in-built optimism of modernisation theory, and the in-built pessimism of dependency theory (concepts discussed in Chapter 2). I argued in the 1970s that some countries in what we then called the Third World might well be able to industrialise, increase labour productivity and increase per capita output (as had Japan) but that this would disrupt the balance of power in the international economy with potential for crisis (Elson 1988). Moreover, no set of regulations and agreements to govern the world economy could be expected to last for ever but would be disrupted by uneven development of productivity that would change the balance of power (Elson 1994: 181). While I did not foretell the subsequent rapid development of China, my understanding of development in international context certainly left space for it.

Marx's analysis of development focussed on paid work (especially waged work) but as a feminist economist I take unpaid work as also important, both for the trajectory of development and the distribution of productivity gains. As discussed in Chapter 1, Nobel prize-winner Sir Arthur Lewis did pay some attention to women's unpaid labour in his influential article *Economic Development with Unlimited Supplies of Labour* (Lewis 1954). He treated the unpaid labour of women in subsistence farming as an additional source of labour for an expanding capitalist sector. He argued that development would bring benefits to women by reducing their unpaid work "because most of the things that women otherwise do in the household can in fact be done much better and more cheaply outside, thanks to large scale economies of specialisation, and also to the use of capital" (Lewis 1954: 404). He was optimistic about the benefits of economic growth for women, arguing that "Women benefit from growth even more than men ....Woman gains freedom from drudgery, is emancipated from the seclusion of the household, and gains at last the chance to be a full human being, exercising her talents in the same way as men" (Lewis 1955: 422). These are views that persist today, underpinning much policy directed to increasing women's labour force participation and to supporting women's economic empowerment. As discussed in Chapter 2, these views were challenged by Ester Boserup (1970) in her analysis of development of the agricultural sector, which claimed women had been excluded from development; but other feminist economists (such as Beneria & Sen 1981) argued that the problem was not exclusion but the terms on which women were included, and called for new visions of what development should be. One such new vision was that of human development, based on concepts of capabilities and entitlements elaborated by Nobel prize-winner Amartya Sen (Sen 1984) and fleshed out in successive *Human Development Reports* produced by United Nations Development Programme. In Chapter 2, I point to some limitations of the human development paradigm and argue that both states and markets would need to be transformed to have any chance of the realisation of human development. I have taken up this question again more recently in my call to ensure that not only is no-one *left behind* in development, but that no-one is *pushed behind* by people, businesses and organisations that wield huge economic power (Elson 2019).

Male bias in development

In a deliberately provocative intervention in debates about women in development in 1991, I argued development is not only an uneven and unequal process but is structured by male bias (see Chapter 3). I drew a comparison with the widely used concept of urban bias, which had served to mobilise analysis and policy to address rural–urban inequality. I did not mean that all men are biased against women, but that the process of development is biased in favour of men, drawing upon and reproducing gender asymmetries which cannot be reduced to differences in preferences and endowments, and which call for remedy. I identified the proximate causes of male bias in everyday attitudes and actions, in theoretical reasoning and in public policy, often masked as gender-neutral but incorporating presumptions that reflect male bias. The underlying foundations of male bias rest in the ways that getting a living is interrelated with raising children, which is in most cases organised in ways that leave women and children with no independent entitlements to resources sufficient for a basic standard of living. Women are pushed into a degree of dependency on male relatives or companions without which survival is hard, and this dependency is 'normalised' as reflecting 'family values' and to be celebrated. It is not only feminist academics who challenge this situation, as an example in Chapter 3 demonstrates, quoting village women in Tanzania complaining that they are dependent on men, and suggesting it would be better if the Council gave every woman one acre for herself. It has now become commonplace to suggest that practices that appear to be gender-neutral are in fact biased, but the phrase that tends to be used is 'gender-bias' not 'male bias'. The sanitised language has been a means to securing wider acceptance of the prevalence of bias but has not prevented a fierce backlash against women's rights and equality in many, many countries in the last decade. Perhaps it is time to insist again on speaking of male bias operating in defence of male privilege, often behind a façade of protection for 'family values' and to insist that what we value are egalitarian families.

Male bias in macroeconomic policy

My 1991analysis of male bias in macroeconomics is presented in Chapter 4. Macroeconomics is concerned with the operation of the whole economy, and focuses in particular on employment, consumption, savings, investment, public expenditure, taxation, exports, imports, growth and inflation. Macroeconomic policy includes fiscal, monetary, exchange rate and trade policies. On the surface these policies appear to be gender-neutral. They do not focus on people but on monetary aggregates. I examined structural adjustment programmes that were prescribed in the 1980s by the World Bank and IMF for developing countries that sought loans to help with balance of payments and debt crises. The programmes typically involved devaluation, reduction of public expenditure and deregulation. I show that they were derived from economic models that ignored the gender division of labour, the unpaid work necessary for producing and maintaining human resources, and the gender division of consumption expenditure.

The failure to consider the gendered structure of the economy was a form of male bias, stemming from modelling the economy from a male perspective.[1] It results in policies that are biased against women and mean that women, especially poor women, disproportionately bear the burden of adjustment. The in-built male bias also means that the adjustment policies fail to achieve their own macroeconomic goals – increase of exports, reduction of budget deficits and balance of payments deficits. Gender inequality is a barrier to an unproblematic adjustment process in which paid labour is reallocated from production of goods which are not internationally tradable to those which are. Women are in fact called upon to provide, through their unpaid work, a safety net that will absorb shocks and dislocations to the economy. Measures that supposedly increase efficiency and productivity all too often transfer costs from the paid economy, where they show up in the national accounts, and the accounts of public agencies and private businesses, to the unpaid economy in households and communities, where most of the work is done by women. Ignoring the implications of macroeconomic policy for the unpaid economy is tantamount to assuming that women's capacity to undertake extra work is infinitely elastic, able to expand to make good any shortfalls in public services and incomes so as to sustain the production and maintenance of human resources. But this is not the case. There is deterioration in health, nutrition and education of women and children that is not transitory but has long run effects for both their wellbeing and for the reproduction and maintenance of human resources upon which economic growth depends. I identified this as a process of depletion[2] and degradation and called for a macroeconomics that includes the unpaid reproduction and maintenance of human resources as well as the paid production of good and services for consumption, investment and export.

With co-authors, I subsequently identified a number of specific biases that underpin male bias in macroeconomic policy. In a joint paper with Nilufer Çağatay on the social content of macroeconomic policies, three forms of bias in macroeconomic policies are identified: deflationary bias, male breadwinner bias, and commodification bias (Elson & Çağatay 2000: 1354–6). Deflationary bias is inherent in the decision to prioritise 'credibility' in financial markets, through high interest rates, tight monetary policies and fiscal restraint, over other objectives. Such policies in fact deter investment and place disproportionate burdens on women living in poverty. Male breadwinner bias emphasises full employment as the most important social goal, ignoring gendered character of

---

1. Bakker (1994) refers to this as a 'strategic silence'.
2. Depletion is mentioned frequently in my subsequent writings as a macroeconomic phenomenon. Depletion is analysed as an aspect of social reproduction by Rai (2024) who mobilizes a wealth of micro-level evidence to show the costs of caring at an individual level .

the labour market, and the barriers to women taking full-time jobs; in addition, it constructs social protection in ways that make women dependent on men. Commodification bias presumes that health, education services and care services, and pensions and insurance, are all delivered more efficiently (i.e. at lower monetary cost) if public services are replaced by private provision for profit. This ignores adverse impacts on quality of services and access to services for users, especially women, and on the terms and conditions of those who provide them, disproportionately women. Operating together these biases pave the way for finance to dominate both production and social reproduction in ways that are particularly onerous for women living in poverty.

Two further biases are identified in the feminist critique of financial governance that I co-authored with Brigitte Young and Isabella Bakker: risk bias and creditor bias (Young, Bakker & Elson 2011: 3). Risk bias is embodied in governance that reduces the extent to which risk is pooled, and measures to protect against it are shared, and instead individualises risk. This disproportionately penalises women because they have fewer assets to fall back on than men, and tend to be perceived as more risky borrowers than men. Creditor bias is embodied in an asymmetrical treatment of creditors and debtors, especially large, powerful creditors and small individual debtors. For example, in the global financial crisis of 2008, big American banks were bailed out, but African American women who were unable to service their home loans had their homes repossessed.

The gendered economy: macro, meso and micro

To understand how biases operate, it is helpful to consider the economy as operating at three levels: macro, meso and micro (see Chapter 5). The macro level of aggregate demand and supply interacts with the micro-level of households and individuals via meso-level institutions of markets and states. I differentiate three different perspectives: that of mainstream 'orthodox' neoclassical economics, that of critical 'unorthodox' economics, and feminist economics.

Neo-classical economics insists that individual behaviour is the foundation of an economy, and that through markets, economies are self-regulating, with demand and supply at both micro- and macro-level brought into balance by price changes. The best macroeconomic policy is to minimize the role of the state. Gender can be taken into account at the micro-level by differentiating between male and female individuals and allowing for differences in their preferences and resource endowments. Neoclassical economists consider that differences in outcomes, such as the gender pay gap, is only a sign of discrimination if a pay gap remains, once adjustments have been made for differences in preferences, such as preferences for unpaid care work, and differences in resource endowments, such as education. Discrimination is regarded as something that lowers profits and as such is commercially irrational. At the meso- and macro-levels orthodox neoclassical economics does not take gender into account.

Critical, heterodox, economics draws on Keynesian, Kaleckian, structuralist and Marxist perspectives, all of which insist that the macroeconomy has a life of its own and is not simply an aggregation of behaviour of individuals. It is based on the perception that there is no guarantee that aggregate supply and demand will be brought into balance by price changes. Macroeconomic problems such as unemployment and inflation are not the result of bad policy but are intrinsic to the operation of the macroeconomy and need to be addressed by public policy. Private contracts are always incomplete because of radical uncertainty, and the meso-institutions of market and state necessarily embody social norms, as do the households and communities which shape individual decision-making, and which are marked by both cooperation and conflict. At the micro- and meso-level, heterodox economics is more accommodating to a view of gender as a structure of power, but at the macro-level, gender is absent.

In an attempt to promote dialogue between heterodox and feminist economists, I collaborated with Nilufer Çağatay and Caren Grown on a project gender and macroeconomics that resulted in two special issues of *World Development* (Çağatay, Elson & Grown 1995; Grown, Elson & Çağatay 2000). In my contributions, I argued that the economy should not only be seen as a class structure (as it is by many heterodox economists) but also as a gendered structure (Elson 1995, 1852). This idea is visualised in Figure 1.1 (based on box 10 in Elson, Evers & Gideon 1997).

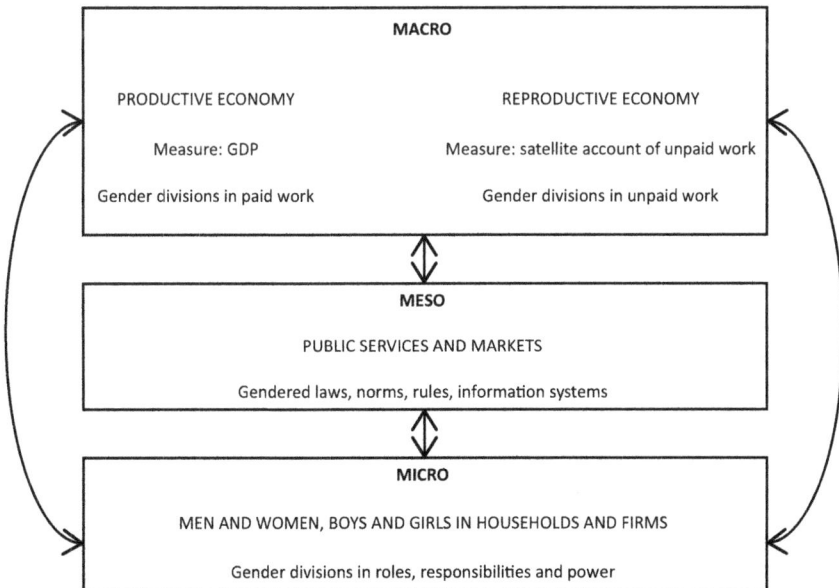

Figure 1.1 The economy as a gendered structure

At the micro-level are people – "economic agents" in the jargon of economics – producing for sale in firms and meeting needs in households. Feminist economics insists we should not treat the households and firms as if they are individuals but recognise that they are structured by gender divisions in roles, responsibilities and power. The behaviour of men and women, boys and girls is not the outcome of exercises in constrained optimisation, given preferences and endowments, but is shaped by gender relations and conflict as well as cooperation. We need gender-disaggregated data that allows us to see what is going on inside households and businesses.

Activities at the micro-level are linked and shaped by meso-level institutions of markets and public services of all kinds. These institutions themselves are not neutral but embody (often in ways not immediately visible) gendered laws, norms, rules and information systems. For instance, labour markets are structured by practices, perceptions, laws, norms and networks which are based on presumptions about what is 'women's work' and what is 'men's work' and operate to devalue tasks that are considered to be women's work. Discrimination is not just a matter of personal prejudice; it is structurally inscribed in labour market institutions (Elson 2023).

At the macro level, the economy is represented as a series of aggregates, measured in the system of national accounts, with GDP the measure of the market value of total output produced by paid work, of the size of the productive economy, underpinned by measures of output in particular sectors (such as agriculture, industry and services, and their sub-sectors) Each sector is characterised by gender divisions of labour, some making intensive use of male labour and some intensive use of female labour. Gender is a barrier to labour substitutability, and different patterns of economic growth will have different gendered implications for employment. What this picture leaves out is the reproductive economy. The ability of money to mobilize labour power for 'productive work' (which produces goods and services for the market) depends on the operation of non-market social relations to mobilize labour power for 'reproductive work' (which provides goods and services needed to reproduce people on a daily and inter-generational basis) (see Chapter 5). The reproductive economy can be included by measuring time use and creating a satellite account of output of the market value of unpaid work[3]. This visualisation provides a snapshot of an economy at a moment in time and can be used as a framework for empirical analysis using data from surveys of various kinds, as has been done by Gideon (1999) and Fontana (2024).

To create a more gender-equal economy, policy needs to address unpaid work, not take it for granted. In a UNDP seminar in 2008, I put forward the idea that

---

3. For a discussion of incorporating feminist ideas into macroeconomic accounting, see Heintz (2019: chapter 2).

policy should recognise unpaid work as a key foundation of the economy, especially by making it visible in national statistics, for instance through time use surveys; it should reduce unpaid work through public investment in water, sanitation, clean energy and care services; and it should redistribute the remaining unpaid work through incentives and support for men and boys to take an equal share. This 3R's framework was adopted by UNDP (Falth & Blackden 2009) and subsequently widely used in policy discussions. I applied it in in the context of developing countries in Elson and Fontana (2014) and to USA in Elson (2017).

The circular flow of resources and the depletion of human capabilities

Over time the interdependence of the productive and reproductive economy does not work smoothly but is marked by dislocations and depletions. Macroeconomic policy takes the 'reproductive economy' for granted and policies are implemented without any consideration of their impacts on the 'reproductive economy' – this is true of both orthodox economics, and many varieties of heterodox economics (as discussed further in Elson 1993). However, the 'reproductive economy' may be unable to sustain health, nutrition, education, and skills when so-called economic reforms cut public and community services, to the detriment of both human wellbeing and improvements in productivity in the productive economy. One way of visualising this is in terms of the circular flow of resources, both labour time and money, in an economy, and highlighting the potential for breaks in this circular flow, especially the depletion of human capacities (Elson 2000: 26; Elson 1998: 203).

Figure 1.2 shows a snapshot of an economy with four sectors, the private sector, the public sector, the NGO sector and the household sector, corresponding to a capitalist mixed economy. The private sector employs paid labour, both formal labour which has written contracts setting out wages and other benefits, such as pensions and sick pay, and informal labour which does not. In low-income and some middle-income countries most people do not have formal contracts, while in high-income most people do, though there has been a growth of informal labour in high income countries. The goods and services produced by formal work is valued at market prices and counted in the Gross National Product (GNP) and in principle so are the goods and services produced by informal work, but due to difficulties in collecting data on informal work, its output is typically undercounted. The public sector also employs both formal and informal labour, though formal labour predominates. Most of the goods and services produced by the public sector are not marketed (with exception of output of some publicly owned enterprises), so for inclusion in GNP, output of public sector is typically valued at the market cost of producing it. The NGO sector (which can

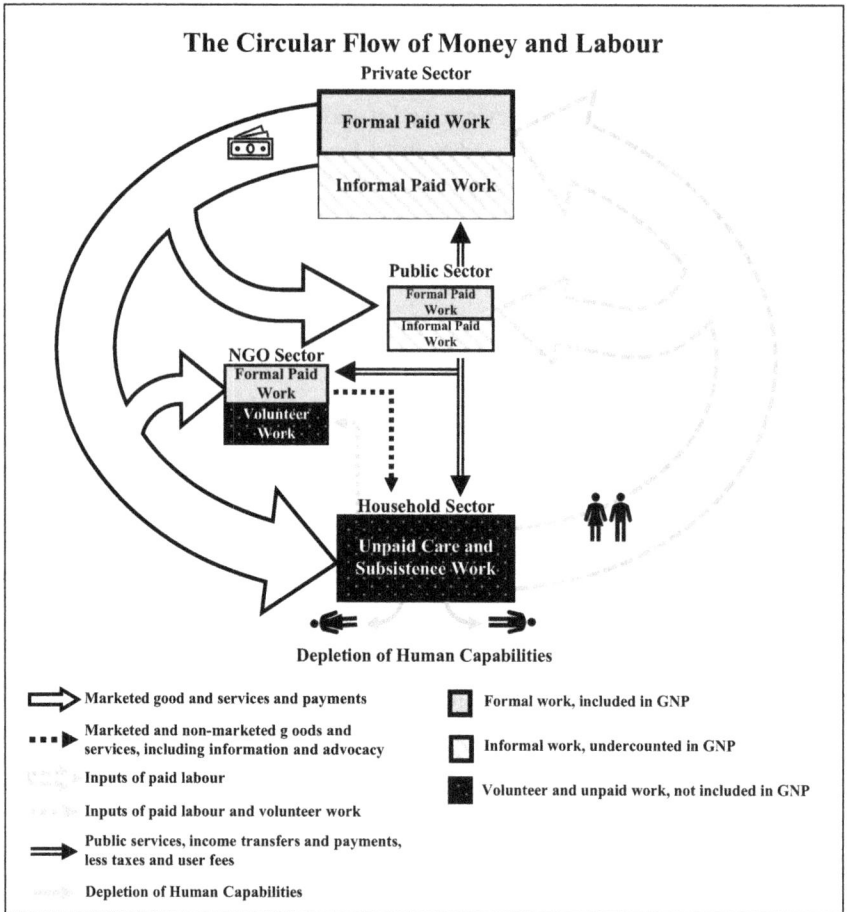

The Circular Flow of Money and Labour

Private Sector

Formal Paid Work

Informal Paid Work

Public Sector

Formal Paid Work

Informal Paid Work

NGO Sector

Formal Paid Work

Volunteer Work

Household Sector

Unpaid Care and Subsistence Work

Depletion of Human Capabilities

Marketed good and services and payments

Marketed and non-marketed goods and services, including information and advocacy

Inputs of paid labour

Inputs of paid labour and volunteer work

Public services, income transfers and payments, less taxes and user fees

Depletion of Human Capabilities

Formal work, included in GNP

Informal work, undercounted in GNP

Volunteer and unpaid work, not included in GNP

Figure 1.2 The circular flow of money and labour

be thought of as comprising all collective organisations, including trade unions, peasant associations, human rights campaigners, and women's organisations, as well as charities) employs formal labour and also relies on unpaid volunteer work, and like the public sector most of its output is not marketed. The goods and services produced by volunteer labour are not included in the GNP, but those produced by paid labour are included, typically valued at market cost. The fourth sector is the household sector, where people are reproduced on a daily and intergenerational basis, using unpaid care and subsistence work. As a matter of principle, most of this unpaid work is not included in the GNP; revisions to the System of National Accounts have allowed for inclusion of some subsistence work, collecting water and fuel, but lack of data means that subsistence production is rarely included in practice. Unpaid care services for household members are in principle excluded from the GNP. All of these sectors are gendered in the ways discussed in the previous section.

The sectors are linked by market flows of wages, goods and services, shown by the arrows on the left-hand side of the figure; and by flows of labour via labour markets shown by the arrows on the right-hand side of the figure. These market flows are not just governed by price incentives, but also by gendered norms and practices. There are also non-market flows from the public sector to the other three sectors of public services and income transfers less taxes and user fees, influenced by markets but governed by gendered configurations of social and political power. There are flows from the NGO sector to the household sector of both marketed and non-marketed goods and services, including information and advocacy. There are flows of labour from households to the NGO sector both via labour markets and volunteer networks. These flows are also gendered, shaped by gender norms and practices, and, most importantly, the people, largely women, whose unpaid care is critical for the reproduction of labour, do not typically own the labour they have reproduced. In a capitalist mixed economy the reproduction of people and the sale of their labour is not organised in the same way as the reproduction and sale of livestock. Such an economy cannot be coordinated by market forces alone.

The smooth continuation of such an economy is called into question by also including, at the bottom of Figure 1.2, arrows showing the depletion of human capabilities, people collapsing because the household sector is unable to reproduce them, because of a lack of the necessary money and goods and services from the other sectors. Market signals alone are unable to secure the smooth continuation of the flows because non-marketed goods and services and unpaid work are also required to sustain people's capabilities. Provision from the public sector and the NGO sector may cover some of these needs but is shaped by macroeconomic policy and configurations of social and political power. Unpaid work in the household cannot be relied on to provide a safety net of last resort and if too many demands are made on it, depletion of capabilities is further exacerbated.

The depletion of capabilities does not by itself necessarily create a crisis for the continuation of a capitalist mixed economy. Indeed, it could be argued to be an intrinsic aspect of such economies. If it leads to a shortage of labour for the private sector, then private sector production may simply move to other locations in other economies where there is an ample labour supply. However, if technological developments mean that the private sector increasingly wants healthy, educated labour, then deep and ongoing depletion will hinder capital accumulation. Moreover, it may lead to challenges to the legitimacy of the configurations of power governing the economy, especially if the NGO sector provides information about the human cost of the depletion and collective campaigns against it. In many ways the depletion of human capabilities is similar to the depletion of the environment, and feminist economists are now exploring these similarities and interconnections (Elson 2025).

Production, social reproduction and economic growth

The circular flow of resources depicts an economy in the short run. Models of economic growth conceptualise the expansion of production over time through investment. I put forward a critique of mainstream models focusing on the way they treat labour as a non-produced input into production and thus ignore the salience of social reproduction and the problems of coordinating production and social reproduction (see Chapter 6).

Looking back, I can see that I slid from using the term 'reproductive economy' to using the term 'social reproduction' without any explicit discussion and sometimes used them interchangeably. 'Social reproduction' is now the term that is widely used in academic writing, though with a range of different definitions about what activities are included in it (only unpaid activities, or also paid activities that produce public services that are not sold on markets, or also paid activities that produce essential goods and services that are sold on markets, such as many paid care services, and commercial production of clothing and food?). If the definition is based on production both unpaid and paid of goods and services that are required for the reproduction of human beings on a daily and intergenerational basis, then there are no clear criteria for where to draw a line. As Folbre (2006) suggests, in a comparable discussion about how to draw the boundaries of the 'care economy', almost the whole economy could be included – not only producing food, but also cooking appliances, energy and steel. I prefer to delineate activities that form part of social reproduction in terms of social relations of production rather than use-values produced. Thus, I consider social reproduction to be a non-market sphere of social provisioning through work which is not driven by profit-seeking, including unpaid work in families and communities, organised unpaid volunteer work, and paid (but non-market work) in public services like health, education and care (Elson 2010: 203).

Bringing social reproduction into the analysis of economic growth challenges the idea that labour is a non-produced means of production. It emphasises that economic growth requires not only investment in technology, equipment and physical infrastructure but also investment in the capabilities of people, their health and skills. Mainstream economics has to some extent recognised this through the concept of 'human capital', and indeed some people do take out loans for investment in their own education and training. But this is only one element of the required investment: social reproduction recognises that investment in capabilities has to take place over the whole of the life course, from birth to death, and that much of this investment is the investment of time in unpaid care for other people. While this investment can be influenced by market incentives, it cannot be reduced to a form of rearing livestock. Social reproduction is governed by social norms, by systems of cooperation and conflict in families and communities, rather than systems of buying and selling in markets. As feminist economists have put it, social reproduction is relatively autonomous (Humphries & Rubery 1984). This means there is no guarantee that the processes of social reproduction will supply labour of the quantities and qualities required for economic growth simply in response to price signals.

The state has always mediated this relation. As forms of production have developed in which the health and education of workers is an important determinant of productivity, investment through unpaid work in families and communities has been complemented by the growth of public services providing education, health and care. However, in market driven economies, there is always the danger of under-investment in human capabilities, and indeed, depletion of human capabilities. This is exacerbated by the ways that investment is defined in the national accounts: spending money on delivery of public services is treated as consumption rather than as investment, even though it improves productivity (Heintz 2019: 67).

The dominance of finance over production and social reproduction

The interaction of production and social reproduction has been further complicated by the growing dominance of finance in economies. This prompted me, in collaboration with Nilufer Çağatay (Elson & Çağatay 1995) to differentiate financial services from other sectors of production, and wealthy rentier households from the majority of households. The wealthy rentier households own financial assets, managed by financial services companies, from which they derive a large part of their income. The majority of households own few financial assets and owe substantial debts to financial services companies. These net debtor households derive most of their income from work, not asset ownership. The wealthy rentier minority do very little unpaid work, instead paying for substitutes, such as domestic workers; and make very little use of public services, instead paying for private services. In contrast, the majority of households rely much more on unpaid work and also on public services. Financial services companies, especially international financial service companies, exercise power over net debtor households, and also over governments who rely on selling government bonds to finance the gap between public expenditure and revenue from taxes. Wealthy households and large and medium businesses pressure governments to reduce their taxes, both through reduction of tax rates, and through a myriad tax concessions, often obscured from view. International businesses and international financial corporations collaborate in a system of international tax avoidance and evasion which deprives governments of revenue to fund public services and benefits the wealth rentier households who can keep their wealth offshore. This wealthy minority, and international financial companies and international businesses are relatively footloose, able to move their operations to other countries with lower taxes and laxer regulations. Local businesses and the majority of households are not footloose in the same way. People from these households do migrate to other countries but in difficult and onerous circumstances, leaving them open to a variety of forms of exploitation.

If governments prioritise the interests of rentier households, their policies will be marked by deflationary bias and commodification bias, and there will inevitably be pressure on women in the majority of net-debtor households to act as provisioners of last resort, expanding, as far as they are able, their unpaid work. Responses that are marked by male breadwinner bias will not address the needs of women for independent entitlements and may further deepen their dependence.

Deregulation has created an international financial system that is fraught with risks, and in times of financial crisis, risks are downloaded from the dealing rooms of financial markets to the kitchens where low-income women strive to provide meals for their families (see Chapter 7). In the Asian financial crisis in the late 1990s, the World Bank and the IMF imposed policy conditions that intensified the pressures on low-income women, while advocating that a few narrowly targeted social safety nets be added on. It would be better to rebuild an international financial system that avoids deflationary bias, male-breadwinner bias and commodification/privatisation bias, and does not preclude democratic public policy dialogues, in which the interests of women in the kitchen could be represented.

This would require reinstating controls on flows of finance into and out of national economies, so that buyers and sellers of financial instruments, such as bonds and equities, have fewer options to be footloose. It is difficult to conduct a democratic public policy dialogue when some of the key actors have no stake in the outcome beyond the next few hours and are able to foreclose discussion by selling their bonds or equities.

Gender responsive budgeting: hopes and limitations

One important area of policy in which women's rights organisation and feminist economists have made efforts to intervene is that of fiscal policy. In 1995 the Beijing Platform for Action, agreed at the UN Fourth World Conference, called for the integration of a gender perspective in budgetary decisions. Women's rights organizations attempted to 'follow the money' and find out who was benefiting and who was not, from government budgets. They pressed governments to back fine-sounding policy statements about gender equality with the budgets necessary for their implementation. They hoped that gender-responsive budgeting would help to transform gender relations. Since then there have been many efforts to get governments to adopt gender responsive budgeting, building on pioneering efforts in Australia and South Africa (see Chapter 8). I contributed to these efforts through developing tools, conducting training with UN agencies, publishing articles and reports, and working with the UK Women's Budget Group, a feminist NGO that conducts gender impact analysis of UK budgets (Elson 2021). The influence of gender responsive budgeting has waxed and waned depending on the changing political complexion of governments. Though many governments have said that they are adopting gender responsive budgeting, few have conducted ex ante and ex post gender impact assessments, including taxes as well as expenditures; many have not gone beyond trying to count the amount of spending allocated to what are considered to be programmes that promote gender equality (often limited to programmes specifically target women). International financial institutions like the IMF and the World Bank have promoted their own version of gender responsive budgeting that focuses on public sector financial management and does not address the way that budgets in many countries are vehicles for austerity policies (Elson 2021).

An important limitation on transformative use of gender responsive budgeting are neo-liberal economic policies, especially though trade liberalisation, competition to attract investment from multinationals, and financial liberalisation, which have brought about a fiscal squeeze (Çağatay 2002). Trade liberalisation reduces revenue from taxes on imports and exports. Competition to attract investment leads to cuts in corporation tax an introduction of tax holidays and other exemptions. Moreover, countries are encouraged to borrow from commercial banks and other financial businesses at floating rates of interest, and when central banks put up interest rates, there is a knock-on effect with rising interest rates on government debt, so that debt service payments take an increasing share of public expenditure. In order to build a reputation for 'sound finance' in international financial markets, many governments have adopted 'fiscal rules' (the most stringent of which are laws that require balanced budgets) which severely limit fiscal space and put downward pressure on public expenditure. All of this makes it much more difficult to expand allocations to the public services and social protection systems that are vital for reducing gender inequality.

To ensure more fiscal space for transformative gender responsive budgeting, the international economic system needs changing, as discussed in Chapter 7. Moreover, to ensure an enlarged fiscal space can be effectively and equitably used, fiscal policy needs to be democratised. Instead of being a top-down technocratic exercise, there needs to be transparency, participation and accountability, drawing on the everyday experience of low-income women, and feminist economics expertise, informed by a human rights perspective (Balakrishnan, Heintz & Elson 2016).

Gender equality, inclusive growth, green and caring economies

Many development agencies call for policies to promote inclusive growth as a response to debt burdens and austerity measures; however, inclusion is not necessarily beneficial (Chapter 9). In the sphere of production inclusion can be forcible, injurious, impoverished, precarious, segregated. Inclusion in the sphere of finance risks exposure to mis-sold financial products, fraud, increasing levels of indebtedness, loss of assets and vulnerability to the depredations of debt collectors. Moreover, many millions of people are not just being left behind by processes of economic growth but pushed behind, to lower living-standards, and in worst cases to premature avoidable death, often driven by pollution of air and water (Elson 2019). Economic growth too often depletes both human capabilities and natural resources.

Is it possible to identify gender-equitable forms of growth that are sustainable and avoid these harms and improve well-being? Reducing gender gaps in employment in jobs that meet ILO standards of decent work is not sufficient, because the gap can fall while at the same time levels of employment are falling – 'equalising down'. Gender gaps in enjoyment of decent work should be reduced by increasing the creation of decent work for both women and men, with a higher rate of expansion for women than for men, a process that may be described as 'equalizing up'. Moreover, it matters what is being produced, what sectors are expanding (those that environmentally sustainable and well-being enhancing?) and what contracting (those that are environmentally destructive and well-being diminishing). An increase in the public provision of affordable housing, clean energy, safe public transport, clean water and sanitation, and health, education and care services can be environmentally sustainable and well-being enhancing, particularly for women as it can reduce women's unpaid work and enable them to access decent paid work. Gender equitable inclusive growth also requires redistribution of the remaining unpaid work so that it is more equally shared between women and men. Both jobs and social protection need to be redesigned to support this. Gender-equitable inclusive growth should be understood as a process that transforms the lives of both women and men, so that each is able to participate equally in paid and unpaid work, in production and social reproduction.

Feminist economists have been putting investment in care at the centre of proposals for a gender-equitable sustainable economy, arguing that spending on care services should be treated as investment in social infrastructure and placed on a par with investment in physical infrastructure, recognising that both generate benefits that extend beyond the individual recipient to wider society, both now and into the future. Investment in social infrastructure is capable of creating millions of good quality jobs (De Henau 2022). In the longer run such investment can improve productivity throughout the economy via channels such as increasing women's labour force experience and attachment and increasing the capabilities of the next generation of workers (Onaren *et al.* 2022). Moreover, investing in the care sector is 30 per cent less polluting in terms of greenhouse gas emissions than investing the same amount in the construction sector (De Henau & Himmelweit 2020).

The interaction of care for people and care for the planet is discussed in Elson (2025) in terms of depletion and degradation versus replenishment and regeneration. To secure replenishment and regeneration we need to create green and caring economies that prioritise well-being rather than financial returns. This requires the creation of new development strategies that reorient our economies, dethroning GDP as the dominant indicator of success; change ownership models, dethroning pursuit of profit as the dominant objective; change the ways governments raise and spend money, dethroning compliance with fiscal rules as the dominant driver of decisions; and change the global financial system, dethroning free movement of money as the dominant operating principle (Elson 2024a).

Gender equality and economic crisis

Financial liberalisation has produced a global economy that is prone to financial crisis, as in Latin America in early 1980s, Asia in late 1990s, and Global North in 2008–09. I analysed the generation of, impact of, and response to crisis in terms of the international interaction of three gendered economic spheres: production, social reproduction and finance (Chapter 10). For example, a key factor in the generation of the 2008–09 financial crisis was the growing dependence of social reproduction in USA on debt, particularly through 'predatory inclusion' of women in the subprime market for mortgage loans. Default on these mortgages, triggered by rising costs of food and fuel, led to a collapse in the value of financial assets derived from them, spilling over into the financial sphere internationally, putting banking systems in jeopardy, leading to a credit crunch for the sphere of production, with global impacts via international trade and finance.

The gendered impact in the sphere of production varied by sector and country. In some, male-intensive sectors like construction and cars were harder hit and men lost jobs; in others export-oriented female-intensive sectors like garments were harder hit and women lost jobs. Faced with growing male unemployment, some governments introduced a fiscal stimulus, focusing on supporting construction and cars. However, there were adverse reactions to rising government debt in the bond markets, pushing up rates of interest on government debt for many governments, and in many countries austerity policies were introduced, leading to increases in female unemployment, as women tend to be disproportionately employed in the public sector.

The austerity policies undermined provision of public services and social protection transfers, even in many European countries where there had been a welfare state. The UK Women's Budget Group estimated that the hardest hit would be lone parents (95 per cent of whom are women) and single women pensioners (UK Women's Budget Group 2010). Unpaid work tended to rise, including through volunteer work in operating food banks, and in more labour-intensive shopping and meal preparation using cheaper ingredients. But the sphere of social reproduction cannot provide an unlimited safety net: there were reports in the UK of more women seeking help for mental health problems due to the increased stress they were under.

The problems caused by economic crisis cannot be adequately addressed by adding a few programmes targeted to low-income women, to strengthen their position in social reproduction and production. Banks in trouble had been saved by tax-payer funded bailouts, when was what needed were deep-seated reforms to end the dominance of finance, and to create a socially-useful financial system that meets the needs of production and social reproduction. In fact, the dominance of finance has been restored and intensified. There is a huge, growing and unsustainable debt burden for many low- and middle-income countries, with payments of interest on debt taking up a larger share of the government budget than key public services like health and education. Feminist economists are now analysing the gender dimensions of the international debt burden and putting forward proposals for debt cancellation (Ruwanpura *et al.* forthcoming). Central banks were innovative in addressing the credit crunch in 2008–09 but fifteen years later addressed supply-side driven inflation by conventional monetary policy that has harmful impacts on production and social reproduction. Feminist economists are now analysing central banks and monetary policy and putting forward proposals for more equitable policies (Powell & Elson forthcoming; Rochon *et al.* 2024; Young 2018).

Impact of feminist macroeconomics on research and policy

An innovative assessment of the impact of feminist macroeconomics on academic research has been conducted by Berik and Kongar (forthcoming). They examined citations in academic journals of my work, and that of my collaborators, Nilufer

Çağatay and Caren Grown, and of two other feminist economists who have further developed feminist macroeconomics Elissa Braunstein and Stephanie Seguino.[4] They found that there were fewer citations in economics journals than in journals in other disciplines. Within economics, there were more citations in mainstream journals than in heterodox journals. About a third of the citations in mainstream economics academic journal were in journals focusing on economic development, and almost half of the citations in heterodox economics journals were in *Feminist Economics*.

Reflecting on explanations for this pattern, Berik and Kongar point to research showing that the marginalisation of feminist scholarship overlaps with the underrepresentation of females within disciplines. Macroeconomists are predominantly male. There are more women in other branches of economics and in other disciplines. They note that in heterodox macroeconomics, the integration of gender inequality into the analysis has largely been conducted by feminist economists. The benefits of a unified research agenda for both feminist economics and Post Keynesian macroeconomics have recently been set out by Onaran and Oyvat (2023) who have shown how this has policy relevance in addressing multiple contemporary crises. However, the reluctance of many heterodox macroeconomists to recognise that labour is a produced, not a non-produced, factor of production remains a barrier.

Perhaps surprisingly there has been growing recognition of the relevance of gender equality to macroeconomy policy at the IMF. For more than ten years some economists at the IMF have been describing gender equality as a 'macro-critical issue', mainly on grounds that gender inequality (especially in the distribution of unpaid work) hinders women's labour market participation and is thus a barrier to economic growth. In 2022 the IMF adopted a Gender Mainstreaming Strategy that calls for an intentional and systematic approach to integrating gender into macroeconomic policies to foster strong, sustainable, and inclusive growth (Goyal and Sahay 2023). IMF economists have published research on gender inequality, including in both paid and unpaid work; and gender equality has been addressed in some IMF operational work, such as in some of the regular Article IV reviews (annual consultations between the IMF and all member governments), and in advice on gender responsive budgeting (Elson 2024b). However, as feminists have pointed out, none of this has provoked a rethink of the kinds of conditions that the IMF attaches to loans, which tend to be harmful to women, especially women living in poverty (Bürgisser 2019;

---

4. Seguino and Braunstein have developed formal models drawing on Keynesian and Kaleckian approaches and have conducted econometric analysis of industrialisation, trade, foreign investment and monetary policy. See Seguino (2021) and Braunstein (2021).

Elson 2024b). The IMF economists who work on gender do not consider how the dominance of finance at the macro-level places severe constraints on public investment to reduce gender equality and do not call into question the requirement for austerity policies. It remains to be seen how far the IMF will continue to address gender equality in face of the displeasure of the Trump Administration which considers this goes beyond the mandate of the IMF.

Feminist macroeconomics has also had an impact in the development of the concept of the care economy, which includes both paid care work and unpaid care work. In my own research I did not frame my analysis in terms of the care economy, but used the concepts of unpaid work, reproductive economy, social reproduction and the reproductive sphere. However, subsequent contributions to feminist macroeconomics focus explicitly on care (Braunstein 2021). The ILO produced a comprehensive report on care work, both unpaid and paid, which extended my 3R framework to a 5R framework to incorporate better *rewards* for paid care workers and *representation* of paid care workers in social dialogue and collective bargaining (ILO 2018). The report emphasised the importance of investing in good quality accessible public care services not only to reduce unpaid care work but also to provide decent paid work for women and commissioned quantitative studies from feminist economists (ILO 2018). UN Women and ILO have produced a Policy Support Tool (UN Women-ILO 2021) showing how estimates of the impact of investment in care services can be produced for any country, choosing the method best suited to that country. The guidance covers not only estimating the impact on women's employment and time use, but also the extent to which the investment is self-financing because of the generation of additional tax revenue.

The concept of the care economy is now widely used in policy discussions in international fora, such as the annual inter-governmental meetings of the UN Commission on the Status of Women. It is a more accessible concept than social reproduction but does not foreground the role of unpaid work in reproducing the labour supply and thus the economic system as a whole, benefiting not only those who receive care, but also those who make profits out of the capacities that care sustains. Moreover, as the concept of the care economy has become popular, the link to investment in good quality public services and jobs is often lost. A range of other policies is now often considered as support for the care economy, including tax breaks for parents who pay for child-care services (which benefits better-off women much more than those with low incomes), and cash transfers to encourage mothers to stay at home to raise children (which supports rather than transforms existing unequal gender norms). Feminist economists need to be vigilant in analysing proposals for policies to support the care economy, especially in the current context of a widespread backlash in many countries against gender equality.

Seguino (2021:348) concludes that 'Twenty years ago, gender was not considered to be an important macroeconomic variable. Today it is.' I agree with this conclusion but caution that we still face many challenges in getting economists, both orthodox and heterodox, to look at economies as gendered structures that need to be transformed, rather than simply adding a new variable to their equations. That transformation needs to go beyond the principles embodied by the 5R's framework to aim for the creation of caring economies that replenish and regenerate both people and planet (Elson 2024a).

References

Bakker, I. (ed.) (1994). *The Strategic Silence: Gender and Economic Policy*. London: Zed Books.

Balakrishnan, R., J. Heintz and D. Elson (2016). *Rethinking Economics for Social Justice: The Radical Potential of Human Rights*. London: Routledge.

de Beauvoir, S. (2009). *The Second Sex*. Translated by C. Borde and S. Malovany-Chevallier. London: Jonathan Cape.

Benería, L. and G. Sen (1981). "Accumulation, Reproduction and Women's Role in Economic Development". *Signs: Journal of Women in Culture and Society* 7(2), 279–98.

Berik, G. and E. Kongar (forthcoming). "Rise and Rise of Feminist Macroeconomics: Who's Recognizing?" In L. Chester and A. Bernasek (eds), *Edward Elgar Handbook on Women and Heterodox Economics: Past, Present, and Future*. Cheltenham: Elgar.

Boserup, E. (1970). *Women's Role in Economic Development*. New York: St Martin's Press.

Braunstein, E. (2021). "Care and the Macroeconomy". In G. Berik and E. Kongar (eds), *The Routledge Handbook of Feminist Economics*, 351–9. London: Routledge.

Bürgisser, E. (2019). "The IMF and Gender Equality: Operationalising Change". https://www.brettonwoodsproject.org/wp-content/uploads/2019/02/Operationalising-Change.pdf.

Çağatay, N. (2002). "Gender Budgets and Beyond: Feminist Fiscal Policy in the Context of Globalisation." Paper presented at the Association for Women's Rights in Development Conference, Guadalajara, Mexico.

Çağatay, N., D. Elson and C. Grown (1995). "Introduction: Gender, Adjustment and Macroeconomics." *World Development* 23(11), 1827–36. https://doi.org/10.1016/0305-750X(95)90003-J.

De Henau, J. and S. Himmelweit (2020). *A Care-Led Recovery from Coronavirus*. London: Women's Budget Group. https://wbg.org.uk/wp-content/uploads/2020/06/Care-led-recovery-final.pdf.

De Henau, J. (2022). "Costs and Benefits of Investing in Transformative Care Policy Packages: A Macrosimulation Study in 82 Countries". ILO Working Paper No. 55. Geneva: International Labour Organization. https://doi.org/10.54394/AKYJ8893.

Elson, D. and R. Pearson (1981). "Nimble Fingers Make Cheap Workers: An Analysis of Women's Employment in Third World Export Manufacturing". *Feminist Review* 7 (spring), 87–107. https://doi.org/10.1057/fr.1981.6.

Elson, D., B. Evers and J. Gideon (1997). "Gender Aware Country Economic Reports: Concepts and Sources". Working Paper No. 1. GENECON Unit, Graduate School of Social Sciences, University of Manchester.

Elson, D. (ed.) (2000). *Progress of the World's Women 2000*. New York: UNIFEM. https://www.unwomen.org/sites/default/files/Headquarters/Media/Publications/UNIFEM/152preface.pdf.

Elson, D. (1979). "The Value Theory of Labour". In D. Elson (ed.), *Value: The Representation of Labour in Capitalism*. London: CSE Books/New York: Humanities Press. Reprinted 2015. London: Verso.

Elson, D. (1988). "Dominance and Dependency in the World Economy". In Ben Crow and Marilyn Thorpe (eds), *Change and Survival in the Third World*. Cambridge: Polity/New York: Oxford University Press. Reprinted in 1995 as "Dominance and Dependency in the World Economy" (abridged). In S. Corbridge (ed.), *Readings in Development Studies*. London: Edward Arnold.

Elson, D. (1993). "Gender-Aware Analysis and Development Economics". *Journal of International Development* 5(2), 237–47. https://doi.org/10.1002/jid.3380050214.

Elson, D. (1994). "Micro, Meso, Macro: Gender and Economic Analysis in the Context of Policy Reform". In I. Bakker (ed.), *The Strategic Silence: Gender and Economic Policy*, 33–45. London: Zed Books.

Elson, D. (1995). "Gender Awareness in Modelling Structural Adjustment". *World Development* 23(11), 1851–68. https://doi.org/10.1016/0305-750X(95)00087-S.

Elson, D. (1998). "The Economic, the Political and the Domestic: Businesses, States and Households in the Organisation of Production". *New Political Economy* 3(2), 189–208. https://doi.org/10.1080/13563469808406349.

Elson, D. (2010). "Gender and the Global Economic Crisis in Developing Countries: A Framework for Analysis". *Gender and Development* 18(2), 201–12. https://doi.org/10.1080/13552074.2010.491321.

Elson, D. and M. Fontana (2014). "Public policies on water provision and early childhood education and care (ECEC): do they reduce and redistribute unpaid work?". *Gender and Development* 22(3).

Elson, D. (2017). "Recognize, Reduce, and Redistribute Unpaid Care Work: How to Close the Gender Gap". *New Labor Forum* 26(2).

Elson, D. (2019). "Push No One Behind". *Journal of Globalization and Development* 9(2), 1–12. https://doi.org/10.1515/jgd-2018-0026.

Elson, D. (2021). "Gender Budgeting". In G. Berik and E. Kongar (eds), *The Routledge Handbook of Feminist Economics*, 459–67. London: Routledge.

Elson, D. (2024a). "Reducing Women's Poverty Through New Development Strategies". Background paper for Expert Group Meeting, Sixty-eighth session of the Commission on the Status of Women (CSW68). https://www.unwomen.org/en/csw/csw68-2024/preparations/expert-group-meeting.

Elson, D. (2024b). "How the IMF discovered gender equality but continued to undermine women's rights". In S. Damodaran, S. Gupta, S. Mitra and D. Sinha (eds), *Development, Transformations and the Human Condition: Essays in Honour of Jayati Ghosh*. New Delhi: Routledge.

Elson, D. (2025). "Caring for People, Caring for the Planet: Depletion and Degradation vs. Replenishment and Regeneration". In *Perspectives on the Care–Climate Nexus*, Southern Centre for Inequality Studies, University of the Witwatersrand, Johannesburg.

Falth, A. and M. Blackden (2009). "Unpaid Care Work", Policy Brief No. 1, Gender Equality and Poverty Reduction. https://www.undp.org/sites/g/files/zskgke326/files/publications/Unpaid%20care%20work%20English.pdf.

Folbre, N. (2006). "Measuring Care: Gender, Empowerment, and the Care Economy". *Journal of Human Development* 7(2), 183–99. https://doi.org/10.1080/14649880600768512.

Fontana, M. (2024). *Assessing the Employment Situation in Five Countries and Promoting a Gender-Responsive Structural Transformation*. UN Women–ILO Consolidated Report. Geneva: International Labour Organization. https://www.ilo.org/publications/assessing-employment-situation-five-countries-and-promoting-gender.

Gideon, J. (1999). "Looking at Economies as Gendered Structures: An Application to Central America". *Feminist Economics* 5(1), 1–28. https://doi.org/10.1080/135457099338120. 06/10/2023.

Goyal, R. and R. Sahay (2023). "Integrating Gender into the IMF's Work". Gender Notes No. 2023/001. https://www.imf.org/en/Publications/gender-notes/Issues/2023/10/06/Integrating-Gender-into-the-IMFs-Work-539801.

Grown, C., D. Elson and N. Çağatay (2000). "Introduction to Special Issue – Growth, Trade, Finance and Gender Inequality". *World Development* 28(7), 1145–56. https://doi.org/10.1016/S0305-750X(00)00032-2.

Heintz, J. (2019). *The Economy's Other Half: How Taking Gender Seriously Transforms Macroeconomics*. Newcastle upon Tyne: Agenda Publishing.

Humphries, J. and J. Rubery (1984). "The Reconstitution of the Supply Side of the Labour Market: The Relative Autonomy of Social Reproduction". *Cambridge Journal of Economics* 8(4), 33–346. https://www.jstor.org/stable/23596643.

International Labour Office (2018). *Care Work and Care Jobs for the Future of Decent Work*. Geneva: ILO.

Lewis, W. (1954). "Economic Development with Unlimited Supplies of Labour". *Manchester School* 22(2), 139–91.

Lewis, W. (1955). *The Theory of Economic Growth*. London: Allen & Unwin.

Onaren, Ö., C. Oyvat and E. Fotopoulou (2022). "A Macroeconomic Analysis of the Effects of Gender Inequality, Wages and Public Social Infrastructure: The Case of the UK". *Feminist Economics* 28(2), 152–88. https://doi.org/10.1080/13545701.2022.2044498.

Onaran Ö. and C. Oyvat (2023). "Synthesizing feminist and post-Keynesian/Kaleckian economics for a purple-green-red transition". *European Journal of Economics and Economic Policies* 20(2), 317–37.

Powell, J. and D. Elson (forthcoming). "Engendering Monetary Policy". *Feminist Economics*.

Rai, S. (2024). *Depletion. The Human Costs of Caring*. Oxford: Oxford University Press.

Rochon, L.-P., S. Rossi, and G. Vallet (eds) (2024). *Central Banking, Monetary Policy and Gender*. Cheltenham: Elgar.

Ruwanpura, K., S. Rao and A. Oduro (eds) (forthcoming). "Gendering the Debt Crisis: Feminist Political Economy Perspectives". Special issue of *Feminist Economics*.

Sen, A. (1984). "Rights and Capabilities". In *Resources, Values and Development*, 307–24. Cambridge, MA: Harvard University Press.

UN Women and ILO (2021). *A Guide to Public Investments in the Care Economy: Policy Support Tool for Estimating Care Deficits, Investment Costs and Economic Returns*. https://www.ilo.org/employment/Whatwedo/Publications/WCMS_767029/lang--en/index.htm

Young, B. (2018). "The Impact of Unconventional Monetary Policy on Gendered Wealth Inequality". *Papeles de Europa* 31(2), 175–86. https://doi.org/10.5209/PADE.63637.

Young, B., I. Bakker and D. Elson (2011). "Introduction". In B. Young, I. Bakker and D. Elson (eds), *Questioning Financial Governance from a Feminist Perspective*, 1–14. London: Routledge.

2
THEORIES OF DEVELOPMENT

Development, understood as a process of economic, social and political transformation that raises the general standard of living, has been a pre-occupation of social science from Adam Smith's *Wealth of Nations* and Karl Marx's *Das Kapital* onwards. No short entry can do full justice to such a huge field. This entry will be confined to the narrower field of contemporary theories of economic development (or lack of development) and to the interventions that feminist economics (or women-focused economics) has made within it.

Development economics, as taught in economics programmes today, dates back almost 50 years, to the setting up of the United Nations Organization with a mandate to promote the development of the poorer regions of the world, the efforts at economic reconstruction after World War II, and the beginning of decolonization, with the independence of India in 1946. It has always had a strong policy focus, concerned to influence policymakers in both national and international economic institutions.

There have been three dominant themes in the theories of economic development advanced in the last 50 years: first, a concern with national processes of accumulation, structural change and economic growth; secondly, a concern with poverty and wellbeing; and thirdly, a concern with the implications of international economic relations for national development. The field of development economics has always been contested, with continuing debates on the relative merits of the state and the private sector as engines of growth; on the relationship between growth, wellbeing and poverty; on the relative efficacy of planning and markets as means of co-ordination; and on the international economy as a facilitator or constraint upon the development of the countries of Asia, Africa, the Middle East and Latin America (once collectively referred to as the Third World, now more often referred to as the South) (for guides to these debates, see Toye 1987; Sen 1983; Lal 1985).

Until 1970, with the publication of Ester Boserup's *Women's Role in Economic Development*, the production of theories of economic development was an almost exclusively male activity, and women were largely invisible within those theories. Boserup's book was followed by a growing body of work by women scholars, some of it in continuation of Boserup's arguments, some of it in counterpoint to Boserup's arguments, but all of it insisting that theories of development have to take into account differences between men's and women's economic lives, and the inequalities of power between men and women.

This entry will first discuss some of the key, pre-Boserup, analyses of economic development, selecting those theories which are particularly relevant to the subsequent discussion of women-focused and feminist contributions to theories of development. A good starting point is Nobel prize-winning economist Arthur Lewis's 1954 article, 'Economic Development with Unlimited Supplies of Labour', in which Lewis draws upon the classical tradition in economics to emphasize the importance of mobilizing the surplus labour which he argued could be found in the 'subsistence' sector, for reinvestment in a 'capitalist' sector, which sought to maximize the surplus product left after the payment of wages. Lewis postulated that the subsistence sector could continue to sustain its customary level of output per head, while also supplying labour to the capitalist sector, for a wage somewhat higher than customary income per head in the subsistence sector. This transfer of labour would continue until the surplus labour in the subsistence sector had all been transferred, thus permitting the capitalist sector to grow rapidly. This process of structural change would, Lewis assumed, in turn raise the general standard of living.

The validity of the Lewis model as an encapsulation of how development takes place has been the subject of continuing debate. Does labour flow voluntarily to the modern sector, attracted by a higher wage than the customary level of income in the subsistence sector? Or is it extracted by coercive means, as argued for instance by Weeks (1970)? Are there any plausible grounds for supposing that the subsistence sector reacts to a transfer of labour out of the sector by redeploying the remaining labour so that its customary level of production per head is maintained? Sen (1975) implies that such redeployment is possible if there is a work-sharing rule in the family-based subsistence sector. But Lal (1983) points out that such behaviour would entail those who remain in the family-based sector giving up some leisure without getting any extra reward in compensation, which he describes as 'perverse'.

Gender relations were not specifically identified in this debate, as either a barrier to the redeployment of labour between sectors or within sectors, or as a source of motivation to work harder or longer, or of a source of power to extract more work without any extra compensation. Lewis himself implicitly assumed that producers in the subsistence sector were men, remarking that 'men will not leave the family farm to seek employment if the wage is worth less than they would be able to consume at home' (Lewis 1955: 409). However, he did identify 'the wives and daughters of the household', as a further source of labour for the capitalist sector, arguing that this would lead to gains 'because most of the things which women otherwise do in the household can in fact be done much better or more cheaply outside, thanks to large scale economies of specialisation, and also to the use of capital. (Grinding grain, fetching water from the river, making cloth, making clothes, cooking the midday meal, teaching children, nursing the sick, etc.)' (p. 404). In other words, he envisaged what feminists subsequently called 'reproductive work' (that is, the unpaid work in households and communities that is necessary to reproduce the labour force and the social fabric) being trans-ferred to the capitalist sector. In his book on the theory of economic growth, Lewis (1955) was in no doubt about the benefits to women: 'Women benefit from growth even more than men. ... Woman gains freedom from drudgery, is emancipated from the seclusion of the household, and gains at last the chance to be a full human being, exercising her mind and her talents in the same way as men' (Lewis 1955: 422). This reflects the widespread optimism of the 1950s that the benefits of economic growth would 'trickle down' to everyone, and an implicit assumption, that the surplus in the capitalist sector would indeed be reinvested in ways that reduce women's drudgery, and allow women to be 'full human beings'.

There was also optimism that every country could enjoy economic growth, which was frequently understood as taking place through a series of stages. The countries which were labelled 'less developed' or, more optimistically, 'devel-oping', were seen as being at an earlier stage of a process through which the richer, more industrialized countries (labelled developed) had already passed. This was explicit in Rostow's (1960) theory of the 'take-off into self-sustained growth' which described development in terms of a passage from a 'stable and traditional society' to a 'dynamic and modern society'.

The theories discussed thus far focused on development as a process of struc-tural transformation and growth, rather than development as an object of policy. However, both Lewis and Rostow recognized that investment was risky, and that there was a need for the state to promote productive reinvestment of profits, including investment by the state itself. Development planning, based on the Harrod-Domar model at the macroeconomic level, and social cost-benefit anal-ysis at the microeconomic level, was widely advocated in the 1950s and 1960s by economists in both the developing and developed countries; and because it was generally recognized that markets fail in coordinating large-scale invest-ment decisions, producing a national plan became a requirement for receiving development aid (for further discussion, see Lal 1983 and Toye 1987).

Such plans very often focused on industrialization ('traditional' was equated with agriculture and 'modern' with industry) and were based upon the protection of domestic industry ('import-substituting industrialization'). The intellectual case for this was made by 'structuralist' economists, who argued that the agricultural structure of Third World economies hindered their development. One of the most important arguments for this was put forward by UN economists Prebisch (1950) and Singer (1950). They argued that the prices of primary products tended to fall relative to those of manufactured products over the long run. Since the exports of the Third World in the 1940s, 1950s and 1960s were made up mainly of agricultural goods, while their imports were manufactured goods, this meant that their terms of trade tended to fall and international trade did not promote their development. Over time, they would have to supply more and more primary products (for example, coffee) in order to import the same quantity of manufactured goods (for example, tractors). The solution was to change the structure of their production by limiting imports of tractors and producing tractors within the country. More broadly, structuralist economists shared the view that state intervention to promote specific sectors of industry and to overcome obstacles to growth was required to sustain development. Pronounced inequalities in land ownership were identified as one important obstacle, and lack of access to new technology was another.

The optimistic vision of development as a passage from traditional (and agricultural) to modern (and industrial), from less developed to developed, which could be brought about by national development planning and protection of national industries was challenged in the 1960s by the opposing vision of the 'dependency school'. A leading proponent of the dependency school was Andre Gunder Frank who proposed that underdevelopment is largely the result of past and continuing economic and other relations between satellite underdeveloped and the now developed metropolitan countries (Frank 1966). This school of thought, which is reviewed in detail by Palma (1978), rejected the dichotomy between traditional and modern sectors, on the grounds that so-called traditional society had already been reshaped by an international process of capitalist development. Moreover, it proposed that the key problem of development in the underdeveloped countries was the dependent and exploitative way in which they were integrated into the international capitalist economy, which was not fundamentally changed by import-substitution industrialization. The argument was buttressed by interpretations of Latin American history which proposed that integration into the international economy had served to transfer surplus out of the underdeveloped countries for investment in the devel oped countries and could not promote autonomous and self-sustaining national development. The answer lay in a complete disengagement from the international capitalist economy.

The dependency school brought the questions of international power and international inequality to the forefront of attention, but its focus on imperialism was not complemented by a focus on 'machismo'. Nor was it clear what practical action could be derived from its analysis or what guidance it provided to organizations struggling to improve the lives of poor people in what was then called the Third World, since underdevelopment was presented as a self-perpetuating structure.

By the 1970s both the growth and modernization paradigm and the dependency paradigm were being challenged. On the one hand, there were plenty of examples where industrial growth had been achieved, but the living standards of poor people had barely improved, and inequality had worsened (such as Brazil). On the other hand, newly industrializing countries (NICS) in Asia (Taiwan, South Korea, Hong Kong and Singapore) were challenging the domination of the developed countries in world markets for manufactured exports, and the mass of people living in the NICS had enjoyed sustained increases in income. In this ferment, women's voices, insisting women's concerns be addressed, began to be heard.

By common consent among development and feminist economists, the pioneer was Ester Boserup (1970) who challenged the optimistic view that capital accumulation, economic growth and modernization necessarily benefited women. In the case of agricultural modernization, she argued that women had been deprived of access to training, land rights, education and technology, by both colonial and post-colonial administrators, who could not conceive of women being farmers in their own right, even though in much of sub-Saharan Africa and South-East Asia women enjoyed a significant autonomous role in traditional agricultural production. This lack of access to resources meant that while men's productivity in farming increased, women's productivity did not. In the case of industrial modernization, she argued that women accounted for a much lower percentage of the industrial labour force in large-scale modern factories than they did in home-based handicraft manufacturing. She pointed to obstacles on the demand side, including labour market regulations, and employers' prejudiced perceptions of women's capacities and work commitment; and on the supply side, she suggested that women had difficulties combining work in the modern sector with their reproductive responsibilities, and were hindered by the view that work outside the home was not proper for women. Above all, women were hampered by their lack of appropriate skills, stemming from their lack of formal education, and confinement with the family. According to Boserup (1970: 214), 'Employment in the modern sector requires not only formal training, but also a certain attitude to work, which may best be described as the capacity to work regularly and attentively. Those who work within the confines of the home are not likely to acquire this attitude'. As a result of all these factors, women had been left marginalized and excluded from modernization. Boserup's remedy for this was investment in more and better education for women-planners must change their view that women were primarily housewives, and train women to compete equally with men in the market place, so that women could be included in economic modernization.

As Kabeer (1994) points out, Boserup's book laid the foundations for a large body of 'Women-in-Development' literature, and a large number of policy initiatives aimed at 'integrating women into development'. Tinker (1990), in describing the making of the field of Women-in-Development, calls Boserup's book, 'the fundamental text for the UN Decade for Women' (1975–85). Boserup's 'marginalization' thesis found support from other authors analysing development from women's perspective. For instance, as Pearson (1992) points out, the idea that development marginalized women was supported by some Latin America researchers, such as Saffiotti (1978) who examined the implications for women's employment of import-substitution industrialization in Brazil. Saffiotti found that during the 1950s and 1960s, while women's industrial employment increased overall, their share relative to men in the industrial labour force declined. In her view this was related to Brazil's dependent position in the world economy, which meant that import-substitution industrialization was reliant upon imported large-scale capital-intensive technology which created jobs for men rather than women.

But by no means all feminists agreed with Boserup. By the end of the 1970s there was a strong body of feminist opinion that identified the problem not in terms of exclusion of women from development but in terms of the ways in which women were incorporated into development. Benería and Sen (1981, 1982) argued that the key concept is subordination rather than exclusion and marginalization; and that women's subordination can take a wide variety of different forms because capitalist modernization takes a wide variety of different forms (plantations, small commercial farms, labour-intensive or capital-intensive technologies, and export-oriented or import-substitution industrialization). Women's disadvantage in new forms of paid work is not primarily the result of traditional cultural practices and prejudices, but of the way in which the new forms of production create insecure and hierarchical job structures. Benería and Sen also criticized Boserup for ignoring the crucial significance of reproductive work, (that is, the unpaid work in households and communities that is necessary to reproduce the labour force and the social fabric) and the need to focus on changing the way that production and reproduction are articulated. Without this, women would always be disadvantaged by having to do the bulk of unpaid reproductive work, as well as work in paid production.

Similar themes were also central to the analysis produced in the late 1970s by the Subordination of Women Group at the Institute of Development Studies, University of Sussex. The SOW Group made a significant contribution by promoting a multidisciplinary approach, in which economists such as Diane Elson, Maureen Mackintosh and Ruth Pearson worked with political scientists, such as Maxine Molyneux, and anthropologists, such as Kate Young, Penelope Roberts and Ann Whitehead, to analyse how both marriage and the market would need to be transformed if the subordination of women were to be ended (Young *et al.* 1981).

They argued that gender subordination takes many forms, and that new forms may be created as old ones fade away. For example, Elson and Pearson (1981) analysed female labour-intensive export-oriented industrialization, not as an inter-sectoral labour transfer, but as an interplay of conflicting tendencies: a tendency to *intensify* the existing forms of gender subordination; a tendency to *decompose* existing forms of gender subordination; and a tendency to *recompose* new forms of gender subordination. While policies to promote the expansion of employment in export factories did not in any simple way liberate women, the interplay of these tendencies opened up a space for women to act collectively to improve their conditions as wage workers and as members of household communities, and to build co-operation and solidarity between women.

The terrain on which feminists had to engage with development theory shifted in the 1980s. Planning for development was replaced by liberalization and privatization. The economics of development became dominated by neoclassical economics which identified the main obstacle to development as policy-induced price distortions, such as over-valued exchange rates, import controls and credit controls. It was argued that deregulation of the economy would remove such distortions and promote both growth and improved standards of living (for a guide to this shift, see Toye 1987). This theory was put into practice via IMF stabilization policies and World Bank structural adjustment policies, which made devaluation, decontrol and deflation conditions for the receipt of the funds that governments of developing countries urgently needed to enable them to service the debt they incurred in the late 1970s in the aftermath of the quadrupling of oil prices.

Nevertheless, a concern with the inter-sectoral transfer of labour continued – but now as a transfer from the non-tradable sector to the tradable sector. (The non-tradable sector includes all public sector and private sector production of goods and services which do not enter international trade – such as education or food for on-farm consumption; the tradable sector includes all production of goods and services which do enter international trade.) This transfer is expected to be brought about by devaluation and deregulation of markets (including import liberalization) (Lal 1988; Edwards 1988). Such a transfer is expected to lead to a reduction in the balance of payments deficit and a higher rate of economic growth (as a result of a lifting of the balance of payments constraint). Unlike the Lewis model, there is no appeal to surplus labour in the macroeconomics of structural adjustment; the development gains are supposed to come not from mobilizing surplus labour, but from reallocating a given stock of fully employed labour (Addison & Demery 1994).

A feminist critique of this theory was presented by Elson (1991) arguing that the theory of structural adjustment implicitly assumes unlimited supplies of female labour, available to make good any shortfalls in provision of public sector non-tradable services (such as health, education, water, sanitation) and to increase production of exports, while at the same time maintaining household food security and the social fabric of family and community networks. Adjustment theory does not confront this implication because it appears to treat labour as a non-produced means of production, and all consumption as discretionary. But since even devotees of structural adjustment do not believe that people can live on fresh air, there is a hidden assumption that whatever is necessary to sustain the given stock of labour will be done. This in practice is largely 'women's work'.

Gendered cultural norms about what is 'men's work' and 'women's work' mean that men's labour tends not to be reallocated to women's work where there is a decrease in what is considered to be men's work and an increase in what is considered to be women's work. Instead, a more likely outcome is unemployment and underemployment for men, and overwork for women. Failure to take this into account in analysing adjustment, argued Elson, results in extra burdens for women, and means that adjustment programmes are unlikely to be able to deliver the growth they promise:

> Ignoring the implications of macro-economic changes for unpaid domestic labour inputs is tantamount to assuming that women's capacity to undertake extra work is infinitely elastic – able to stretch so as to make up for any shortfall in income and resources required for the production and maintenance of human resources. However, women's capacity for work is not infinitely elastic and breaking point may be reached. There may simply not be enough female labour time available to maintain the quality and quantity of human resources at its existing level. This may not have an immediate impact on the level and composition of gross national output, but in the longer run a deterioration in health, nutrition and education will have adverse impacts on output levels.
> (Elson 1991: 179)

There is thus an underlying continuity between theories of development which postulate a transfer from the subsistence or traditional or agricultural sector to the capitalist or modern or industrial sector, and theories of adjustment that postulate a transfer of labour from the non-tradable sector to the tradable sector. Similar questions arise: how will the transfer take place; is extra labour time required and, if so, how is it mobilized; what barriers might obstruct the productive use of labour and the reinvestment of profits so as to increase productivity and living standards? The critique of structural adjustment theory produced by feminist economics has some similarities with parallel critiques by structuralist economics: both emphasize discontinuities and non-substitutability as well as the role of power and cultural norms in structuring the use of resources. However, as Elson (1993) argues, structuralist economics prioritizes social relations of class and ignores the social relations of gender.

In the 1990s there has been a growing concern in feminist contributions with moving beyond critique to the construction of alternative models and analytical tools. For instance, Palmer (1991, 1992) has suggested that price distortions can be caused by gender discrimination as well as by inappropriate government controls. She identified four sources of gender-based price distortion: gender discrimination in access to resources or outlets for produce; the additional tasks women face (and men do not) in reproduction and family maintenance (which Palmer characterizes as a 'reproduction tax' on women which distorts their choice of activities); unequal terms of exchange between men and women within households; and a distribution of income within households that does not provide women with the same incentives as men to respond to new opportunities introduced by structural adjustment programmes. Palmer argued that adjustment programmes do not focus on reducing gender-based price distortions and may even worsen them. She suggested that the persistence of gender-based price distortions will weaken the supply response, especially in smallholder-based agricultural economies, so that adjustment programmes will fail to achieve their growth objectives. Her conclusion was that adjustment programmes should be redesigned to include reduction of gender-based distortions. In particular, fiscal policy should be designed to reduce the 'reproduction tax'.

Further contributions have come from a project on gender, adjustment and macroeconomics which promoted dialogue between feminist economics and non-orthodox macroeconomists (see Çağatay et al. 1995). For instance, Darity (1995) constructed a two-sector model of a gender-segregated low-income agrarian economy, and used it to show how a devaluation of the currency, which raises the relative price of export cash crops, means extra demand for women's labour and extra income for their husbands who control the sale of the crop. The key to women benefiting from an expansion of the cash crop sector is a reduction in the degree of power men exercise over women's labour, and a more equal sharing of the proceeds.

In contrast, Erturk and Çağatay (1995) focused on the investment behaviour of firms and savings behaviour of households in industrializing economies, drawing upon empirical research on patterns of economic development to identify some 'stylized facts' about the degree of feminization of the paid labour force and the extent of women's unpaid household work. They assumed that a rise in the feminization of the labour force stimulates investment by making available a new pool of low-cost and malleable labour, while a rise in the extent of women's unpaid household work is equivalent to an increase in savings because it reduces expenditure on marketed goods. The interaction of these two effects is examined in relation to recovery from economic crisis and recession, and it is concluded that recovery will be dampened if the positive impact of feminization of the paid labour force on investment is weaker than the positive impact of an intensification of women's household work on savings.

Both of these models are highly simplified (as all formal models must be) but they are important as heuristic devices which begin the task of showing how gender-sensitive variables, which capture reproduction as well as production, and power as well as choice, can be incorporated in analysis of how growth and structural change takes place (or fails to take place).

As well as new concepts and models for analysing production and growth, feminist writers have also insisted on the importance of new visions of what development should be. Particularly important have been the writings of an autonomous interregional organization of women from the South – DAWN, standing for Development Alternatives with Women for a New Era – which was set up just prior to the 1985 UN Conference of Women in Nairobi. DAWN emphasized not only gender equality, but also class and race equality, and international equality between countries, and put forward a critique of both states and markets (Sen & Grown 1987; Sen & Heyzer (eds) 1994). There were some parallels between DAWN's concern to articulate a new vision of development and the concept of human development articulated in the *Human Development Report*, published annually since 1990 by the United Nations Development Programme, and drawing its conceptual framework from the concepts of capabilities and entitlements developed by Amartya Sen (Sen 1984). Feminist economists generally welcomed this approach to development theory but were concerned to ensure that it became more gender-sensitive, and to ensure that some critical ambiguities in the concept of human development were resolved in a way that empowered women (DAWN 1995; Elson 1997).

The *Human Development Reports* themselves did become more gender-aware in their analysis and presentation of statistics, devoting an issue (1995) to the struggle for gender equality, and presenting measures of the economic value of women's unpaid reproductive work, and two new indexes of development, the gender-related development index and the gender-empowerment measure. However, the concept of human development has often been narrowly interpreted by international aid agencies as meaning simply an emphasis on investing in health and education as well as in infrastructure and equipment – investment in human capital as well as in physical capital. In this way, human development has been assimilated into the dominant model of adjustment and liberalization, and labour is still viewed as a factor of production and development a process of inter-sectoral reallocation of this factor, and the enhancement of its productivity (see, for instance, World Bank 1991).

Moreover, while the *Human Development Reports* themselves have stressed that people should not be regarded as simply factors of production (the means to an end) but as ends in themselves, Elson (1997) points out there is a lack of clarity in the Reports about the conditions under which this is possible. In particular, the fact that markets may be coercive as well as enabling is not fully confronted. DAWN (1995) argues for redefining and engendering human development, stressing values of self-realization together with sharing and reciprocity (DAWN 1995: 23). The challenge for feminist economics is to help translate this into a practical strategy. This will require more analysis of how both states and markets (national and international) can be transformed; of how new forms of property right that emphasize stewardship rather than ownership can be created; and of how forms of mutually supportive organization of production and reproduction can be created. A fruitful approach may be to reconceptualize development not as a transfer of labour between sectors, but as an interactive and contradictory process, in which there is potential (albeit often suppressed) for the transformation of labour from the object to the subject of the process, and for the creation of the conditions for women to truly be agents of their own development.

References

Addison, T. and L. Demery (1994), 'The Poverty Effects of Adjustment with Labor Market Imperfections', in S. Horton, R. Kanbar and D. Mazumdar (eds), *Labor Markets in an Era of Adjustment*, 147–93. Washington, DC: World Bank.

Benería, L. and G. Sen (1981), 'Accumulation, reproduction and women's role in economic development', *Signs: Journal of Women in Cultural and Society* 7(2), 279–98.

Benería, L. and G. Sen (1982), 'Class and gender inequalities and women's role in economic development – theoretical and practical implications', *Feminist Studies* 8(1), 157–76.

Boserup, E. (1970), *Women's Role in Economic Development*. New York: St Martin's Press.

Çağatay, N., D. Elson and C. Grown (eds) (1995), *Gender, Adjustment and Macroeconomics*. Special Issue of *World Development* 23(11).

Darity, W. (1995), 'The formal structure of a gender-segregated low-income economy', *World Development* 23(11), 1963–8.

DAWN (1995), *Markers on the Way: The DAWN Debates on Alternative Development*. Barbados: Women and Development Unit, University of West Indies.

Edwards, S. (1988), 'Terms of trade, tariffs and labor market adjustment in developing countries', *World Bank Economic Review* 2, 165–85.

Elson, D. (1991), 'Male Bias in Macroeconomics: The Case of Structural Adjustment', in D. Elson (ed.), *Male Bias in the Development Process*, 164–90. Manchester: Manchester University Press.

Elson, D. (1993), 'Gender aware analysis and development economics', *Journal of International Development* 5(2), 237–47.

Elson, D. (1997), 'Economic Paradigms Old and New: The Case of Human Development', in A. Berry, R. Culpepper and F. Stewart (eds), *Global Governance and Development Fifty Years After Bretton Woods*, 50–71. London: Macmillan.

Elson, D. and R. Pearson (1981), 'The Subordination of Women and the Internationalisation of Factory Production', in K. Young, C. Wolkowitz and R. McCullagh (eds), *Of Marriage and the Market: Women's Subordination in International Perspective*, 144–66. London: CSE Books.

Erturk, K. and N. Çağatay (1995), 'Macroeconomic consequences of cyclical and secular changes in feminization: an experiment in gendered macromodeling', *World Development*, 23(11), 1969–77.

Frank, A. (1966), 'The development of underdevelopment', *Monthly Review*, 18(4), September, 17–31.

Kabeer, N. (1994), *Reversed Realities: Gender Hierarchies in Development Thought*. London: Verso.

Lal, D. (1983), *The Poverty of 'Development Economics'*. London: Institute of Economic Affairs.

Lal, D. (1985), 'The misconceptions of "development economics"', *Finance and Development* 22 (June), 10–13.

Lal, D. (1988), 'A simple framework for analyzing various real aspects of stabilization and structural adjustment policies', *Journal of Development Studies* 25 (April), 291–312.

Lewis, W. (1954), 'Economic development with unlimited supplies of labour', *Manchester School* 22(2), 139–91.

Lewis, W. (1955), *The Theory of Economic Growth*. London: Allen & Unwin.

Palma, G. (1978), 'Dependency: a formal theory of underdevelopment or a methodology for the analysis of concrete situations of underdevelopment', *World Development* 6(7/8), 881–924.

Palmer, I. (1991), *Gender and Population in the Adjustment of African Economics: Planning for Change*. Geneva: ILO.

Palmer, I. (1992), 'Gender Equity and Economic Efficiency in Adjustment Programmes', in H. Afshar and C. Dennis (eds), *Women and Adjustment Policies in the Third World*, 69–83. London: Macmillan.

Pearson, R. (1992), 'Gender Issues in Industrialisation', in T. Hewitt, H. Johnson and D. Wield (eds), *Industrialization and Development*, 222–47. Oxford: Oxford University Press.

Prebisch, R. (1950), *The Economic Development of Latin America and its Principal Problems*, New York: United Nations.

Rostow, W. W. (1960), *Stages of Economic Growth*, Cambridge: Cambridge University Press.

Saffiotti, H. (1978), *Women in Class Society*, New York: Monthly Review Press.

Sen, A. (1975), *Employment, Technology and Development*, Oxford: Clarendon Press.

Sen, A. (1983), 'Development: Which way now?', *Economic Journal*, 93, 745–62.

Sen, A. (1984), *Resources, Values and Development*, Oxford: Blackwell.

Sen, G. and C. Grown (eds) (1987), *Development, Crises and Alternative Visions: Third World Women's Perspectives*, New York: Monthly Review Press.

Sen, G. and N. Heyzer (eds) (1994), *Gender, Economic Growth and Poverty: Market Growth and State Planning in Asia and the Pacific*, New Delhi: Kali for Women,

Singer, H. (1950), 'The Distribution of gains between borrowing and investing countries', *American Economic Review*, 40 (2) (Papers and Proceedings), 470–85.

Tinker, I. (1990), 'A Context for the Field and the Book', in I. Tinker (ed.), *Persistent Inequalities: Women and World Development*, Oxford: Oxford University Press, 27–53.

Toye, J. (1987), *Dilemmas of Development*, Oxford: Blackwell.

United Nations Development Programme (1990–98), *Human Development Report*, Oxford: Oxford University Press.

Weeks, J. (1970), 'The political economy of labor transfer', *Science and Society*, 1, 463–80.

World Bank (1991), World Development Report, Oxford: Oxford University Press.

Young, K., C. Wolkowitz and R. McCullagh (eds) (1981), *Of Marriage and the Market: Women's Subordination in International Perspective*, London: CSE Books.

3

MALE BIAS IN THE DEVELOPMENT PROCESS: AN OVERVIEW

Books about women in development have been a necessary stage in making gender relations visible in the development process, but posing the issue in terms of women in development has several limitations. It facilitates the view that 'women', as a general category, can be added to an existing approach to analysis and policy, and that this will be sufficient to change development outcomes so as to improve women's position. It facilitates the view that 'women's issues' can be tackled in isolation from women's relation to men. It may even give rise to the feeling that the problem is women rather than the disadvantages women face; and that women are unreasonably asking for special treatment rather than for redress for injustices and for removal of distortions which limit their capacities. It tends to encourage the treatment of women as a homogeneous group with the same interests and viewpoint everywhere. It is necessary to move on from 'women in development' to approaches that emphasise gender relations.

Gender relations are the socially determined relations that differentiate male and female situations. People are born biologically female or male, but have to acquire a gender identity. Gender relations refer to the gender dimension of the social relations structuring the lives of individual men and women, such as the gender division of labour and the gender division of access to and control over resources. An emphasis on gender highlights the fact that work is gendered; that some tasks are seen as 'women's work', to do which is demeaning for men; while other tasks are 'men's work', to do which unsexes women. An emphasis on gender relations encourages a questioning of the supposed unity of the household and facilitates the posing of questions about the relative power of women and men.

There is a wealth of evidence demonstrating the differences in power between women and men throughout the world. It is not that women are powerless victims or that no women are in positions of power over men, but rather that, relatively speaking, women are less powerful than men of similar economic and social position. A graphic example is the risk of sexual violence faced by any woman who finds herself alone in a public place at night. The rich woman whose car has

THE DIANE ELSON READER

broken down is in the same position as the poor woman waiting for a bus. They are both at risk because they are breaking a gender norm, the norm that 'respectable' women should not be alone at night in public places. In breaking this norm they can be perceived as legitimate targets, as 'asking for it'. Men too may risk violence on the streets, but mugging has a quite different significance from rape.

A gender approach has greater flexibility than a women-in-development approach. For instance, an emphasis on gender relations tends to permit greater awareness of the different ways that different women experience gender. Though rich and poor women both face a common danger of rape if they are alone in a public place after dark, poor women have more of an interest in improvements in public transport than do rich women.

The asymmetry between male and female gender can be expressed in terms of the language of gender subordination: the idea that women as a gender are subordinate to men as a gender. But this language focuses on structures rather than agents. It can obscure individual responsibility and suggest the presence of immovable social forces in whose operation we can only acquiesce. It can even be used to justify the denial of equal opportunities to women, as in the case of *Equal Opportunity Commission v. Sears, Roebuck & Co.* in the USA (Kessler-Harris 1987).[1] Women active in grass-roots feminist activities, such as Women's Aid and Rape Crisis Centres, have suggested to me that it is also a language which is too academic, too sanitised, too polite. It is time to stop talking about gender subordination and start talking about male bias.

Male bias

Talk of bias can be simply emotive, so it is certainly necessary to think carefully about criteria for use of the term. There are some precedents for using it in examining development issues, most notably the term 'urban bias' (Lipton 1977). Whatever reservations one has about the explanatory power of 'urban bias', there is no doubt that it served to mobilise analysis and policy to address the important question of rural-urban inequality. An essential contribution to its mobilising ability was the way it combined the flavour of condemnation of the word 'bias' with appeals to objective criteria and empirical evidence. It is in the same spirit that I shall use the term 'male bias'.

By *male* bias I mean a bias that operates in favour of men as a gender, and against women as a gender, not that all men are biased against women. Some

---

1. Sears, Roebuck & Co. argued that they were not guilty of discrimination against women. Rather, the gender structure of society meant that women did not offer themselves for certain types of job.

men have contributed substantially to the diagnosis and understanding of male bias and have campaigned to overcome it. Some women show little understanding of the operation of male bias and do much to perpetuate it. To emphasise this point, in what follows I shall draw on the work of a male economist, A. K. Sen, who has provided some useful conceptual tools for the elucidation of male bias. Nevertheless, on the whole women are more likely to recognise the significance of male bias, and to wish to combat it, than are men. But this is a matter of differences in the experience of women and men, not of differences in some essential femininity or masculinity.

What is bias? It is asymmetry that is ill-founded or unjustified. There is no problem in demonstrating gender asymmetry in the outcomes of development processes, in the lived experience of women and men throughout the world; the arguments are about the extent to which such asymmetry is ill-founded and unjustified. No attempt will be made here to review the enormous literature depicting gender asymmetry in developing countries. A useful overview of the literature and summary of key features of gender relations in the major regions of the Third World is provided by Brydon and Chant (1989). Compilations of statistical evidence can be found in United Nations publications, from organisations like the International Labour Office (ILO/INSTRAW 1985) and the Department of International Economic and Social Affairs (UN 1986). But there remains a question of interpretation. How far do the asymmetries represent male bias, and how far difference and complementarity?

Male bias in development outcomes

The first point that must be tackled is the issue of the benchmark against which bias in development outcomes is to be judged. What counts as lack of bias? Equal treatment of equals? But equal in what respects? Different people in different situations have different needs and different talents. Removing bias does not mean complete standardisation and removal of all differences. One approach to defining bias is in terms of differences which are not the result of differences in endowments and preferences. This is the procedure favoured by neo-classical economists setting up models of the labour market and the household (for example, Becker 1981). Such models tend to downplay the prevalence of bias through using oversimple, uncritical notions of endowments and preferences.

Aptitudes that are often ascribed to endowments, such as women's supposedly 'nimble fingers', may be due to the upbringing women have received at home and at school, which trains them in sewing and in repetitive sorting tasks (like tidying up and separating grains of rice from stones and husks), and emphasises the virtues of patience and endurance of routine (Elson & Pearson 1981). It is virtually impossible to separate out endowments from acquired characteristics for a wide range of attributes (Block & Dworkin (eds) 1977). Levels of nutrition before birth can have an impact on subsequent achievements. Characteristics that are unproblematically genetic endowments, such as eye colour, are those which are least interesting from the point of view of explaining social outcomes. Part of the problem of male bias is that it tends to hamper women from acquiring those characteristics which are well-rewarded in the market; and that it tends to hamper social scientists from understanding the limitations of notions of male and female endowments of aptitudes or talents.

If innate aptitudes cannot be taken for granted, neither can well-defined individual preferences. Sen argues that family identity may exert such a strong influence on the perceptions of rural Indian women that they find it unintelligible to think in terms of their own preferences and welfare. Instead, they think in terms of the welfare of their families (Sen 1987). This is a theme which has also run through much feminist literature on women's consciousness in developed countries. Part of the problem of male bias is that it tends to hamper women from forming well-defined notions of what they want; women submerge their own interests beneath those of men and children.

Instead of judging bias against endowments and preferences, it may be judged against rights and capabilities (Sen 1984: ch. 13). Equal rights have been a rallying cry for many women's movements, and in many countries women have won a substantial measure of legal equality. But even in countries where equal rights for women are enshrined in the constitution, women find enormous difficulties in exercising those rights. Key rights for poor rural women, such as rights to land, have no practical purchase because land rights are vested in household heads: that is, in men, unless there are no adult males in the household (Jiggins 1988). Key rights for poor urban women, such as equal pay, have no purchase because women are concentrated in the informal sector where legislation does not reach, or in female ghettos in the formal sector where there is no male standard with which to establish equality (Joekes 1987). Moreover, entitlement systems, governing who can have use of what, which regulate market transactions, typically do not regulate intra-household resource distribution (Sen 1987). Thus, an emphasis on rights has to be supplemented by an emphasis on socially conferred capabilities – what are women in practice able to do? Are they able to be well-nourished; to enjoy good health and long lives; to read and write; to participate freely in the public sphere; to have some time to themselves; to enjoy dignity and self-esteem? How does women's enjoyment of these capabilities compare with that of men? Do women face constraints which are not faced by men? In so far as women enjoy fewer and more circumscribed capabilities than do men, then there is male bias in development outcomes. Constraints on women operate to men's advantage in the short run, as in bargaining within the household (discussed below). Male bias exists even if women do not manifest any lesser satisfaction with their lot in life than do men. As Sen points out: "There is much evidence in history that acute inequalities often survive precisely by making allies out of the deprived. The underdog comes to accept the legitimacy of the unequal order and becomes an implicit accomplice. It can be a serious error to take the absence of protests and questioning of inequality as evidence of the absence of that inequality" (Sen 1987: 3). Sen's argument has force with respect to any kind of inequality, and in emphasising male bias I do not intend to imply that it is the only important form of bias. Class bias, regional bias, urban bias, racial and ethnic bias, are all important; and the different kinds of bias are imbricated with one another, forming differentiable but not separated aspects of a whole lived situation for any individual. Thus all women do not face the same kind and same degree of male bias; and they may enjoy the fruits of other kinds of bias, or share the deprivations, with men in the same class, region, ethnic group.

What perhaps is unique about male bias is that those who are disadvantaged by it live daily in intimate personal relationships with those who are advantaged by it. The relationship between women and men living together in households has been usefully depicted by Sen (1985, 1987) in terms of co-operative conflicts. Women and men gain from co-operating with one another in joint living arrangements in so far as this increases the capabilities of the household as a whole; but the division of the fruits of co-operation is a source of conflict. Women are at a disadvantage in bargaining over the division of the fruits of co-operation because their fall-back position tends to be worse. That is, if no bargain is struck, and women are on their own, without husband, father, brother or other male relative to co-operate with, they tend to be worse off, in terms of capabilities, than if they agree to strike a bargain and enter into some kind of co-operation with men. The evidence of the poverty of female-headed households is overwhelming testimony to the weakness of women's fall-back position. However, co-operative conflicts between people of different genders are more than simple bargaining problems because of the gender differentiation in the specification of preferences discussed earlier. As a result of an upbringing shaped by male bias, women tend not to have such sharp perceptions as men of their own interests, needs, rights or deserts. And this perpetuates male bias, because the co-operative arrangement arrived at is likely to be less favourable to those individuals with less well-defined perceptions of their own interests.

Male bias is contradictory in that while it preserves the subordination of women as a gender to men, it also has costs for society considered as a whole. For instance, male bias distorts resource allocation by denying women adequate access to productive inputs. This lowers women's productivity and reduces total output in comparison with what could be achieved if resource allocation were free of gender distortion (Palmer 1988). Thus male bias is a barrier to the achievement of development objectives such as growth of output. So why don't more men show eagerness to overcome male bias? Perhaps it is because the disadvantages of relinquishing male power are more immediately apparent, while the distribution of the gains is uncertain and the transition period may be painful. If women's productivity is enhanced because male bias in resource allocation is reduced, total output may rise, but so may women's bargaining power. The total size of the cake may increase, but men's share of it may fall.

The proximate causes of male bias in development outcomes

The proximate causes of male bias in development outcomes can be analysed in terms of male bias in everyday attitudes and actions, in theoretical reasoning, and in public policy. The underlying supports of male bias are to be found in the particular ways in which getting a living is integrated with raising children.

Male bias in everyday attitudes and actions may be the result of prejudice and discrimination at the conscious level, but this is not necessarily the case. Bias may be deeply embedded in unconscious perceptions and habits, the result of oversight, faulty assumptions, a failure to ask questions. For instance, women's contribution to family income tends to be overlooked because much of it is unpaid or takes the form of repetitive services rather than products that can be massed together in an unmistakable sign of contribution made. As a result, women tend to be regarded as less deserving than men when it comes to intra-household distribution (Sen 1987). Such unconscious bias is not unreachable and unchangeable. People can be brought to recognise it through education, consciousness-raising groups, politicisation, social change. Domitila Barrios de Chungara, a women's leader and miner's wife in a tin-mining community in Bolivia, explains how she went about doing this:

> But in spite of everything we do, there's still the idea that women don't work, because they don't contribute economically to the home, that only the husband works because he gets a wage. We've often come across that difficulty.
>
> One day I got the idea of making a chart. We put as an example the price (>1 washing clothes per dozen pieces and we figured out how many dozens of items we washed a month. Then the cook's wage, the babysitter's, the servant's. We figured out everything that we miners' wives do every day.Adding it all up, the wage needed to pay us for what we do in the home, compared to the wages of a cook, a washerwoman, a babysitter, a servant, was much higher than what the men earned in

the mine for a month. So that way we made our *compañeros* [husbands] understand that we really work, and even more than they do in a certain sense.   (Johnson & Bernstein (eds) 1982: 235)

However, conscious and unconscious male bias in thought and action is frequently buttressed by economic and social structures which make such practices seem rational, even to those who are disadvantaged by them. Thus it can seem entirely rational for mothers to allocate more food to sons than to daughters when food is short, in circumstances where sons are more valuable, socially and materially, than daughters; and where future survival of the household depends crucially on survival of sons to adulthood, then it can seem entirely rational to prioritise their needs and neglect those of daughters. Such behaviour is acclaimed by neo-classical economists as evidence that their harmonious 'joint utility' models of the household are correct (Rosenzweig 1986), though it can equally well be explained in terms of a co-operative conflicts model (Folbre 1986). But the important point is that although actions that perpetuate male bias are rational from the point of view of a highly constrained individual, they do not testify to the overall rationality, much less desirability, of the social system. Rather, they suggest that the constraints on individuals need to be changed through some collective process. In the absence of such a process, individual women will certainly find it rational to do things that perpetuate male bias. This has been recognised by careful thinkers about individual choice and well-being, such as Sen, who points out that:

> Deprived groups may be habituated to inequality, may be unaware of possibilities of social change, may be hopeless about upliftment of objective circumstances of misery, may be resigned to one's fate, and may be willing to accept the legitimacy of the established order. The tendency to take pleasure in small mercies would make good sense given these perceptions, and cutting desires to shape (in line with perceived feasibility) can help to save one from serious disappointment and frustration.   (Sen 1987: 9)

Male bias in theoretical reasoning may often not be so immediately apparent because the reasoning is presented in terms which appear to be gender neutral. Rather than talking about women and men, and sons and daughters, use is made of abstract concepts like the economy, the formal sector, the informal sector, the labour force, the household. Or the argument is conducted in terms of socio-economic categories which, on the face of it, include both women and men, such as 'farmer', and 'worker'. It is only on closer analysis that it becomes apparent that these supposedly neutral terms are in fact imbued with male bias, presenting a view of the world that both obscures and legitimates ill-founded gender asymmetry, in which to be male is normal, but to be female is deviant. This is more immediately apparent in analysis conducted in terms of socio-economic groups, where we soon read of 'farmers and their wives' and 'workers and their wives' but never of 'farmers and their husbands' and 'workers and their husbands', despite the fact that large numbers of women are farmers or wage-earners in their own right.

Let us examine this more closely using the example of the category 'farmer'. Though this appears to be a gender-neutral category, it is used in a way that implies farmers are men; this suggests that major decision-making and farm management is undertaken by men, while women serve as unpaid family labour, helping their husbands. While this may be true of some areas, and some types of farming, we have enough case study data to know that it is certainly not universally true. Many countries in sub-Saharan Africa have large numbers of women who farm in their own right, either because of a high incidence of female-headed households in rural areas (as in Botswana, Lesotho, Sierra Leone and Zambia, for instance), or because there is a traditional demarcation of crops into men's crops' and 'women's crops' (as in Cameroon, Ghana and Malawi) (FAO 1986). Outside Africa, women are more likely to be managing post-harvest activities, such as processing, storage and marketing, than managing production of staple crops; or managing livestock-related activities or horticulture. But whatever the differences in the particular activities undertaken, the point remains that many women in agriculture do undertake management responsibilities.

The picture of farmers as men disadvantages women farmers and hinders attempts to improve agricultural productivity. When there is an implicit assumption that farmers are men, it is not surprising if new agricultural technology and inputs flow mainly to men – and there is a wealth of evidence that this is what has happened in developing countries over the last three decades. Despite the attempts of concerned researchers to make rural women 'visible' to policymakers in the 1970s, most rural projects up to the early '80s still addressed women through welfare and home economics programmes for farmers' wives. Governments still fail to collect comprehensive, reliable and unbiased statistics on the contribution women make to agricultural production (Safilios-Rothschild 1987). But we know from village-level studies that when resources are redirected to women there are increases in agricultural productivity and efficiency (Jiggins 1987; Staudt 1987).

To see the male bias in analysis which is conducted in terms of abstract categories, we have to examine the implicit assumptions structuring the definition and use of the abstract categories. Is there a hidden assumption about the homogeneity of sectors of the economy regardless of gender? For instance, is it assumed that surplus labour can be withdrawn from agricultural production because those left behind will be able to make up any shortfall, without considering the division of agricultural tasks into 'men's tasks' and 'women's tasks'? This does seem to be the implicit assumption in many dual-sector models of development – including Sen's (Sen 1966). Ignoring the gender division of labour may result in failure to consider the overloading of women and reduction in agricultural productivity that male migration from the rural sector may induce. Is there a hidden assumption about the costs of reproduction of labour power and who bears them? Most models of the economy treat labour, like land, as an unproduced factor of production. In effect, there is an implicit assumption that the necessary inputs of time and effort required to ensure its continuing supply will be forthcoming even though these inputs are unpaid. These inputs are, of course, disproportionately supplied by women in their roles as wives, mother and daughters, ministering to the needs of other family members. Time budget studies from around the world show that these activities are undertaken by most women in addition to activities that are counted as 'economic' (Goldschmidt-Clermont 1987). Women have far less leisure than men because of this 'double day'. Ignoring women's unpaid domestic work obscures both the burdens women bear and the constraints this work places upon women's capacity to respond to opportunities for paid work. There is no intrinsic reason why the work of caring for others should not be shared equally between women and men. But a reduction in this asymmetry is unlikely while male bias continues to deny the economic contribution such work makes.

Is there a hidden assumption about the benevolence of the ties that bind households together? The household is in some sense a social unit, but can we assume it is a unity? The models of the household constructed by neo-classical economists do assume unity, implying, for instance, that the welfare of household members can be judged on the basis of aggregate household income, and that extra income accruing to one household member will 'trickle down' to others. But a growing volume of case-study evidence supports alternative models, such as Sen's co-operative conflict model. They suggest a picture of a home divided over income and expenditure decisions (Dwyer & Bruce (eds) 1988). Households are in some sense pooling and sharing organisations but to imply that this pooling and sharing is unproblematic is to reveal male bias. There is considerable evidence to suggest that while women typically pool and share their income, especially with their children, men are more inclined to reserve part of their income for discretionary personal spending (*ibid.*). Uncritical theorisation of existing forms of family life is a barrier to securing real reciprocity. (Overcoming male bias does not mean the disintegration of pooling and sharing of resources between women and men. Rather, it means more extensive pooling and sharing and a disintegration of unjust gender asymmetries in family relationships).

When supposed gender neutrality masks male bias, this serves to obscure the distribution of costs and benefits of development processes between men

and women. It also serves to obscure the barriers that gender asymmetries constitute to the successful realisation of many development policy objectives. To
overcome such bias, it is not enough to affix 'women' as an afterthought. For
that tends to obscure the differences between different groups of women, and
to perpetuate the gender blindness of analytical concepts. What is needed is
a gender-aware conceptualisation in the first place. Otherwise, male bias will
remain even though 'women' are present.

Male bias in development policy is encouraged by male bias in everyday attitudes and practices and by male bias in analysis, reinforced by male bias in politics.
Until the late 1970s women were hugely invisible to policy-makers, whose perspective might be summed up in the old Russian proverb: 'I thought I saw two people
coming down the road, but it was only a man and his wife'. Women were treated
merely as dependents of men. Development objectives were disaggregated on a
household basis and it was assumed that resources targeted to men would equally
benefit dependent women and children. For a variety of reasons, including the
advocacy of 'women in development' experts, and the breakdown of family support systems leading to increases in the numbers of femaleheaded households in
dire poverty, by the end of the '70s women had become visible to policy-makers –
but as recipients of welfare benefits rather than as producers and agents of development. There was a proliferation of special women's projects, many of which failed
to become self-supporting because of lack of gender awareness in their design,
perpetuating the idea of women as a drain on the public purse (Buvinic 1986).

In the 1980s more attention has been paid to women as agents of development, but as agents of social development whose caring and nurturing could
substitute for expenditure on health, education and social services (Antrobus
1988; Dwyer & Bruce (eds) 1988). Moreover, there remains the problem of
male bias in the policy process itself. With few exceptions, women's interests
are marginalised in the formulation and implementation of economic policy
(Moser 1989). Women's voices play little part. At the grassroots level, there are
frequently factors that inhibit women from speaking out in public meetings. A
study of women and village government in ten villages in Tanzania in 1981 found
that village officials gave the following reasons for women's low attendance at village meetings: women are still too shy to attend public meetings; women are too
busy at home to come; it is not the woman's job to roam and survey the village
and attend things like meetings – it is her job to watch the house; women can't
speak Kiswahili; women are uneducated; women don't understand the discussions; it's difficult for a woman to get a pass from the house to come; only one
person from a household need come, so it is always the man; women don't need
to come because we ask the men to tell them what we have discussed; women are
not used to sitting together with men; there are still some men here who don't
like to see women in meetings (Wiley 1985: 170).

In the corridors of power there are relatively few women. The experience of women's bureaux and ministries of women's affairs is particularly discouraging, as they tend to be underresourced, overstretched and cut off from the economic policy-making process (Gordon 1984). Development objectives are defined in practice in ways that are more beneficial to men than to women. Thus in practice it is not more food output *per se* that tends to be sought, but more of the kind of food output which is produced under the direction and control of men (for examples, see Mblinyi 1988); not more private trading *per se* but more of the kind of private trading undertaken by men – large scale and capital intensive – rather than the kind of trading undertaken by women – localised and with a quick turnover (for an example from Ghana, see Loxley 1988).

That is not to claim that male policy-makers deliberately define objectives in terms that benefit men more than women, but rather that they tend to see as in the general interest policies that in practice are male-biased, and to perceive policies that reduce gender asymmetry as female-biased.

The underlying supports of male bias

I have discussed the proximate causes of male-biased development outcomes in terms of male bias in everyday attitudes and decisions, in theoretical analysis, and in the process of defining and implementing public policy. Underlying these individual and collective acts are structural factors that circumscribe and shape them. The key structural factor is not the way in which getting a living is organised, nor the way that raising children is organised, but the way these two processes are interrelated.

The crucial question is how children, and those people engaged in raising children, get their living. Do they have an entitlement to the necessary resources in their own right? Or are they dependent on other family members to secure access to the required resources? It would be possible for children and those engaged in caring for them to have an adequate independent entitlement through independent access to a basic minimum income paid to all members of society regardless of the work they do;[2] or through independent access to adequate earning opportunities coupled with adequate child care facilities But this would require the integration of getting a living and raising children not being confined to the family; it would require integration through social provision and the mediation of organisations in the public sphere; it would require access to a basic minimum

---

2. Such an entitlement differs from most existing welfare state provisions by being unconditional and paid to individuals. For more discussion of this issue, see the Bulletin of the Basic Income Research Group.

income as of right, to be independent of family circumstances. Such an entitlement is extremely rare. In practice, most children and those caring for them are either dependent on other family members for access to income or resources, or, when there is no one to depend on, they suffer poverty and deprivation because of difficulties in combining child care and income-generating activities. Relief may be available through charities or state welfare schemes but this relief is generally not an absolute entitlement and creates a new form of dependence. The opportunity to earn an income through selling labour or products in the market may seem to offer independence to women. But in practice this independence is open only to a small minority. For the market does not provide adequate and affordable child care facilities for most women, and does not guarantee them an adequate income. On the whole, markets tend to lead to the concentration of income in the hands of those who start off with most resources. Unless markets are socially regulated they offer only the semblance of independence for women, and not the reality (Elson 1989). The lack of an independent and secure entitlement creates a bias operating against those people who have the task of child care and weakens their bargaining position in the co-operative conflicts of the family.

The desire for an independent entitlement is not confined to well-educated feminists. A study of ten villages in Tanzania in the early 1980s reports the following comments as typical of those made by village women about their situation:

> 'Now we are sitting in meetings, but my husband can still beat me if I complain. We are still dependent on men.'
> 'Women are still the same because the money belongs to the husband still.' 'A man can still refuse you anything because he owns all the things.'
> 'Our main problem here is that the men are drinking our money and we have no way to get more.'
> 'In my opinion it would be better if the Council gave every woman one acre for herself.'   (Wiley 1985: 171)

The lack of an independent entitlement for children and those who care for them tells against women. It gets women 'locked in' to child care. There are some phases of raising children which physically have to be undertaken by women – pregnancy, childbirth, breast-feeding – but the rest could be undertaken by men too. However, if lack of an independent entitlement forces women into dependence for these phases of child-rearing, phases which are particularly difficult to combine with income-earning, then women are likely to get locked in to all the other phases. Dependence and its associated lack of bargaining power at one stage are transmitted to later stages. The winners of a co-operative conflict in one round have enhanced bargaining power for the future. The transmission can also work intergenerationally, perpetuating asymmetry over time (Sen 1987).

It is biology that creates the initial link between women and children; but it is the socially determined lack of entitlement that turns this link into the underpinning of male bias.

Overcoming male bias is not simply a matter of persuasion, argument and changes in viewpoint in everyday attitudes, in theoretical reasoning and in the policy process. It also requires changes in the deep structures of economic and social life, and collective action not simply individual action. It requires profound changes in the way that raising children and getting a living are integrated, so as to make maternity economically autonomous. Marriage clearly cannot do this; and existing forms of market opportunity and state provision have not done it either.

References

Antrobus, P. (1988), 'Consequences and responses to social and economic deterioration: the experience of the English-speaking Caribbean', Workshop on Economic Crisis, Household Strategies, and Women's Work, Cornell University.

Becker, G. (1981), *A Treatise on the Family.* Cambridge, MA: Harvard University Press.

Block, N., and Dworkin, G. (eds), (1977), *The IQ Controversy.* London: Quartet Books.

Brydon, L., and Chant, S. (1989), *Women in the Third World.* Aldershot: Edward Elgar.

Buvinic, M. (1986), 'Projects for women in the Third World: explaining their misbehaviour', *World Development* 14(5).

Dwyer, D., and Bruce, J. (eds) (1988), *A Home Divided: Women and Income in the Third World.* Stanford, CA: Stanford University Press.

Elson, D., and Pearson, R. (1981), "'Nimble fingers make cheap workers": an analysis of women's employment in Third World export manufacturing', *Feminist Review* 7.

Elson. D. (1989), 'The impact of structural adjustment on women: concepts and issues', in B. Onimode (ed.), *The IMF, the World Bank mid the African Debt,* vol. 2: *The Social and Political Impact.* London: Zed Books.

Folbre, N. (1986), 'Cleaning house: new perspectives on households and economic development', *Journal of Development Economics* 22.

FAO (1986), *Report of the Workshop on Improving Statistics on Women in Agriculture* 21–23 October, Rome.

Goldschmidt-Clermont, L. (1987), *Economic Evaluations of Unpaid Household Work: Africa, Asia, Latin America and Oceania.* Geneva: International Labour Office.

Gordon, S. (1984), *Ladies in Limbo.* London: Commonwealth Secretariat.

ILO/INSTRAW(1985), *Women in Economic Activity: A Global Statistical Survey (1950–2000).* Geneva: International Labour Office.

Jiggins, J. (1987), '*Gender-Related Impacts and the Work of the International Agricultural Research Centers*', CGIAR Study Paper No. 17. Washington, DC: World Bank.

Jiggins, J. (1988), 'Women and land in sub-Saharan Africa', Rural Employment Policies Branch, Employment and Development Department, International Labour Office, Geneva.

Joekes, S. (1987), *Women in the World Economy: an Instraw Study.* New York: Oxford University Press.

Johnson, H. and Bernstein, H. (eds) (1982), *Third World Lives of Struggle.* London: Heinemann.

Kessler-Harris, A. (1987), '*Equal Opportunity Commission v. Sears, Roebuck & Co.*: a personal account', *Feminist Review* 25.

Lipton. M. (1977), *Why Poor People Stay Poor – Urban Bias in World Development.* London: Temple Smith.

Loxley, J. (1988), *Ghana: Economic Crisis and the Long Road to Recovery*. Ottawa: North-South Institute.

Mbilinyi, M. (1988), 'Agribusiness and women peasants in Tanzania', *Development and Change* 19, 549–83.

Moser, C. (1989), 'Gender planning in the Third World: meeting practical and strategic gender needs', *World Development* 19(11).

Palmer, I. (1988), 'Gender Issues in Structural Adjustment of Sub-Saharan African Agriculture and Some Demographic Implications', Population and Labour Policies Programme, Working Paper No. 166. Geneva: International Labour Organisation.

Rosenzweig, M. (1986), 'Program interventions, intra-household distribution and the welfare of individuals: modelling household behaviour', *World Development* 14(2).

Safilios-Rothschild, C. (1987), 'Women in Agriculture: the need for sex-segregated data', in Ministry of Agriculture and Fisheries of the Netherlands, *Operational Strategies for Reaching Women in Agriculture*. The Hague.

Sen, A. K. (1966), 'Peasants and dualism with or without surplus labour', *Journal of Political Economy* 74, 425–50.

Sen, A. K. (1984), *Resources, Values, and Development*. Oxford: Blackwell.

Sen, A. K. (1985), *Women, Technology, and Sexual Divisions*. Geneva: UNCTAD and INSTRAW.

Sen, A. K. (1987), 'Gender and co-operative conflicts', [mimeo.]. Helsinki: World Institute of Development Economics Research.

Staudt, K. (1987), 'Uncaptured or unmotivated? Women and the food crisis in Africa', *Rural Sociology* 52(1).

UN (1986), *World Survey on the Role of Women in Development*. New York: Department of International Economic and Social Affairs.

Wiley, L. (1985), 'Tanzania: the Arusha Planning and Village Development Project', in C. Overholt, M. Anderson, K. Cloud, and J. Austin (eds), *Gender Roles in Development Projects*. West Hartford: Kumarian Press.

4

MALE BIAS IN MACRO-ECONOMICS: THE CASE OF STRUCTURAL ADJUSTMENT

Macro-economic problems, such as large balance of payments deficits, high inflation rates and very low growth rates, have devastated many countries in Asia, Africa, Latin America and the Caribbean in the 1980s. These problems have been caused by a mixture of internal and external factors. The governments in many of these countries have pursued inappropriate policies, and the external economic environment has sharply deteriorated. Higher oil prices, lower prices for primary products exported by less developed countries, and increases in the real rate of interest on international commercial loans have resulted in rising demand for, and falling supply of, foreign exchange. Many less developed countries (LDCs) have had no choice but to seek assistance from the International Monetary Fund (IMF) and the World Bank.

As a condition of this assistance, countries have to undertake programmes of economic stabilisation and structural adjustment. These programmes aim to reduce inflation; increase the rate of growth of output and exports; and increase productivity and efficiency. Typically, they involve devaluation, a reduction in public expenditure, decontrol of prices and of the allocation of imports and foreign exchange, and attempts to improve incentives for the production of goods which are internationally tradable and to switch resources away from the production of goods which are not internationally tradable.

There is no doubt that policy changes are needed in many LDCs, but there is considerable controversy about the validity of the IMF and World Bank diagnosis and policy prescriptions (for example, Onimode (ed.) 1989). The need for complementary policy changes in developed countries has been urged by many critics (for example, Cornia, Jolly & Stewart (eds) 1987) but, of course, the IMF and World Bank have no leverage over these countries. Here it will be argued that one serious deficiency of the IMF/World Bank approach is its disregard for gender, which leads to male bias.

Stabilisation and structural adjustment programmes are formulated on the basis of macro-economic concepts; that is, concepts that look at the economy as a whole rather than individual firms or households. Such concepts appear to be gender neutral. But a closer examination reveals them to be imbued with male bias. This male bias at the conceptual level predisposes such programmes to male bias in operation and outcome. Comprehensive evidence about the gender impact of stabilisation and structural adjustment programmes is not yet available, not least because of male bias in statistical information about the economy (Elson & Fleming 1988). More evidence will be available in the near future from studies being undertaken by the Commonwealth Secretariat and the World Bank/UNDP research programme on the Social Dimensions of Adjustment in Sub-Saharan Africa. The incomplete and fragmented evidence currently available certainly suggests that there are substantial grounds for concern that such programmes tend to result in an unfair distribution of the burdens of stabilisation and structural adjustment as between women and men. This has short-term benefits for men in terms of preserving male privilege, but longer-term costs in so far as it hampers the achievement of sustainable and equitable adjustment for both men and women. Here it is argued that the effectiveness of the programmes in achieving such a goal is likely to be weakened by male bias. Male bias in macro-economics is not only bad for women, it is also bad for the prospects of setting in train a process of sustainable development.

The macro-economics of structural adjustment: from non-tradables to tradables

Macro-economic trends and macro-economic thinking are usually presented in a language which appears to be gender neutral. No specific mention is made of gender or of the sexual division of labour. The focus of attention is not on people at all but on monetary aggregates, such as the gross national product; tradables and nontradables; imports and exports and the balance of payments; savings and consumption and investment; public expenditure and the budget deficit; or on impersonal concepts such as productivity and efficiency.

It may be argued that the absence of gender awareness in macro-economic analysis is immaterial and does nothing to disadvantage women, or to hamper the achievement of sustainable adjustment. Such analysis is concerned with fluctuations in the level of output and in rates of growth; and in changing the balance between different sectors of the economy: things, it may be argued, which have nothing to do with gender. However, this apparent gender neutrality masks a deeper gender bias. There is a hidden set of assumptions underlying macro-economic thinking which is deeply imbued with male bias. This hidden set of assumptions concerns human resources, their allocation to production, and their own reproduction and maintenance. It is assumed that human resources may be treated as if they were a non-produced factor of production, like natural resources; and as if they were costlessly transferable between different activities, in the way that a piece of land may be used for growing one crop one year and a different crop the next. These assumptions permit many macro-economic models to be constructed without any formal reference to human resources at all. But though there may be no variable in the equations labelled L for labour, and no axis on the diagram labelled L for labour, nevertheless drawing any policy conclusions from such models requires assumptions about human resources.

The usual macro-economic framework for analysing structural adjustment is constructed simply in terms of two categories of goods, tradables and non-tradables.[1] It is assumed that the primary resources of land and labour can either be used to produce goods and services which are internationally tradable; or to produce goods and services which are not internationally tradable and which are produced and consumed only within national boundaries. The prices of internationally tradable goods are assumed to be determined on international markets, and are assumed to be beyond the control of any one LDC, so that they can be taken as externally given. The prices of non-tradables are determined by supply and demand within the LDC economy. Examples of tradable goods are crops like rice and wheat; manufactures like clothing and machine tools; services like tourism and telecommunications. Tradables may be exports or efficient import substitutes: that is, goods that could be imported but which are produced within a country at costs which are internationally competitive. Many LDCs produce import substitutes at costs which are above the costs of imports because of policies to protect domestic industries. These high-cost import substitutes are non-tradables. Other examples of non-tradable goods are subsistence crops which are grown by farming households for their own consumption; construction, from housing to dams and roads and power stations; personal services and small-scale trading; and public services like health and education, and police and armed forces.

Using this framework, World Bank economists diagnose the problem as one of policy-induced price distortions leading to overproduction of non-tradables and

---

1. This framework was originally produced to analyse how to deal with the balance of payments problems of the Australian economy (see Salter 1959). It was subsequently adapted for analysing IMF stabilisation policies and World Bank structural adjustment policies (see Lal 1984).

under-production of tradables.[2] This produces balance of payments deficits and a shortage of foreign exchange which hampers growth. Structural adjustment thus consists of switching resources from the production of non-tradables to the production of tradables. The model suggests that the way to do this is by changing the relative prices of the two categories of goods, making tradables relatively more expensive, so as to give an incentive to produce them rather than non-tradables; and to cut down on consuming them so as to save foreign exchange. A range of policies is recommended to achieve this, including devaluation, raising the prices paid to farmers, withdrawal of food subsidies, and cut-backs in public expenditure. This conclusion is reached on the basis of a type of reasoning that economists call comparative statics. That is, the pattern of output associated in a particular model with one set of relative prices is compared with the pattern of output associated with another set of relative prices, and it is inferred that by changing the relative prices, the output pattern can also be changed. The actual process of switching is not analysed. At the root of this neglect lie certain assumptions about the utilisation and reproduction of human resources.

It is assumed that there are no structural barriers to transferring labour from one sort of production to another. It may take time for households to realise that they can make more money producing tradables than non-tradables, but in the absence of government-imposed 'distortions', they will fairly quickly make the switch. It is also assumed that there is no need to take into account any costs of change. The conceptual framework explicitly assumes full employment in the sense that it assumes a given amount of labour and merely adjusts its allocation. There is no question of structural adjustment necessitating an increase in total labour input or a rise in unemployment, just a better utilisation of existing total labour time. Any transitional costs (considered solely in terms of consumption losses) will be compensated for by the end result. The possibility of social and personal disintegration during the transition is not considered – it is assumed that households and people will not fall apart under the stress of the decisions that adjustment requires.

These fundamental assumptions are open to a number of criticisms (for example, Bienefeld 1988; Cornia, Jolly & Stewart (eds) 1987), the gravest of which is that if the transitional costs are great enough, some people will not survive in order to enjoy their compensation in the post-transition stage. Here we focus on the gender implications of these assumptions, contending that three kinds of

---

2. This diagnosis offers an unduly restrictive view of the nature of the structural problems of LDCs, which many social scientists would see as more fundamentally determined by the social relations of production, both national and international. The distinction between tradables and non-tradables is itself open to question, and is likely to vary geographically within a country, owing to variations in transport costs to the border. The concept of price distortion is equally problematic. However, further discussion of these important issues is beyond the scope of this chapter.

male bias are at work: male bias concerning the sexual division of labour; male bias concerning the unpaid domestic work necessary for producing and maintaining human resources; and male bias concerning the social institution which is the source of supply of labour – the household.

The sexual division of labour

The model just considered ignores the barrier to labour reallocation which is presented by the sexual division of labour. By the sexual division of labour we mean not just the pattern of work allocation between women and men that can be empirically observed at any moment of time, but also the social practices that constitute some sorts of work as suitable for women but unsuitable for men, and other sorts of work as unsuitable for women but suitable for men. A change in the relative returns of different kinds of work will not be enough to reallocate labour if it requires men to do work which is constituted as 'women's work' or women to do work which is constituted as 'men's work'. This is not to claim that the sexual division of labour is unchanging and immutable, but that, in general, such change requires more than a shift in relative remuneration and tends to entail a redefinition of the work both technically and organisationally and culturally (Goldstein 1989).

One defence of the implicit treatment of labour as ungendered might be that gender has no practical significance for switching from non-tradables to tradables, but this is not true in the case of structural adjustment in LDCs. There are at least two areas of considerable practical significance: production of labour-intensive manufactures for export; and production of crops for export. The first is of more significance in Latin America, Asia and the Caribbean, while the second is of more significance in Africa. It is, of course, open to question whether the promotion of such exports will lead to *sustainable* development – it is a high-risk strategy vulnerable to fluctuations in the international market (Bienefeld 1988; Elson 1988; Elson & Fleming 1988). But detailed consideration of this point is beyond the scope of this chapter.

The encouragement of the production of labour-intensive manufactures for export is an important component of the switch from non-tradables to tradables in many countries in Asia, Latin America and the Caribbean. Taking no account of gender leads to the belief, expressed by the Chief of the Trade and Adjustment Policy Division in the World Bank, that 'it is relatively easy to retrain and transfer labour originally working in, say, construction or commerce for employment in the export ... of, say, radios or garments' (Selowsky 1987). All the available studies of such production show that it is not just labour-intensive, it is female labour-intensive. This is not simply the result of women having a preference for such work, or men not considering the wages high enough. Many studies have shown that employers have a preference for employing women, particularly young and single women, for such work. A vivid example is given in a study of a Brazilian plant making electronic components (Hirata 1989). Here the management had tried, and abandoned, employing men on the night shift to carry out jobs done by women in the day. The men were unable to match the productivity of the women. The reason, in management's view, was that the men lacked the patience and concentration of the women. Women were regarded as having greater endurance and the ability to carry out tasks which were 'painful for a man', as well as having a 'better sense of touch in their fingers'. Many firms are unwilling to make the experiment of employing men, even in the face of pressure from governments that see male unemployment as much more important than female unemployment, and are anxious for more jobs to be created for men (see Jackson & Barry (1989) for a discussion of this in the case of Ireland). The views of the management of the Brazilian plant seem to be the 'commonsense' of manufacturers around the world.

Underlying this 'commonsense' tends to be the view that women are 'naturally' suited to labour-intensive assembly operations. This view can be found in more sophisticated form in the literature on human capital in which it is assumed that labour is differentiated by different endowments of innate skills and aptitudes. If women have higher productivity than men in labour-intensive assembly jobs, then this is explained by women's greater endowment of relevant aptitudes (nimble fingers, perhaps?). Feminists reject this naturalistic approach, arguing instead that women have acquired the attributes that generate their higher productivity in their training both at home and at school for life as dutiful daughters, wives and mothers (Elson & Pearson 1981; Kergoat 1982).

Such gender differentiation means that while it is relatively easy to transfer women from construction and commerce to radios and garments, this is not the case for men. The only situation in which it seems at all plausible that the expansion of labour-intensive export manufacturing will increase the number of jobs for men is when technological changes lead to reorganisation of production and a demand for more technical skills, for which women are typically not given training (for an example of this in the electronics industry in Scotland, see Goldstein 1989). Thus the assumption that changes in the relative returns of tradable and non-tradable activities will serve to reallocate labour to labour-intensive manufacturing for export depends for its validity on the assumption that there is plenty of female labour available for factory work, and that this labour can be mobilised simply by changes in relative wages. Studies of the integration of women into export industries show the process is more complex. Several other changes are also necessary to create a factory work-force of young women: social resistance to young unmarried women working outside the home may have to be overcome; suitable transport and accommodation may have to be provided; legislation may have to be changed to permit continuous night work for women (for a discussion of the complexities of constructing a female labour force, see Pearson 1988). The evidence to date seems to suggest that meeting these conditions requires either of two contrasting situations. The first is when there is an absolute deterioration in the returns to alternative ways of getting a living so that they no longer offer enough to live on; for example, rural poverty pushing women into garment factories in Bangladesh (Feldman 1988). The second is when there is rapid accumulation and growth, and employers, especially multinationals, are so eager to expand that they will offer wages and conditions superior in absolute terms to anything else available to most young women, packaged as a new, modern, enticing life-style; for example, the expansion of the electronics industry in Malaysia and Singapore (Foo & Lim 1989). It is, of course, the first case that is relevant in those LDCs with severe macro-economic problems. Both suggest it is not simply relative wages that matter, but absolute improvements or deteriorations in living standards: more important than relative wages is the overall state of accumulation. Case studies of both situations suggest that the incorporation of women into the factories is not accomplished through an impersonal labour market but through social networks, which, in the case of recruitment of young women in Asia, are frequently between employers and the parents of the prospective employees.

Granted that women can be pushed or pulled into the export factories, as barriers are swept aside under the pressure of necessity or the desire for social mobility, there is still a further question. Is an increase in the time that women spend in export factories the result of a substitution of this work for other work; or is it additional work, increasing women's total labour time? It could well be additional work, a second shift, undertaken in addition to unpaid domestic work as wives, daughters, mothers. Unlike many other kinds of work, such as handicrafts and farming, factory work cannot be undertaken at the same time as reproductive work. Children can be supervised while carpets are woven or crops picked, but not during work in a garment factory or on an electronics assembly line. Few of the studies of women in export factories have gathered much evidence on time spent on domestic tasks. One recent study in the Philippines which did concern itself with this issue found that domestic work still accounted for between twenty-seven and thirty-two hours a week for married women employees, which was fitted in through a reduction in leisure time (Miralao 1984). In Singapore, there has been mounting concern at labour shortages caused by married women leaving factory work because they cannot cope with the burden of factory work combined with child care and housework (Heyzer (ed.) 1988b: ch. 13). Even if the woman factory worker is herself relieved of domestic work for others, as in the case of many daughters, the domestic work she formerly undertook is likely to fall on the shoulders of other women – her mother or younger sisters (Salaff 1981). It is unlikely that much unpaid domestic work is reallocated to men dismissed from employment in work that is newly unprofitable: all the evidence tends to show that the sexual division of labour in the household is resistant to change. Taking care of children, and sick and old people, cooking, cleaning, shopping – all this is 'women's work' and a man taking responsibility for it is in danger of losing his dignity, of being 'unmanned', in many parts of the world. Enduring idleness while looking for a proper 'man's' job is the option men are steered towards.

Explicitly recognising the sexual division of labour means questioning the benign picture of structural adjustment presented in the model we have considered. Gender barriers to the reallocation of labour are likely to mean unemployment for men displaced from non-tradable activities, and extra work for women as factory work is added to unpaid domestic work (Heyzer (1988a) suggests that this has happened in the Philippines). This extra work is not recognised because unpaid domestic labour is not counted as work. However, it may be argued that, in return, women who work in export factories get an income of their own, and that this brings higher status, greater independence and more bargaining power within the household.

The precise benefits which women derive from earning an income of their own have been the subject of considerable debate, the details of which are beyond the scope of the present argument. In my view, the benefits, though they may be great, are incapable of fully emancipating women from gender subordination (Elson & Pearson 1981); and the extent of the benefits depends very much on the context in which women enter into the labour market. In situations of economic crisis, women are often forced into 'distress sales', selling their labour on very disadvantageous terms in an overcrowded market, in which wages and conditions of work are worsening, in order to ensure survival for themselves and their children. Recent evidence from Latin America suggests that rising female participation rates in urban areas represent such distress sales rather than the opening up of new liberating opportunities for women (Joekes 1987; Berger 1988).

A different set of problems presents itself when we consider women's participation in smallholder export crop production in sub-Saharan Africa. Although as conventionally measured, female participation rates in economic activity are low there, we know that women make a major contribution to crop production, both as unpaid family workers and as own-account workers, farming in their own right (Elson & Fleming 1988). Production is typically organised through a sexual division of labour that covers both tasks and crops. Certain tasks, such as land preparation are 'men's jobs', while other tasks such as transplanting and weeding are 'women's jobs', the tasks following in sequence in the crop cycle. Certain crops are 'men's crops' while other crops are 'women's crops', though the same crop may be a 'male crop' in one place and a 'female crop' in another place (Davison 1988a: 12–13). Cash crops, particularly those grown for export, tend to be men's crops, while subsistence food crops tend to be women's crops. However, there are exceptions: for example, cotton is largely in the hands of women in the Sahel; one-third of farmers producing cocoa in Ghana are women (Davison 1988a; Elson & Fleming 1988). The sexual division of labour in tasks cuts across the sexual division of responsibility for different crops: men clear the land for women's crops; women transplant, weed and help with harvesting of men's crops. But men control the proceeds from selling men's crops, while women control the use of women's crops, which are generally used to feed their families, though surpluses may be sold on local markets.

Thus women do not generally earn an income of their own from work they do on crops marketed by their husbands. The extent to which women benefit from such work depends on how their husbands spend the proceeds. There is evidence that many women lack confidence that the benefits of increased work on their husbands' cash crops will trickle down to them. Case studies show the reluctance of women to put more work into production of crops controlled by their husbands: in the case of rice in the Gambia (Dey 1980), in Northern Cameroon (Jones 1983) and in other rice-growing countries such as Madagascar, Senegal and Ivory Coast (Longhurst 1987); tea production in Tanzania (Mbilinyi 1988a and b) and Kenya (Davison 1988b); and tobacco production in Nigeria (Babalola & Dennis 1988). In the Communal Areas of Zimbabwe, a recent study found that 'Even in households in which there is a shortage of labour, women, if faced with loss of control over the product of their labour, will continue to withdraw it from household production in order to meet their needs and those of their children for cash income' (Pankhurst & Jacobs 1988: 212).

The sexual division of labour in crop production could thus present a barrier to the reallocation of labour from non-tradable to tradable crops. Higher prices for producers of export cash crops give an incentive for greater production to the person controlling the proceeds from their sale, but not necessarily to all those whose labour is necessary for increased production. It may be argued that there is no need to consider this possibility because, however, reluctant wives may be, husbands have the power to compel them to supply the extra labour required. This is likely to be true in some cases. But we might note that reliance on this argument does compel recognition of male power over women and is incompatible with a model suggesting that labour reallocation is a matter of new choices in response to different incentives, rather than the extraction of additional work through unequal power relations. In other cases (similar to the Gambian rice case discussed by Dey 1980), women have sufficient autonomy to resist demands for extra work on their husbands' crops, and the result will be a disappointing output response to increased crop prices. In some situations, women may through joint action secure a direct payment to them of part of the proceeds, as happened in the cases discussed by Mbilinyi (1988a) and Davison (1988b). In the latter case, the Kenyan Tea Development Authority already paid women directly for the amount of tea they picked, but a substantial yearly bonus related to the total amount of tea delivered by a household was paid only to the male owner of the tea land. Just before the award of the annual bonus in 1983, women began to organise a protest: 'A group of the most out-spoken women went to the local committee of the KDTA, angrily protesting that they rarely saw the annual bonuses because their husbands spent the cash on beer, meat and other items for their exclusive use. The women pointed out that they provided much of the labour for tea production, and demanded a share of the annual bonus. Their collective protest was successful' (Davison 1988b, 168). This problem could easily be avoided if marketing boards as a matter of course made payments directly to women for their contribution to production. This was suggested in Tanzania but was resisted by both local development planning agencies and international development agencies as too radical: as one official put it, 'Whatever happens, we do not want a revolution. If women have their own money, why will they marry?' (Mbilinyi 1988a).

Ensuring that women would be direct recipients of higher crop prices would not solve all potential problems of adjustment. Women who farm on their own account and produce cash crops for export face other difficulties: lack of access to other inputs they need, such as fertilisers, credit and extension services; extra demands on their time for domestic tasks such as water collection and health care (to be discussed in the next section); and the danger of losing access to land as men take over more land, attracted by the new incentives – something which has already happened in a number of countries following the introduction of irrigation (Carney 1988).

The examples we have considered show that the sexual division of labour will constrain the extent to which labour can be reallocated in the course of structural adjustment. Failure to give explicit consideration to the gender differentiation of labour may mean that structural adjustment policies, based on the kind of macro-economic framework discussed, fail to achieve their objectives. In so far as the gender barriers are overcome, this cannot be attributed simply to changes in the structure of incentives, but to women's relative lack of power which constrains them not simply to reallocate their time but to increase the total input of hours of female labour.

The reproduction and maintenance of human resources

The fact that adjustment implies an increase in female work time may be ignored because much of the time involved is unpaid time spent in the reproduction and maintenance of human resources. This time is not regularly accounted for in production statistics and thus remains 'invisible' in the national accounts that provide the statistical counterpart of macro-economic models (Elson & Fleming 1988). Macro-economic models ignore this work, treating labour as if it were a non-produced natural resource.

When challenged, economists do not deny that human resources require inputs of caring and cooking, of nurturing and nursing; and do not deny that responsibility for providing these inputs lies chiefly with women. But macro-economic thinking assumes that it is perfectly correct to proceed as if such activities were not required because they would be undertaken regardless of changes in the level and composition of national income. This assumption may be based either on the idea that reproduction and maintenance of human resources is undertaken for love, not money, and is therefore not responsive to economic changes (Roston (1983) argues that Keynes's macro-economics is based on this assumption); or on the idea that changes in the level and composition of national income have no impact on the relative costs and benefits of maintaining and reproducing human resources. This assumption would be more consistent with neo-classical economics, which does assume that the reproduction and maintenance of human resources is responsive to economic signals (for example, Becker 1976). Both the Keynesian and the neo-classical view are one-sided. Unpaid domestic labour is not carried out entirely for love, disregarding the economic costs and benefits; but neither is it simply another economic activity. The process of the reproduction and maintenance of human resources is different from any other kind of production because human resources are treated as having an intrinsic value, not merely an instrumental value. Women may to some extent weigh up the costs and benefits for themselves of the amount of services they provide without pay to other family members, but they do not regard their children as just another crop, to be tended if the benefits are high enough, and to be left to rot untended if the benefits become too low. Women may be forced through poverty to leave their children untended, but this is a source of intense anguish, not simply another rational economic decision.

The difference between human resources and other resources does not mean that macro-economic thinking can safely ignore unpaid domestic labour. This neglect would only be justified if there were no interdependence between unpaid domestic work and the paid work that economists do include in the gross national product; or if macro-economic changes had no implications for the amount of unpaid domestic work that has to be done. This is far from being the case. Paid and unpaid work compete for women's time; and in the conditions typical in countries attempting to stabilise and adjust their economies, there is pressure on many women to increase both their paid and unpaid labour input.

One of the main factors increasing the amount of time women must devote to the sustenance of human resources is the cut-back in the production of public-sector non-tradables such as health and education services, water and sanitation services, and rural transportation. Cut-backs in public expenditure are supposed to free labour for work in production of tradables and are a key feature of structural adjustment programmes. From this viewpoint, it is not undesirable that women teachers in the Philippines are leaving teaching, because of deteriorating conditions of work and pay, for employment overseas as maids (Heyzer 1988a).

Declines in public expenditure per capita on health and education services during the 1980s have been documented for a considerable number of LDCs (Cornia, Jolly & Stewart (eds) 1987). Where there were not absolute declines, there tended to be marked deceleration in growth rates. There has been some debate about how far these cuts should be attributed to the conditions laid down by the World Bank and IMF, how far to mismanagement by LDC governments and how far to the recession of the early 1980s. Ultimately, this must remain a matter of judgement. The precise contribution of these three factors does not matter for the point being made here, which is that such cut-backs, whatever the cause, have implications for unpaid domestic labour that macro-economic analysis ignores. If fewer of the services required for the sustenance of human resources are provided by the public sector, then women have to make up some of the shortfall.

As yet there is little detailed documentation of this because statistics are not regularly collected on unpaid domestic labour. Recent work on Zambia indicates some of the potential effects (Evans & Young 1988). In Zambia, real per capita expenditure on health fell by sixteen per cent between 1983 and 1985. For the majority of Zambian people, the only alternative to health services provided by the state are those that have been traditionally available in the community and household. The result of health expenditure cut-backs has been to shift more of the burden of health care to the community and household-which in practice means women. In the rural areas, the decline in health provision has had a direct effect on services which are particularly important to women and children, such as immunisation and mother-and-child health clinics. People now have to travel farther to get treatment and drugs, and wait longer in queues. Women interviewed for the study said they themselves could not afford to be ill because of the time it would take away from their work. They reported having to spend more time caring for other household members when they are sick. If husbands or children have to attend hospitals, shortages of equipment and personnel mean that women are expected to go with them to provide meals and care for the duration of the treatment. One woman reported missing the entire planting season for this reason (Evans & Young 1988), a perfect example of the interdependence between the labour that macro-economic models do include and that which they ignore.

The example just discussed highlights the ambiguity of terms like 'cost', 'productivity' and 'efficiency'. What is regarded by economists as increased efficiency may instead be a shifting of costs from the paid economy to the unpaid economy. It may appear that the cost per patient in hospital has been reduced and the efficiency of hospitals increased, when in reality there has been a transfer of the costs of care for the sick from the paid economy to the unpaid economy of the household. The financial costs fall but the unpaid work of women in the household rises. This is not a genuine increase in efficiency: it is simply a transfer of the costs from the hospital to the home.

Such a transfer of costs has been explicitly advocated under the banner of promotion of self-help practices by exponents of 'Adjustment with a Human Face': 'there is scope for decentralising many activities in health, nutrition, child care, sanitation, etc., to the family (or community) level ... while such an approach may increase time costs for women, it will place extremely modest monetary costs on the household; and will lead to substantial savings in the public sector ...' (Cornia 1987: 174). The implication is that increased time-costs for women do not matter, a result perhaps of the belief that women have lots of spare time.[3] This has been criticised by feminists, who point to the enormous pressure on the time of most women, especially poor women (Antrobus 1988; Elson 1988).

Another time-pressure comes from rises in the price of food. Such rises are the result of a combination of withdrawal of food subsidies, devaluation and increases in the prices paid to farmers, all typically components of structural adjustment programmes. The aim is to provide more incentives for farmers to produce tradables and to reduce government budget deficits. An underlying assumption is that households that buy food will adjust their expenditure patterns, spending less on other things in order to buy food and switching from dearer foods to cheaper foods.[4] But cheaper foods require more input of women's unpaid labour: coarse grains and root crops take a longer time to prepare than wheat products; home-baking takes more time than buying bread. Research on Sri Lankan food consumption patterns has found that time-saving has been a significant factor in the switch from rice consumption to bread consumption in urban areas (Senauer, Sahn & Aiderman 1986). Shopping also takes longer when prices rise, as women have to shop around to find the cheapest source, and buy smaller quantities more often.

Ignoring the implications of macro-economic changes for unpaid domestic labour is tantamount to assuming that women's capacity to undertake

---

3. This belief is fostered by models of the household which conflate leisure time and time spent on unpaid domestic labour. Such models are frequently used in neo-classical economic analysis.
4. There are gender constraints on such expenditure switching, which are discussed later in the chapter. Here we focus on the time implications.

extra work is infinitely elastic – able to stretch so as to make up for any short-fall in incomes and resources required for the production and maintenance of human resources. However, women's capacity for work is not infinitely elastic and breaking point may be reached. There may simply not be enough female labour time available to maintain the quality and quantity of human resources at its existing level. This may not have an immediate impact on the level and composition of gross national output, but in the longer run a deterioration in health, nutrition and education will have an adverse impact on output levels. The assumption of a given quantity and quality of labour, which is invariant as switching from non-tradables to tradables proceeds, will be revealed as untenable.

Data assembled by UNICEF provide evidence that women's unpaid labour has not been able to absorb all the costs of switching (Cornia, Jolly & Stewart (eds) 1987). Special studies of ten countries (Botswana, Ghana, Zimbabwe, the Philippines, South Korea, Sri Lanka, Brazil, Chile, Jamaica and Peru) show that the nutritional status of children has deteriorated in all but two, while infant and/or child mortality statistics have ceased to improve at previous rates, and have shown a deterioration in three of the ten.

There has been very little research at the micro-level into exactly how women are juggling with the competing demands on their time in the context of structural adjustment. Heyzer (1988a) reports the findings of one small-scale village study in East Java, Indonesia, which investigated the implications for poor women of the Indonesian devaluation of 1986, and associated policy changes. Rising prices placed heavy burdens on poor women: longer hours of field work for those with some land; the necessity for those without land to offer themselves as hired workers at low wages in whatever job was available; as well as the continuing daily grind of collecting fuel and water, cooking, looking after children, etc. The overall result was a longer and harder working day for women. Male out migration had risen rapidly, and most of the women did not know exactly where their husbands were. All the women interviewed spoke of worry, tiredness and stress as they struggled to make ends meet.

A study of an urban low-income community in Guayaquil, Ecuador (Moser 1989), found that women had been forced to allocate more time to income-earning activities and to unpaid participation in the provision of community services, such as housing improvements and health care, as the economy had undergone structural adjustment and stabilisation programmes in a deteriorating international economic environment. Their working day (paid and unpaid) continued to be between twelve and eighteen hours, but they had been forced to reduce the time allocated to looking after their families. An increasing burden was falling on the shoulders of their elder daughters, who had less time for school work. The sexual division of labour which designates reproduction and maintenance of human resources as female tasks had not changed. Total input of female labour time had increased, though since adult women already worked very long hours, much of the extra input was coming from school-age daughters. In about thirty per cent of the 141 households surveyed, women were managing to cope; in about fifty-five per cent, women were just hanging on, mortgaging the futures of their sons, and especially daughters, in order to survive; in about fifteen per cent, women were exhausted, their families disintegrating, their children dropping out of school and roaming the streets, becoming involved in street gangs and exposed to drugs. As Moser concludes, 'Not all women can cope under crisis and it is necessary to stop romanticising their infinite capacity to do so'.

What Moser's valuable study graphically shows is that the process of reallocating labour from non-tradables to tradables may place severe stress upon, and even lead to the disintegration of, the process of human resource production and maintenance that macro-models assume can safely be taken for granted. Complacency about human resource production and maintenance is fostered by the models of the household that form the micro-level underpinning of most macro-economic models.

Gender divisions and household expenditure

Conventional economic analysis assumes that the household may be treated as a unity. The macro-economy is an aggregation of household units, firms and the public sector. Labour and goods are supplied by households, which also buy goods and hire labour. The unity of the household may be theorised in one of three different ways. In an illuminating critique of such theories, Sen has labelled them the glued-together family, the despotic family and the super-trader family (Sen 1983).

The first two assume that the household can be treated as if it were an individual with a single set of objectives – this is known as the assumption of a joint utility function or unified family welfare function (Evans 1989). The difference between them is that the theory of the glued-together family does not allow for differences between individuals and, in effect, treats all household members as identical, whereas the theory of the family ruled by a despot does allow for variation within the household. In the latter case, individual family members do have differing objectives, but a despotic head of household takes decisions for them, and they just fall into line. Much of the analysis by economists of households in developing countries makes use of the despot assumption,[5] but with

---

5. The assumption of a despotic male household head may also be attractive to feminists – but the weakness of such an assumption is that it leaves to women only the role of passive acquiescence, and fails to take account of women's active role in household decision-making, and their strategies of resistance to male power.

the added twist that the despot is benevolent, and altruistically takes decisions that will maximise the welfare of all family members, not just his own. (It is usually assumed that the benevolent despot is male – indeed, Evans has found one author who explicitly claims that the household decision-maker will 'feel the disutility of labour, say of his wife, as much as that of his own' [*ibid.*].)

The super-trader model allows for a multiplicity of decisionmakers within the household, each pursuing his/her individual objectives, and makes household unity the outcome of these individual decisions (Becker 1981). In effect, the household is treated as if it were a market with household members buying and selling from each other. The division of labour and distribution of income between different household members is treated as resulting from individual choices freely exercised – there is no room for notions of inequality of power. Such a model is unable properly to take account of children, since they are born into households and cannot in any sense be regarded as choosing to join them.

Despite the variation between them, the outcome of all three approaches is a vision of the household as a unity. The result is also generally an uncritical approach to the household as an institution which maximises the welfare of all its members, either through the altruism of the benevolent dictator, or through the freely exercised choices of its members to exchange goods and services with one another. The household is celebrated as a pooling and sharing institution which strengthens its members in their interconnections with the rest of society. Such a vision supports a view of the household as capable of absorbing any transitional costs of adjustment, and as an institution that can safely be taken for granted by designers of structural adjustment programmes.

However, there is now available a wealth of theorising (Sen 1983; Folbre 1986a and b) and evidence (Beneria & Roldan 1987; Blumberg 1988; Dwyer & Bruce (eds) 1988) which undermines this complacency. The household is a site of conflict as well as of cooperation; of inequality as well as of mutuality; and conflict and inequality are structured along gender lines.

This does not mean that women are passive victims within the household and play no decision-making role. Rather, it means that women do not enjoy the same decision-making power as men: their bargaining power is weaker. The fundamental reason for this is that their fall-back position is weaker. If no bargain can be struck and the household disintegrates, women are generally in a worse position than men, both economically and socially. Female-headed households are usually among the poorest households. Women on their own, without a male 'protector', in the shape of husband, brother or father, frequently face social denigration and physical violence.

Evidence from a large variety of case studies suggests that women play an active role in decision-making about the reproduction and maintenance of human resources, and typically bear the responsibility for managing household income and expenditure to secure the day-to-day welfare of household members. The problem is that they do not control access to all the resources they require to discharge these responsibilities. They are dependent on men's goodwill. A recent case study of low-income households in Mexico City vividly depicts the stress and anxiety frequently attendant upon women's role as manager of household resources. As Dona Soledad put it:

> He gives me the gasto [housekeeping allowance] all right, but I must see that everything is fine, that nothing is lacking, good food for him, yes, the best pieces are for him ... He usually wants beer ... He says: '... bring me some beer. I'll pay you later!' He never does. On Thursday I am without a cent and I have to ask my comadrita to complete the week [borrow from a woman friend]. He collects his money on Saturday and that day I get the gasto, and start returning what I owe. You know, to manage the allowance is a difficult job, prices are going up and we must buy food, no matter what. And if something goes wrong, or he gets angry at me, he may even cut off the allowance of that week!
> (Beneria & Roldan 1987: 121)

African women's lack of confidence that income accruing to men will trickle down to them and their children has already been discussed above. When adjustment is necessary to changing external circumstances, it is women who must manage the adjustment so as to minimise damage to household members. But in doing so, women are generally in a situation of responsibility without power. This is particularly acute with respect to the determination of household expenditure.

When the household is viewed as a unity, it is assumed that income of household members is pooled and is spent in such a way as to maximise their joint welfare. However, the wealth of evidence assembled by Dwyer and Bruce (eds) (1988) and Blumberg (1988) from case studies in all major regions of the Third World, makes clear that such procedures are far from being the norm: not all income is pooled, some is kept for personal discretionary spending, and men and women actively strive over the use of pooled income and have differing expenditure priorities. This is not just a feature of Third World countries but is just as true of richer countries, as work by sociologists makes clear (Whitehead 1984; Pahl 1980). A general finding is that women's income is almost exclusively used to meet collective household needs, whereas men tend to retain a considerable portion of their income for personal spending. A key source of male bargaining power within the household is determining what proportion of their income to pass on to other household members. Family interaction over the use of income is fraught with friction, and family members are frequently ignorant of the magnitude of each other's earnings.

There are a wide variety of systems of organisation of household expenditure, but in understanding their dynamics, the crucial distinction is between discretion over how much of one's income to allocate to household as opposed to personal needs, and discretion over exactly what to buy for dinner tonight, or whether to give priority to a son's need for new shoes or a daughter's need for a new dress. Typically, the first type of discretion is enjoyed by men, while the second type of discretion is endured by women. This is true whether the household expenditure system is organised through a male earner making a housekeeping allowance to a non-earning wife (as in the Mexican example above); or through a common fund to which both husbands and wives contribute earnings to finance all household expenditure; or through a system of separate budgets and responsibilities, as occurs in much of rural sub-Saharan Africa, where women are typically responsible for providing food, while men are responsible for paying for items like clothing, medical and educational expenses and taxes. It is important to stress that personal spending money for male adults cannot be assumed to be residual, determined by what is available when household needs have been satisfied. In some cases discussed in Dwyer and Bruce (eds) (1988), it appears to be a priority, and the amount allocated to household expenditure is residually determined by the difference between male income and personal spending. The good husband is one who strictly limits his personal spending, but his prerogative to enjoy such spending remains.

The process of adjusting expenditure to rising prices of food and other basic items is thus constrained by gender divisions within the household. It may not be easy to maintain decent standards of health and nutrition and clothing and schooling by switching expenditure from non-basic items like alcohol, tobacco and entertainment when these items are part of male personal spending. As yet, little research has been done on the adjustment of household expenditure in the context of structural adjustment, but the forebodings expressed here are confirmed by Moser's study of low-income households in Guayaquil, which found that expenditure adjustment was embedded in domestic conflict and violence. The system in most households was a daily housekeeping allowance. While the allowance had tended to rise, the amount had not kept pace with inflation. Moreover, forty-eight per cent of the women interviewed said that there had been an increase in domestic violence, claiming that it always occurred when they had to ask for more money. Some women specifically linked this with the desire of men to maintain their own personal expenditure on alcohol and other women. With younger men, there was a growing problem of drug addiction; during the field work period, a young man addicted to cocaine killed himself after a row with his wife about his spending most of his income on drugs (Moser 1989). Economic stress and unemployment are particularly conducive to male use of hard drugs, and tobacco and alcohol; and addiction is one reason why men may resist a reduction in their personal expenditure. Another reason is ignorance: Dwyer and Bruce (eds) (1988) cite case studies suggesting that men simply do not know the level of prices or appreciate the level of needs of other members of I he household, because they do not do the shopping and spend little time at home. A further reason is disagreement about what level of provision is required, particularly for children: a study of poor families in Mexico City found that husbands and wives disagreed about what is the minimum acceptable standard of children's clothing and schooling, and about what is urgently required and what can be deferred (Beneria & Roldan 1987). A more subtle point is made by Sen (1985), who suggests that women tend not to have as strong a sense of self and self-worth as men, and tend to identify with the needs of their children.

An examination of the process of adjusting expenditure within the household to cope with an economy-wide switch in resource allocation highlights the neglected issue of the stress and anxiety of adjustment. This does not only affect women, but it affects women with peculiar force because of their responsibility for provisioning the household, unmatched by control over the allocation of household income. Besides the costs in time, discussed in the previous section, there are costs in terms of sleepless nights, deteriorating health and deteriorating human relationships.

The examples considered here show that there are gender barriers to the reallocation of expenditure within the household that constrain the extent to which the costs of adjustment can be absorbed without a deterioration in the quality of human resources. It is not simply a matter of income foregone during the switching process, or even of extra work having to be done; it is a matter of the disintegration of people's lives.

Conclusions

Models of structural adjustment which depict the problem as something that can be solved by changing relative prices so as to switch resources from non-tradables to tradables in fact rely on an increase in the provision of a non-tradable that is not explicitly included: an increase in women's time and effort in the reproduction and maintenance of human resources. The process of switching, which is regarded as sufficiently unproblematic as to require no detailed analysis, is only unproblematic in so far as women are willing and able to act as the 'shock absorbers' of the system. Failure to specifically address the role of this important non-tradable is a form of male bias, compounded by a failure to perceive how unequal gender relations may themselves prevent adjustment from working in the way envisaged, by limiting women's willingness and ability to absorb the shocks.

Any worthwhile form of structural adjustment must be equitable and sustainable. It must not deplete and degrade resources, particularly human resources.[6] This requires a view of macroeconomics that includes the reproduction and maintenance of human resources alongside conventionally included goods and services. It requires a national accounting system that accounts for unpaid labour as well as paid labour. It requires a diagnosis of the structural problems of development that includes gender barriers, as well as price distortions. It requires a strategy for tackling gender barriers as well as for improving the functioning of prices and markets. A full elaboration of this will not be undertaken here, but it is clear that the core of the strategy would be to channel more resources to women and to enhance women's organisational capacity.

Equitable and sustainable adjustment cannot be achieved simply by getting the prices right so as to switch resources from non-tradables to tradables. It requires increased investment.[7] There is growing evidence that investment channelled to women may have a higher rate of return and do more to increase productivity, to improve children's welfare and to improve the use of natural resources, than investment channelled to men (Herz 1988; Dwyer & Bruce (eds) 1988). There is also growing evidence that women's ability to make the best use of resources is enhanced by participation in extra-familial organisations. Such participation improves women's bargaining power within the household and within the public sphere from which women have been so often excluded, and transforms their consciousness of their rights and abilities (*ibid.*). Outstanding and well-known examples are the Self-Employed Women's Association in India, and the Grameen Bank in Bangladesh. But effective action can also be taken on a very small-scale, localised and spontaneous basis, as is shown by the example, discussed earlier, of a group of Kenyan women mobilising to demand their rightful share of the proceeds of tea production. The issue now is to what extent are those with economic and political power prepared to channel resources directly to women, rather than hope for resources channelled to men to trickle down to women and children? To what extent are those with economic and political power prepared to restructure gender relations, as well as other social institutions such as markets and bureaucracies? For how long will equitable and sustainable adjustment

---

6. The idea of sustainable development has been popularised with particular reference to the depletion of natural resources and environmental degradation. These concerns are also linked to gender awareness (see Agarwal 1986), but to discuss them is beyond the scope of this chapter.

7. The evidence for this is now emerging from studies of the impact of World Bank structural adjustment programmes. Those countries that have been claimed as 'success stories', like Turkey and Ghana, have enjoyed massive inflows of foreign aid, which have enabled them to increase their investment. Many World Bank economists now agree that ability to switch resources and increase production of tradables depends not just on incentives but also on investment.

continue to be constrained by male bias, vividly expressed in the fear that 'whatever happens, we do not want a revolution. If women have their own money, why will they marry'?

References

Agarwal, B. (1986), *Cold Hearths and Barren Slopes: The Woodfuel Crisis in the Third World.* California: Riverdale.

Antrobus, P. (1988), 'Consequences and responses to social and economic deterioration: the experience of the English-speaking Caribbean', Workshop on Economic Crisis, Household Strategies and Women's Work, Cornell University.

Babalola, S. O., and Dennis, C. (1988), 'Returns to women's labour in cash crop production: tobacco in Igboho, Oyo State, Nigeria', in J. Davison (ed.) (1988), *op. cit.*

Becker, G. (1976), *The Economic Approach to Human Behaviour.* Chicago, IL: University of Chicago Press.

Becker, G. (1981), *A Treatise on the Family.* Cambridge, MA: Harvard University Press.

Beneria, L., and Roldan, M. (1987), *The Crossroads of Class and Gender.* Chicago, IL: University of Chicago Press.

Berger, M. (1988), 'Women's responses to recession in Latin America and the Caribbean: a focus on urban labor markets', Workshop on Economic Crisis, Household Strategies and Women's Work, Cornell University.

Bienefeld, M. (1988), 'Structural adjustment and its impact on women in developing countries', Discussion Paper submitted to CIDA, RC/ Project 839/11109.

Blumberg, R. L. (1988), 'Income under female vs. male control', *Journal of Family Issues* 9(1).

Carney, J. (1988), 'Struggles over land and crops in an irrigated rice scheme: The Gambia', in J. Davison (ed.) (1988), *op. cit.*

Cornia, G. (1987), 'Social policymaking: restructuring, targeting, efficiency', in G. Cornia, R. Jolly, and F. Stewart (eds) (1987), *op. cit.*

Cornia, G., Jolly, R., and Stewart, F. (eds) (1987), *Adjustment with a Human Face.* Oxford: Clarendon Press.

Davison, J. (ed.) (1988), *Agriculture, Women and Land.* Boulder, CO: Westview Press.

Davison, J. (1988a), 'Land and women's agricultural production: the context', in *ibid.*

Davison, J. (1988b), 'Who owns what? Land registration and tensions in gender relations of production in Kenya', in *ibid.*

Dey, J. (1980), 'Gambian women: unequal partners in rice development', *Journal of Development Studies* 17(3).

Dwyer, D., and Bruce, J. (eds) (1988), *A Home Divided: Women and Income in the Third World.* Stanford, CA: Stanford University Press.

Elson, D. (1988), 'Gender aware policymaking for structural adjustment', unpublished report for the Commonwealth Secretariat.

Elson, D., and Flemming, S. (1989), 'Women's contribution to the economy and structural adjustment', unpublished report for the Commonwealth Secretariat.

Elson, D., and Pearson, R. (1981), '"Nimble fingers make cheap workers": an analysis of women's employment in Third World export manufacturing', *Feminist Review* 7.

Elson, D. and Pearson, R. (eds) (1989), *Women's Employment and Multinationals in Europe.* London: Macmillan.

Evans, A. (1989), 'Gender issues in rural household economics', Institute of Development Economics, Discussion Paper No. 254.

Evans, A., and Young, K. (1988), 'Gender issues in household labour allocation: the case of Northern Province, Zambia', ODA ESCOR Research Report.

Feldman, S. (1988), 'Crisis, Islam and gender in Bangladesh: the social construction of a female labor force', Workshop on Economic Crisis, Household Strategies and Women's Work, Cornell University.

Folbre, N. (1986a), 'Hearts and spades: paradigms of household economics', *World Development* 14(2).

Folbre, N. (1986b), 'Cleaning house: new perspectives on households and economic development', *Journal of Development Economics* 22.

Foo, G., and Lim, L. (1989), 'Poverty, ideology and women export factory workers in Asia', in H. Afshar and B. Agarwal (eds), *Women, Poverty and Ideology*. London: Macmillan.

Goldstein, N. (1989), 'Silicon Glen: women and semiconductor multinationals', in D. Elson and R. Pearson (eds) (1989), *op. cit.*

Herz, B. (1988), 'Briefing on women and development'. Berlin: World Bank/IMF Annual Meeting.

Heyzer, N. (1988a), 'Economic crisis, household strategies, and women's work in South East Asia', Workshop on Economic Crisis, Household Strategies and Women's Work, Cornell University.

Heyzer, N. (ed.) (1988b), *Daughters in Industry*. Asian and Pacific Development Centre, Kuala Lumpur.

Hirata, H. (1989), 'Production relocation: an electronics multinational in France and Brazil', in D. Elson and R. Pearson (eds) (1989), *op. cit.*

Jackson, P., and Barry, U. (1989), 'Women's employment and multinationals in the Republic of Ireland: the creation of a new female labour force', in *ibid.*

Joekes, S. (1987), *Women in the World Economy: An INSTRAW Study*. New York: Oxford University Press.

Jones, C. (1983), 'The mobilisation of women's labour for cash crop production: a game theoretic approach', *American Journal of Agricultural Economics* 65(5).

Kergoat, D. (1982), *Les Ouvrieres*. Paris: Editions Le Sycomore.

Lal, D. (1984), 'The real effects of stabilisation and structural adjustment policies', World Bank Staff Working Papers No. 636, Washington DC.

Longhurst, R. (1987), 'Policy approaches towards small farmers', in G. Cornia, R. Jolly, and F. Stewart (eds) (1987), *op. cit.*

Mbilinyi, M. (1988a), 'The invention of female farming systems in Africa: structural adjustment in Tanzania', Workshop on Economic Crisis, Household Strategies and Women's Work, Cornell University.

Mbilinyi, M. (1988b), 'Agribusiness and women peasants in Tanzania', *Development and Change* 19, 549–83.

Miralao, V. A. (1984), 'The impact of female employment on household management', in G. W. Jones (ed.), *Women in the Urban and Industrial Workforce: Southeast and East Asia*. Canberra: Australian National University.

Moser, C. (1989), 'The impact of recession and structural adjustment policies at the micro-level: low income women and their households in Guayquil, Ecuador', *Invisible Adjustment*, vol. 2, UNICEF.

Onimode, B. (ed.) (1989), *The IMF, the World Bank and the African Debt*. London: Zed Books.

Pahl, J. (1980), 'Patterns of money management within marriage', *Journal of Social Policy* 9(3).

Pankhurst, D., and Jacobs, S. (1988), 'Land tenure, gender relations, and agricultural production: the case of Zimbabwe's peasantry', in J. Davison (ed.) (1988), *op. cit.*

Pearson, R. (1988), 'Female workers in the First and Third Worlds: the greening of women's labour', in R. E. Pahl (ed.), *On Work*. Oxford: Blackwell.

Roston, M. (1983), 'Early neoclassical economics and the economic role of women', Social Science Working Paper, Open University, Milton Keynes.

Salaff, J. (1981), *Working Daughters of Hong Kong*. Cambridge: Cambridge University Press.

Salter, W. (1959), 'Internal and external balance: the role of price and expenditure effects', *Economic Record*, August.

Selowsky, M. (1987), 'Adjustment in the 1980s: an overview of issues', *Finance and Development* 24(2), 11–14.

Sen, A. K. (1983), *Resources, Values and Development*, ch. 16: 'Economics and the family'. Oxford: Blackwell.

Sen, A. K. (1985), 'Women, technology, and sexual divisions', UNCTAD and INSTRAW, Geneva.

Senauer, B., Sahn, D., and Aiderman, H. (1986), 'The effect of time on food consumption patterns in developing countries: evidence from Sri Lanka', *American Journal of Agricultural Economics* 68(4).

Whitehead, A. (1984), '"I'm hungry mum": the politics of domestic budgeting', in K. Young, C. Wolkowitz, and R. McCullagh (eds), *Of Marriage and the Market*. London: Routledge & Kegan Paul.

5

MICRO, MESO, MACRO: GENDER AND ECONOMIC ANALYSIS IN THE CONTEXT OF POLICY REFORM

Economists traditionally divide economics into a supply side and a demand side and look at the functioning of economies at the micro-level of supply and demand interactions between individual economic agents, and at the macro-level of aggregate supply and demand. More recently, some economists have explicitly introduced into the analysis a third level, the meso, between the macro and the micro. Meso analysis concerns itself with the structures that mediate between individuals and the economy considered as a whole, by providing economic signals, costs and benefits, and typically focuses on markets, private-sector firms, and public-sector services.

This chapter examines how concepts of the micro, the macro, and the meso are used by orthodox and critical economists in discussions of economic policy reform, and the extent to which these concepts recognize gender. We also consider some feminist strategies for enabling economic analysis at these three levels to contribute towards the empowerment of women, rather than the perpetuation of their subordination.

The advocacy of economic policy reform: micro, macro, and meso in the neo-classical perspective

The dominant analysis of economic policy reform is based on neo-classical economics. From this perspective, there is no inherent reason why an economy based on voluntary contracts between individuals should experience any persistent problems. Such an economy should be self-regulating, in the sense that supply and demand are quickly brought into equality at micro- and macro-levels through the mediating structure of the market mechanism (that is, the economy tends towards general equilibrium). Such an economy should also be efficient, in the specific sense that it results in outcomes where no one can be made better off without someone else being made worse off (that is, the economy tends towards

Pareto optimality).[1] Finally, the economy should also experience dynamic development, as voluntary contracts between individuals mediated by the market mechanism supposedly encourage initiative and innovation, and the best use of scarce resources.

In the neo-classical paradigm, micro-, meso-, and macro-levels are fully integrated, and simply represent pictures of the economy at varying levels of detail. The macro-level looks at the economy in terms of total marketed output (domestic private-sector and public-sector production plus imports) and total expenditure (consumption plus private investment plus government expenditure plus exports). These aggregates are understood as a coherent result of the activities of millions of individuals (micro-level) integrated by the institutions of the meso-level. The private-sector institutions operating at the meso-level, the institutions of the market mechanism and the firm, are understood as the outcome of voluntary contracts by individuals who wish to create institutions to economize on the costs of conducting transactions (see Hodgson 1988 for a critical explanation). What is economically rational at the individual level also appears to be economically rational at the level of society as a whole.

If things are not working out like this, and there are problems of budget and balance-of-payments deficits, inflation and unemployment, then the main problem is argued to lie in the wrong sort of public policies at macro- and meso-levels. Public policy is conceptualized as an intervention in the economy from the outside, an intervention made not by individuals but by the state, acting not via voluntary contracts but by legislative commands. The wrong sort of public policy leads to imbalances at the macro-level between aggregate supply and demand brought about by the wrong sort of fiscal and monetary policy; by giving individuals the wrong sort of economic signals at the meso-level it leads to imbalances at the micro-level between supply and demand for particular goods and services. This creates inefficiency and undermines dynamic development. The wrong sort of public policy also prevents an economy from being able to adapt easily to change, particularly to 'external shocks' coming from the international economy, such as rises in interest rates, falls in the terms of trade, and falls in inflows of finance.

Changes therefore need to be made in state intervention at macro- and meso-levels. Typically, the reforms recommended include cutbacks in aggregate public expenditure and the money supply, to reduce aggregate demand and a whole series of changes at the meso-level, to remove so-called 'distortions' in the economic signals transmitted to individuals and the economic costs and benefits they enjoy. These will include changes in prices (for instance, via devaluation,

---

1. This does *not* necessarily mean a situation where everyone's basic needs are satisfied. Pareto optimality is consistent with a very unequal, as well as a very equal, distribution of income.

trade liberalization, and withdrawal of subsidies) and in infrastructural services (such as transport, training, education and health services.)

The state tends to be conceptualized as absent from the micro-level, which is seen as a private sphere of economic individuals. However, the very ability of a person to function as an economic individual – that is, an individual able to enter into voluntary contracts to exchange goods and services – is constituted by the state. A gender-aware perspective is much more likely to recognize this, because it will be concerned with economic woman as well as economic man. The ability of women to enter into economic contracts is constrained by the way that state legislation typically constructs women as less than full citizens.

A key example of this in the context of economic policy reform in many developing countries is the way in which the ability of women to enter into credit contracts is constrained by women's lack of rights to family assets. All too often, women cannot sign contracts in their own right and require a male guarantor (father, brother, husband). There is no such thing as a purely private level of the economy.

A related key issue in economic policy reform, but one which is often neglected, is how the reforms change the rights enjoyed by individuals. Where this *is* considered, it tends to be in terms of an enhancement of individual property rights brought about by privatization. But privatization typically also reduces individual social rights of employees and certainly reduces the collective rights of citizens over economic assets.

Individual social rights can also be reduced in the course of economic policy reform by shifts of employment from the 'formal' to the 'informal' sector; by erosion of customary use rights to land by commercialization of land; and by direct legislative changes to withdraw or restructure state-provided services and benefits and to abolish employee rights, such as minimum-wage legislation and the right to strike (Standing 1989; Elson 1991).

For example, removal of rights is very often undertaken in the name of removing 'distortions' from markets. However, unequal distribution of wealth and income is not considered a 'distortion', and reduction of the property rights of the rich and powerful does not tend to feature on the current agendas of economic policy reform.[2] Rather, it is the poor and weak who are most likely to find their social rights regraded as 'distortions'.

The family,[3] one might think, should logically be regarded as belonging to the meso-level – it is, after all, a social institution that brings people together and

---

2. Land reform is rarely included, even though there are strong reasons to suppose land reform would in many cases improve the efficiency of resource use.
3. I shall use the terms 'family' and 'household' in the rather unquestioning way that economists do. For discussion on the complexities of these social groupings and the problems of where to draw bounds, see IDS Bulletin (1991).

mediates between them. In economic analysis, however, the family is usually assigned to the *micro-level*. Indeed, neo-classical analysis treats the family as if it were an individual: in technical terms it is assumed that the family has a joint utility function, and that an altruistic head of household makes decisions on behalf of the family that maximize the joint activity of its members. This means that, provided the 'right' economic signals reach a family via state agencies, markets, and firms, the division of labour and distribution of income within a family is bound to be 'optimal', simply reflecting the different tastes and skills of family members. (This is known in the literature as the 'new household economics'; for critical discussion, see Evans 1989, and Folbre 1986.)

At the micro-level, the neo-classical approach can accommodate gender difference, and even some degree of gender inequality. Economic agents can easily be characterized as 'male' or 'female', in a way that macro-economic aggregates cannot. But gender differentiation must be conceptualized as a matter of differences in the preferences and resource endowments (including skills) of individuals, if the fundamental neo-classical characterization of human beings as utility maximizers with well-defined choice sets and preference orderings is to be preserved. The key problem for women is then judged to be discrimination against them, in a variety of transactions, by other economic agents. But discrimination is judged to be in itself generally economically irrational, leading to lower monetary returns for the discriminating agent. Thus commercialization is seen as generally acting in ways advantageous to women by undermining prejudice.[4] From this point of view, economic policy reforms which strengthen commercialization and the profit motive are seen as likely to work to women's advantage.

At the meso- and macro-levels, neo-classical analysis excludes gender. Mediating structures and monetary aggregates cannot be identified as 'male' or 'female', and so gender analysis is seen as out of place. Indeed, meso institutions and macro-policy instruments tend to be seen as 'gender neutral' (see also Elson 1991). If these institutions and instruments operate in ways that are detrimental to women, then this is fundamentally due to the characteristics of individuals at the micro-level, and in particular to prejudice against women. The appropriate policy response is equal-opportunities legislation, education to combat prejudice, and 'safety nets' for women needing gainful employment – not a restructuring of meso institutions and a rethinking of macro-policy reforms. Gender has a place only at the micro-level, in the analysis of the responses of individuals to the reforms.

---

4. Occasional arguments are presented to suggest that discrimination may be 'rational' and will persist. See, for instance, Birdsall & Sabot (1991: 10–11).

The critique of economic policy reform: micro, macro, and meso in the perspectives of critical economists

There is a variety of economic analysis critical of current forms of economic policy reform, drawing on Keynesian, Kaleckian, structuralist and Marxist perspectives. Critical perspectives stress that what is rational for the individual economic
agent is not necessarily rational for the system as a whole. The macro-level of the
economy has a life of its own and is not simply an aggregation which synthesizes
the preferences and endowments of the individuals who make up the economy.
The reason it has a life of its own is that money and the market mechanism do
not simply integrate the actions of many individuals, in the way that general equilibrium theory supposes. Money and the market mechanism also disintegrate,
fragment, and segment individual actions. In particular, there is no guarantee
that supply and demand for goods will be brought into line by price changes, with
money acting simply as a medium of exchange. If agents think prices will change
in the future, it makes sense for them to hold on to money itself, rather than use
it to buy something right now (see Bhaduri 1986, for further explanation).

Once this is taken into account, the economy can be seen as something with the
potential to generate its own problems, such as unemployment, inflation, debt, and
declining productivity. Economic crisis is not just the result of the wrong policies
and 'external shocks.' Indeed, the 'external shocks' themselves can be seen as resulting from inherent dysfunctions of the international economy. A corollary of this
is that the macro-level should not just be analysed on a country-by-country basis.
It should be analysed at a global, as well as a national level. Policy reform should
extend to the international system of trade and payments (see Helleiner 1992).

Critical perspectives also challenge the idea that the institutions of the firm and
the market mechanism can simply be derived from the utility-maximizing decisions of individuals (argued in depth by Hodgson 1988). One strand of analysis
emphasizes that these institutions embody co-operative conflicts, that is, situations in which individuals do stand to make gains from co-operating (for example,
producing something together on the basis of a wage contract) but have different
and conflicting interests in the distribution of the benefits (see also Drèze & Sen
1989). Partly as a way of coping with this, meso-institutions embody social norms
and networks that help shape the behaviour of individuals and the ideas they
have about what it is appropriate to want and to do. Without such social norms
market economies could not function, because voluntary contracts between
individuals are always incomplete. This is because life is radically uncertain, and
try as we might to cover all contingencies, the unexpected is always liable to crop
up. The outcome will always depend on the degree to which people feel bound
to act in certain ways even though there is not a clause in the contract to cover

it, on what labour market analysts call 'custom and practice', on shared general understandings and mutual trust (see Hodgson 1988).

Similar sorts of analysis have also been extended to the family, which has been seen as a social institution that is an area of co-operative conflict in which behaviour is constrained by social norms. In the work of some economists, the analysis also extends to calling into question the fundamental characterization of human beings as economic agents. It may be argued that the experience of subordination makes people less likely to have a well-defined preference function. The experience of subordination inclines people to shape their preferences to what is available, rather than reach out for what they want. Social norms constrain the choices that people make about the division of labour in the family. A notable example of this type of analysis of the family may be found in Sen 1990.

This perspective easily lends itself to an analysis of gender inequality at the micro-level that is much more critical than that offered by the neo-classical paradigm. Rather than see the gender division of labour and income in the family being seen as the optimal outcome of free choices, it may be seen as the profoundly unequal accommodation reached between individuals who occupy very different social positions with very different degrees of social power. Individuals may be conceptualized not just as biologically male and female but as socially gendered (as in Sen 1990). Most critical economics, however, shares with neo-classical economics a lack of gender analysis at the meso- and macro-levels. Although individuals are conceptualized as gendered in the critical economics of the family, markets and firms are not generally conceptualized as gendered in a comparable way, even though they may operate in ways that are particularly constraining and disadvantageous to women.

At the macro-level, gender is absent altogether; the discourse is all about monetary aggregates. Many critical economists are puzzled about how gender analysis can be introduced at a level of economic analysis which is completely impersonal. However, feminist critical economics has begun to show us how we can demonstrate that not only is the personal political, the impersonal is political too!

Feminist critical economics and the critique of economic policy reform

Feminist critical economics[5] argues that the operation of economic reform at micro-, meso-, and macro-levels is male-biased, serving to perpetuate women's relative disadvantage, even though the forms of that disadvantage vary between

---

5. Feminist economics is only just beginning to build itself and make its presence felt in economics as a discipline. Some of the work of those who define themselves as feminist economists draws on the mainstream neo-classical paradigm; other feminist economists draw on a variety of critical approaches, a notable example being Folbre (forthcoming).

different groups of women and are disrupted and change in the course of policy reform. Most economic theory, whether orthodox or critical, is also male-biased, even though it appears to be gender-neutral. The male bias arises because theory fails to take adequate account of the inequality between women as a gender and men as a gender, Neo-classical economics is fundamentally disabled from doing this because of its 'choice-theoretic' framework of analysis. Critical economics opens up the possibility of theory which is not male-biased, and of economic policy reforms which are not male-biased, because it does not regard micro-, meso-, and macro-levels of the economy as integrated and regulated by a choice-theoretic logic. Feminist critical economics starts from these possibilities.[6]

Most feminist critical work to date has concentrated on the micro-level. The feminist critique of economic policy reform has concentrated on investigating the impact of economic policy reform at the level of the family and the individual, utilizing a bargaining-based critical theory of the family, and arguing that the burdens placed on poor rural and poor urban women are incommensurate with any benefits they may possibly obtain (see, for example, Beneria & Feldman 1992).

It is necessary to go beyond this and to analyse how male bias is constituted at the meso- and macro-levels, at the level of mediating institutions and monetary aggregates. One way of doing this is to investigate how social institutions and monetary relationships which are not themselves intrinsically gendered nevertheless become bearers of gender.[7] The family is an intrinsically gendered institution, in that the conjugal relation that constitutes it is gender ascriptive. Marriage is a social relation between a person of the male and a person of the female gender. Kin relations are gender ascriptive—the discourse of kin indicates the gender of the persons referred to (sister, brother, nephew, niece, grandmother, grandfather).

Commercial relations between buyer and seller, and employer and employee, are not intrinsically gendered in this way. Neither are the relations between users and providers of public services. But although they are not gender ascriptive, these relations are bearers of gender, in the sense that they are permeated through and through by gender in their institutional structure. As one study of Brazilian factories concluded, the supposedly objective economic laws of market competition work through and within "gendered structures" (Humphrey 1987: 219).

At the meso-level, the operation of markets, firms, and public-sector agencies is gendered via the social norms and networks which are functional to the smooth operation of those institutions. Social cohesion between men is enhanced by the exclusion of women. Social discipline in hierarchical organizations is enhanced

---

6. These issues are explored at greater length in Elson (1993a and 1993b).
7. The distinction between social relations which are intrinsically gendered ('gender ascriptive') and those which are not, but which are nevertheless bearers of gender, is due to Whitehead (1979).

by the systematic subordination of women. Critical institutional economics has tended to stress the social benefits of customs which fill the gaps in incomplete contracts, in order to stress that economic acts cannot be understood simply in terms of contracts and cash nexuses. But although such customs may be beneficial in allowing economies to continue to function, the benefits tend to be very unequally distributed. Shared social understandings and mutual trust tend to be expressions of the hegemony of the powerful. Thus, although women may formally be able to participate in markets, they tend to find themselves excluded from the traditional business–social networks, where vital exchanges of information occur and 'goodwill' is built up.[8] Similarly, although women may formally be able to participate in paid employment in the private sector, they tend to find themselves excluded from the teams of skilled and professional workers who obtain the higher incomes.[9]

Economic policy reform often involves the emergence of new meso-level institutions. Rolling back the state means the emergence of new markets and new firms. Reforming public-sector services means the emergence of new types of public-sector agency. Unless explicit thought is given to the design of these new institutions, they will tend to instigate new instances of male bias.[10] Women will be excluded from or disadvantaged in their operations. The shared social understandings on which they rest will be expressive of male hegemony. Even though the policy reforms may not be male-biased by design, they will be male-biased by omission.

At the meso-level, therefore, we can introduce gender analysis via an examination of how the social norms and networks which are needed for the successful operation of both commercial and public-service institutions are bearers of gender.

At the macro-level the crucial thing to consider is the role of money. Money mobilizes human effort via prices and wages; and the output of effort that it mobilizes gets counted in the gross national product, and in other monetary aggregates such as savings, investment, public expenditure, public revenue, imports and exports. But money's mobilizing power is incomplete. It is not able to mobilize directly all the resources that go into reproducing and maintaining the capacity for effort (labour-power) in any economy which is based on wage labour rather than slave labour. The ability of money to mobilize labour power for 'productive work' depends on the operation of some non-monetary set of social relations to

---

8. As was found by a study of women entrepreneurs in Kenya, Ghana, Jamaica and the Solomon Islands (Commonwealth Secretariat 1990).

9. This is established in fascinating detail in a study of technical workers in Britain by Cockburn (1985).

10. For discussion of male bias in state agencies, see Agarwal (1988).

mobilize labour power for 'reproductive work.' These non-monetary social relations are subordinate to money in the sense that they cannot function and sustain themselves without an input of money; and they are reshaped in response to the power of money. Nevertheless, neither can the monetary economy sustain itself without an input of unpaid labour, input shaped by the structure of gender relations. Male bias in gender relations means that the burdens of 'reproductive work' fall mainly on women. There is an interdependence between the economy of monetized production and the non-monetized 'reproductive' economy. One implication of this 'incompleteness' of monetary relations is that money and all its forms (prices, wages, rates of interest, and so on) become bearers of gender, expressing male bias both in quantitative terms (as in the differential between male and female wages) and in qualitative terms (as in the differential between paid work which is recognized as productive and unpaid work which is not). Money is not gender-neutral. Women's access to money is structured by gender relations. Such access tends to disrupt non-monetized gender relations, but it results in new forms of gender relations, in which male bias is expressed in monetary form.

The interdependence between the economy of monetized production and the non-monetized economy of 'reproductive work' is a delicate balance, constrained by the fact that basic needs must be met to sustain human beings and human communities, and that monetized production is subject to inherent dislocations and crises. History shows that this interdependence in market economies cannot be successfully regulated by individual contract and monetary relations. It has always required the mediation of the organizations of the state and the community, the provision of public services and community mutual aid, to avoid destitution and social breakdown, and to enhance human development in ways that promote increases in productivity in the monetized economy. It has always required ways of transferring resources that do not entail buying and selling, but operate through taxes and subsidies, gifts and grants.

A feminist critique of economic policy reform at the macro-level can be developed in terms of an analysis of how economic policy reform treats the interdependence between the 'productive economy' and the 'reproductive economy', between making a profit and meeting needs, between covering costs and sustaining human beings. Overwhelmingly, the design of economic policy reform focuses on the 'productive economy.' Macro-policy is generally designed to bring the *level* of aggregate monetized demand in line with the level of aggregate monetized supply, and to change the *structure* of monetized demand and supply so as to favor the production of goods and services traded internationally (tradables) as compared with those that are only domestically traded (non-tradables).

Macro-policy generally takes the 'reproductive economy' for granted, assuming it can continue to function adequately no matter how the 'productive economy' is disrupted. Current forms of economic policy reform that emphasize rolling back the state and liberating market forces give scant consideration to how this will impact on the 'reproductive economy'. There tends to be an implicit assumption that the 'reproductive economy' can accommodate itself to whatever changes macro-policy introduces, especially to withdrawals of public services and subsidies and declines in public-sector employment and to rises in prices and taxes. Since it is women who undertake most of the work in the 'reproductive economy', and in the organization of community mutual aid, this is equivalent to assuming that there is an unlimited supply of unpaid female labour, able to compensate for any adverse changes resulting from macro-economic policy, so as to continue to meet the basic needs of their families and communities and sustain them as social organizations.

This is the point at which macro-economics is male-biased. It is not that macro-policy reforms are deliberately designed to favour men. Nor is the key issue that male-biased social traditions prevent women from taking advantage of macro-policy reforms that could work in their favour. The key issue is that macro-economics has a one-sided view of the macro-economy: it considers only the monetary aggregates of the 'productive economy'. It ignores the human resource aggregates of the 'reproductive economy', the indicators of population, health, nutrition, education, skills. This one-sided view of the macro-economy is male-biased because the sexual division of labour means that women are largely responsible for the 'reproductive economy' as well as contributing a great deal of effort to the 'productive economy'.[11] This male bias cannot, however, simply be changed by theoretical analysis and research. It requires changes in the way that national and international economies function, so that human development is taken as a priority – a point made in UNDP 1990. For this to happen, it is not enough to introduce targeted poverty-alleviation programmes ('safety nets'). Rather than bind the wounds after they have been inflicted, it is better not to inflict the wounds in the first place.

Conclusions

One way forward would be to campaign in order that all programmes for macro-economic policy reform include not only targets for monetary aggregates and policy instruments for achieving them but also targets for human development

---

11. The functioning of the 'reproductive economy' does, of course, require inputs of cash and public services. Indeed, these are vital in improving productivity in the development of human capacities.

and the policy instruments needed for delivering them. The relation between the policy instruments and the targets should be analysed in gender-disaggregated terms that recognize inputs of unpaid labour as well as paid labour.[12] We need to ask what kinds of institutions will mediate between changes in fiscal and monetary policy and exchange rate policy and individuals. What benefits and what costs are different groups of women and men expected to experience? Has the interdependence between the 'productive economy' and the 'reproductive economy' been taken into account? For instance, has the programme of expenditure cuts been designed in a way that will sustain or undermine the ability of women to respond to new price incentives in agriculture and job opportunities in export-oriented manufacturing, without jeopardizing human development targets?[13]

The integration of human development targets into macro-economic policy reform programmes will also facilitate a view of human beings as ends, not just means, as persons with social rights, not factors of production with prices. Programmes for economic policy reform should be required to specify whose rights (distinguishing rights of men and of women) will be changed, and how. This way of introducing gender-awareness into the design of economic policy reforms is likely to benefit some men as well as women insofar as it introduces consideration of needs and rights into the process of reform alongside dollars and deficits. It combats a male bias in policy reforms which is far from being deliberately introduced by those who design reforms, but which is the result of oversights and omissions facilitated by a one-sided concern with monetary variables. It emphasizes that the key issue we need to address in attempts to engender macro-economic policy reform is not pre-existing customs and traditions which discriminate against women, but one-sided emphasis by reformers on paid work in the 'productive economy', and a neglect of unpaid work in the 'reproductive economy'.

References

Agarwal, B. (ed.) (1988) *Structures of Patriarchy*. London: Zed Books.
Beneria, L. and S. Feldman (eds) (1992) *Economic Crises, Persistent Poverty and Women's Work*. Boulder, CO: Westview Press.
Bhaduri, A. (1986) *Macroeconomics: The Dynamics of Commodity Production*. Basingstoke: Macmillan.

---

12. This requirement goes beyond the prescriptions of the Human Development Report (1990), which surprisingly fails to recognize the vital role of unpaid labour as a producer of human capacities and one-sidedly emphasizes public-sector services.
13. A study of economic policy reform in Zambia found that cutbacks in health expenditure were hampering women farmers, who were having to spend more time looking after sick relatives, and less time farming (Evans & Young 1988).

Birdsall, N. and R. Sabot (eds) (1991) *Unfair Advantage: Labour Market Discrimination in Developing Countries*. Washington, DC: World Bank.

Cockburn, S. (1985) *Machinery of Dominance: Women, Men and Technical Know-How*. London: Pluto Press.

Commonwealth Secretariat (1990) *Women in Export Development*. London: Commonwealth Secretariat.

Drèze, J. and A. K. Sen (1989) *Hunger and Public Action*. Oxford: Oxford University Press.

Elson, D. (1991) 'Appraising Recent Developments in the World Market for Nimble Fingers: Accumulation, Regulation, Organisation'. Paper presented at Workshop on Women Organising in the Process of Industrialisation, Institute of Social Studies, The Hague.

Elson, D. (1993a) 'Feminist Approaches to Development Economics' (mimeo). Department of Economics, University of Manchester.

Elson, D. (1993b) 'Gender-Aware Analysis and Development Economics', *Journal of International Development* 5(2).

Evans, A. (1989) *Gender Issues in Rural Household Economics*, Institute of Development Studies Discussion Paper No. 254.

Evans, A. and K. Young (1988) Gender Issues in Household Labour Allocation: The Case of Northern Province, Zambia, ODA ESCOR Research Report. London: Overseas Development Agency.

Folbre, N. (1986) 'Hearts and Spades: Paradigms of Household Economics', *World Development* 14(2).

Folbre, N. (forthcoming) *The Logic of Patriarchal Capitalism*. London: Routledge.

Helleiner, G. K. (1992) 'The IMF, the World Bank and Africa's Adjustment and External Debt Problems: An Unofficial View', *World Development* 20(6), 779–92.

Hodgson, G. (1988) *Economics and Institutions*. Cambridge: Polity Press.

Humphrey, J. (1987) 'Gender, Pay and Skill: Manual Workers in Brazilian Industry', in M. Mitter (ed.) *Women, Work and Ideology in the Third World*. London: Tavistock.

IDS Bulletin (1991) Special Issue: 'Researching the Household: Methodological and Empirical Issues', *IDS Bulletin* 22(1).

Sen, A. K. (1990) 'Gender and Co-operative Conflicts', in I. Tinker (ed.) *Persistent Inequalities: Women and World Development*. Oxford: Oxford University Press.

Standing, G. (1989) 'Global Feminisation through Flexible Labour', *World Development* 17(7).

UNDP (1990) *Human Development Report*. Oxford: Oxford University Press.

Whitehead, A. (1979) 'Some Preliminary Notes on the Subordination of Women', *IDS Bulletin* 10(3).

6

TALKING TO THE BOYS: GENDER AND ECONOMIC GROWTH MODELS

Introduction

The last ten years have seen a blossoming of critical research on gender and macro-economic processes, theories and policies; the next ten years present us with the challenge of building on this to try to start transforming practice and move towards the use of macro-economic policy as an instrument for empowering rather than burdening women. This will not be easy. There will be obstruction from gender based coalitions of men, intent on blocking changes, even though greater gender equality promises benefits for society as a whole (Folbre 1994, 1995). There will be obstruction from class-based coalitions of men and women, intent on preventing any active use of macro-economic policy to change the outcome of market processes. There will be a need to tackle the international dimensions of macro-economic policy, and to work simultaneously on national and international levels, in order to contest the constraints that international bond markets currently place on macro-economic policy.

We shall have to work simultaneously on improving conceptual understanding, improving our empirical knowledge, and constructing a process of institutional change. This chapter is written in the belief that in doing all these things we shall have to act both 'in' and 'against' the established modes of macro-economic theory, empirical enquiry and policy processes. If we only work on the 'inside' we run the risk of merely achieving small improvements in the formulation of models or collection of statistics which do not actually transform women's lives.

If we only work on the 'outside', we run the risk of simply communicating with those who already share our viewpoint, and of not engaging with actual processes of macro-economic policy making. A great deal can be done at the grassroots level in terms of transforming women's livelihoods through the creation of new economic institutions that have gender-aware principles of operation. But macro-economic processes and policies are national and international processes and policies – and require intervention at that level. This requires some kind of engagement with those on the 'inside', to show both where we think they are wrong, and also what we think should be done instead. It requires some willingness to get to know and speak the language of the 'insiders' – economists, statisticians, Ministries of Finance and Governors of Central Banks. There is always a danger with this kind of engagement that one gets incorporated, and becomes an 'insider' oneself. From talking to the boys (most people involved in the macro-economic analysis and policy formulation are male), one may become oneself 'one of the boys'.

A way of guarding against this is to emphasise ways of transforming the conceptual tools rather than the integration of women into the existing paradigm; and to emphasise the democratic transformation of public debate and policy processes and not simply the incorporation of new forms of expertise.

This chapter explores these issues with respect to the most basic macro-economic growth model. It is couched in non-technical language in the sense of not using complex mathematical or diagrammatical notation, in order to communicate to the wide readership of this book. It could be expressed in more technical language for the economics profession, if that seemed likely to improve the chances of communicating with that audience, though in fact the gist of the argument can be expressed without using either complex maths or diagrams. What maths and diagrams do is make more precise the limits to outcomes and policy options, and the trade-offs we may face. This precision is, of course, only precision within the confines of a particular set of assumptions, and will be a spurious precision if the assumptions are an inadequate representation of the processes we wish to investigate. All models are by their nature abstractions – but this is their strength, not their weakness. The weakness comes not from making abstractions *per se* but from making inappropriate abstractions.

Formal economic models whether stemming from neo-classical, structuralist or Marxist versions of economics, are closed systems. They, by their very nature, set bounds. Because of this, they can be misused to suggest that there are no alternatives to some particular policy. But they can only properly be used to investigate the implications of accepting a particular set of assumptions about variables, parameters, behaviour and technology. Their very boundedness is useful in forcing us to think clearly about which parameters we need to change in order for different policies and different outcomes to be feasible.

The coherence of formal models is a one-sided abstraction, because economic processes do not jump cleanly from one equilibrium to another. But by making us think hard about limitations and priorities, they can help us avoid macro-economic policies that are unsustainable and lead to economic crises, which disempower women as much as do badly designed adjustment policies.

Some people may query the usefulness of discussing growth models at all. Shouldn't we be criticising economic growth rather than modelling it, they may say? To which I would reply that the two things are not incompatible. Moreover, it is useful to engage with simple growth models because they form the conceptual framework of many medium-term macro-economic policies. This does not mean an endorsement of aggregate growth of national output as the only important macro-economic objective; nor an endorsement of any and every pattern of growth. Indeed, growth models themselves may generate a critical understanding of growth processes. Harrod's original purpose in devising his widely used model of growth was to develop a critique of the assumption that a full employment balanced growth path can be taken for granted (Walters 1995). He was concerned about the problem of what the most recent *Human Development Report* called 'jobless growth' (UNDP 1996: 2).

That same *Human Development Report* identifies four other undesirable types of growth: ruthless growth, where the fruits of economic growth mainly benefit the rich; voiceless growth where growth is not accompanied by an extension of democracy or empowerment; rootless growth, which causes peoples' cultural identity to wither; futureless growth, where the present generation squanders resources needed by future generations. Nevertheless, the Report concludes that more economic growth, not less, will generally be needed in the next century. But it will need to be directed to supporting human development, reducing poverty, protecting the environment and ensuring sustainability (UNDP 1996: 1).

Here we shall focus on simple growth models not because we are assuming that growth of aggregate national output is a good thing irrespective of the pattern of growth, but because such models crystallise in a simple form some influential ways of thinking about savings, investment, productivity and output and employment. We shall look at ways of making use of such models as a departure point in order to raise potentially transformatory questions about economies as gendered structures, and about the interaction of production and social reproduction. We shall also identify an agenda for empirical research arising out of this discussion.

The Harrod–Domar growth model: basic considerations

The most simple model of growth, which every student of development studies generally comes across in one form or another, is the Harrod–Domar model. This is a synthesis of work originally undertaken separately by Harrod (1939, 1948) and Domar (1946) to create a model which can be used to answer questions such as – if the policy objective is to achieve a rate of growth of national output of 5 per cent a year, how much will the country need to save and invest? The model suggests that the answer depends on the productivity of investment. Its reasoning is summed up in the conclusion that the annual growth of output is equal to the annual share of savings in national output divided by the incremental capital-output ratio (which measures the amount of output produced by a given addition to the capital stock in a year). To raise the rate of growth it is necessary to raise the rate of saving and/or to raise the productivity of capital. This is based on the assumption that all savings are invested and result in additions to the capital stock, and that the capital stock is fully utilised. It also assumes that there is no shortage of labour to utilise the capital stock, and no large-scale unemployment which might lead to hesitation in the investment of savings by depressing demand expectations.

The basic version of the model was modified to introduce exports, imports and foreign sources of saving by Chenery and Strout (1966). This resulted in what is generally known as the 'two gap' model, which is used as the basis for evaluations of the foreign aid requirements of a country by national governments and donor agencies, (see for example, Ministry of Foreign Affairs, Netherlands, 1994). The 'two gap' model forms the basis of the Revised Minimum Standard Model used by the World Bank to make projections of growth and balance of payments deficits for countries undergoing structural adjustment (Tarp 1993). In this chapter, however, we shall confine our attention to the basic version of the Harrod-Domar model, as expounded in textbooks such as Gillis *et al.* (1992), in order to highlight a number of issues which arise irrespective of whether the national economy is relatively 'closed' or relatively 'open' to the international economy. These are issues to do with savings, investment and productivity, issues which as Amartya Sen has argued, were at the heart of development economics when it was first constructed as a separate discourse in the 1940s and 1950s (Sen 1983); and which continue to be urgent and unresolved issues, despite the attempts of the neo-classical counterrevolution in development economics to shift the emphasis from the macro analysis of capital accumulation to the micro analysis of prices (Toye 1987).

The Harrod–Domar model is constructed at a high level of abstraction and does not specify the pattern of ownership of the capital stock; or the processes through which savings are mobilised, investments are made, and capital stock is used in production; or the distribution of the output provided. Domar, in fact, constructed his version of the model with a planned economy in mind, whereas Harrod had in mind a market economy, with savings and investment and production largely in the private sector. The assumption of full capacity utilisation on which the synthetic version of the model is built is in fact more plausible for a 'mixed' economy with a large public sector and a 'Keynesian' public policy or for a centrally planned socialist economy; because in these types of economy there is less likely to be a deficiency in aggregate demand. Those making investment decisions in such an economy do not have to worry too much about the risk of lack of demand because there is a relatively soft budget constraint, and a state which stands ready to act as buyer of last resort. (However, such economies may well be prone to other problems such as inflation or low productivity.)

Many criticisms may be made of the Harrod–Domar model as a basis for development policy (for an early and effective example, see Streeten 1968). For instance, as well as ignoring problems of deficient demand, it ignores problems of inter-sectoral input-output relations, and problems of lack of sufficient skilled labour. However, these last two deficiencies can in principle be remedied by disaggregating the model, using an input-output table; and by extending the concept of investment to include investment in health, nutrition and education to develop the skills and capacities of workers. Here, we shall focus on the gender blindness of the Harrod–Domar model. As with all aggregate growth models, the Harrod–Domar model pays no attention to gender relations (Walters 1995). However, thus gender blindness is not a benign gender neutrality, because the omission of consideration of gender relations in relation to saving, investment, productivity and growth serves to consolidate and perpetuate gender inequality. In the next two sections we discuss strategies for introducing an awareness of gender into the model.

Gender disaggregation

It may seem that the way to introduce gender into the basic growth model is by disaggregating the economy into a male economy and a female economy, with male and female streams of savings, investment and output. Certainly from the perspective of neo-classical economics, gender disaggregation is the obvious move to make. This is the procedure advocated by Collier (1990, 1994) in dealing with a different type of model – the small dependent economy model of structural adjustment, in which resources are switched from non-tradables to tradables. Collier sets out his reasons as follows:

> Gender is one of many ways in which data can be disaggregated and the rationale for doing this is twofold. First, in earning income, women often face different constraints, from men. Since structural adjustment is largely about changing constraints, if those facing women and men are sufficiently different, it is illuminating to treat the genders as distinct groups rather than studying gender-undifferentiated averages. Second, women and men often have radically different propensities to consume particular public services and so budgetary changes can have powerfully gender-differentiated effects. It should be stressed that gender is not a topic in itself but rather a possible disaggregation to be borne in mind when studying a topic. Sometimes gender disaggregation will

not add enough to be worthwhile. However, for some topics it will be useful and for others essential. A corollary of this rationale for an analysis which distinguishes between women and men is that, generally, there is not a small, self-contained set of 'women's issues' which can be appended to an otherwise unaltered analysis. Rather, the claim is that many standard issues in resource allocation become better illuminated when the analysis is disaggregated by gender.

(Collier 1990: 149–50)

Walters (1995) writing from a Keynesian perspective is not so sure that disaggregation is the best way of proceeding:

Of course, disaggregation is possible. At the simplest level, representative agents in different economic circumstances would carry different parameter values within a disaggregated model. However, a mechanical disaggregation based on the fact that all economic agents are biologically male or female would be inappropriate. Gender disaggregation should correspond to our understanding of how gender relations impose constraints on the overall behaviour of macro models; the analogy is disaggregation by class. In Keynesian macro-economic models, based on class, the models are driven by the aggregate level of spending which becomes a function of the distribution of income between workers and capitalists. This is a structural, rather than an individualist disaggregation. It is based on the different economic functions of workers and capitalists and corresponds to the institutional division between firms and households. Any disaggregation by gender should be based on a similar understanding of the way in which gender as a social institution impinges on or constrains the behaviour of the macroeconomy.

(Walters 1995: 1870)

The caution displayed by Walters seems justified when one considers how gender is understood in the gender-disaggregation analysis conducted by Collier (1988, 1990, 1994; Collier *et al.* 1991). This analysis locates gender primarily in terms of the 'physiological asymmetry of reproduction' and the impulse of boys to copy men and girls to copy women. Biology and preferences are the ultimate foundations of gender inequality.

The basic problem with disaggregation is that it focuses on the separate characteristics of men or women (whether individuals or groups) rather than the social institutions of gender as a power relation. It can thus lead to the analysis of women in isolation from men (and vice versa); or the female economy in isolation from the male economy. The danger is that it does not draw sufficient attention to the reciprocal determination of the characteristics of women and men as economic agents; and the reciprocal determination of the characteristics of male or female sectors of production. Nevertheless there is much to be gained in empirical research in a multisectoral framework in distinguishing between male-intensive and female-intensive sectors of the economy. A greater empirical understanding of the comparative sectoral pattern of the employment of men and of women is extremely useful for any analysis of inter-sectoral resource transfers, such as are implied by structural adjustment (Elson *et al.* 1997).

The strategy of gender disaggregation does not however do very much to transform perceptions of how a national economy functions. It would be useful to consider strategies which pose the issue of the economy itself as a gendered structure, rather than as a gender-neutral structure within which men and women undertake different activities.

Gendered parameters

One strategy for doing this at the abstract level of a simple growth model is to conceptualise the parameters of the model as 'bearers of gender'. This entails recognising the matrix of gender relations as an intervening variable in all economic activities, whether undertaken by men or women, in male-intensive or female-intensive sectors of the economy. In the context of the simple Harrod–Domar growth model, this means introducing gender relations as an intervening variable that can influence the productivity of investment and the propensity to save. Unequal gender relations could operate to reduce the productivity of investment – in technical terms to raise the potential value of ICORs (Incremental Capital Output Ratios) above the level that would prevail with more egalitarian gender relations.

There is certainly a wealth of evidence which demonstrates male bias in the use of productive resources. Male bias disadvantages women in access to and control of credit and land; in the creation and dissemination of new technologies; and in the acquisition of health, strength and skills. Male bias disadvantages women in credit, labour and product markets and intra-firm labour processes, marginalising women from decision-making processes; in access to and control of infrastructural services (energy, water, transport, buildings) and in intra-household arrangements for the organisation of both production of commodities and the social reproduction of people. Male bias excludes women's voices from the policy processes in which public expenditure patterns are determined. There is a large literature on all these forms of male bias which leaves no doubt that they are widespread and have significant impact on women's well-being (Agarwal 1988; Tinker 1990; Birdsall & Sabot 1991; Young 1993; Kabeer 1994; Elson *et al.*

1997). But in addition, gender inequality, just like class inequality, is likely to be a barrier to the most effective and productive use of human resources to meet human needs.

Quantitative evidence can be cited to illustrate this point with respect to control over the use of resources by small-scale producers. For example, Ongaro (1988) looked at the adoption of new farming technology in maize production in Kenya in the 1980s and investigated the impact of gender relations on the use of technology by comparing the effect of weeding on yields in female-headed households and male-headed households. It was found that in female-headed households the weeding undertaken raised yields by 56 per cent, whereas in male-headed house holds the increase in yield was only 15 per cent. After controlling for other differences between the two types of household, the study concluded that the most likely explanation was a systematic difference in effort due to differential entitlement structures, with women in female-headed households having more incentive to weed more effectively because they controlled the proceeds of their own work whereas the women in male-headed households did not.

Output is also lost because women small-scale producers do not have the same access as men to productive inputs, including education. For instance, Moock's (1976) investigation of the efficiency of women as farm managers in Kenya found that their performance compared very well with that of men, but that their access to resources was more restricted. On the basis of the coefficients in Moock's study, it has been calculated that if the woman farmers had the same access to inputs and education as the men farmers in the sample, yields could be increased by between 7 and 9 per cent. Another study covering beans and cowpeas as well as maize suggests even bigger increases in yields, of around 22 per cent, would be possible if women farmers had the same access to inputs and education as men farmers (Saito et al. 1994). Similar results have been found for Burkino Faso, where a recent study suggests that the intra-household reallocation of resources from men to women could increase the value of household output by 10–20 per cent (Aiderman et al. 1995).

Similar findings are reported in a study of small-scale urban retailers in Peru (Smith & Stelcher 1990). This established that women were as effective managers of resources as men. However, firms with a smaller amount of capital tended to have much higher returns to capital, and a much higher proportion of female-owned firms had low amounts of capital. Directing increments of capital (via reforms of credit) to female-owned firms would therefore tend to raise the overall rate of return to capital (and *ipso facto* reduce the investment required to achieve any given rate of growth).

Similar arguments can be made with respect to eliminating discrimination against women in labour markets. Such discrimination has been treated in economic analysis mainly as an equity issue, but can also be seen as socially inefficient. A pioneering study by Tzannatos (1992 Part 1: 15) has demonstrated that if gender discrimination in patterns of occupation and pay in Latin America were eliminated not only could women's wages rise by about 50 per cent, but national output could rise by 5 per cent.

In counterpoint to this, it is certainly possible to construct scenarios in which gender inequality might lead to increased profitability of investment through extracting more effort from women. There are cases where such tendencies can be discerned. A study of gender and industrial reform in Bangladesh has found that between 1983 and 1990, the average weekly hours worked in urban formal sector manufacturing by women workers increased from 41.3 to 55.9. For men, the increase was from 48.9 to 53.2, so that by 1990 women were working on average longer hours than men despite having more unpaid work in social reproduction than men (Zohir 1996). However, such long hours of work for women are likely to reduce labour productivity through ill-health and stress. Exploitation of women workers certainly leads to a bias in the distribution of income against women and towards employers (who are usually men). But profitability and productivity are not the same thing. It is possible for lower profitability to be combined with higher productivity. If women's hours of work were reduced and discrimination against women ended, the social return in terms of output per unit of investment would tend to be higher, but the private returns to owners of capital might tend to fall. The latter would then have an interest in perpetuating gender inequality even though there would be gains in terms of final output.

Societies may be temporarily locked into a particular path-dependent set of unequal gender and class relations which are conducive to the persistence of behaviour patterns that create adverse trade-offs between equality and productivity. There are clearly parallels here with the debates on productivity and democratic or participatory economic institutions (see for instance Bowles *el al.* 1993). Much depends on whether people's preferences and institutional structures are believed to be exogenous or endogenous. Insofar as preferences and institutions are endogenous, then there is much more scope for dynamic institutional transformations which can move societies out of vicious circles into virtuous circles in which equality and efficiency are mutually reinforcing rather than at odds; and production is organised through cooperative rather than exploitative institutions. The key issue then is how such dynamic transformations can be accomplished. The view taken here is that what is required is not 'investment *in* women' but investment *with* women in institutional changes which change preferences, perceptions, norms and rights. In considering the costs of this investment it must be remembered that perpetuating gender inequality is also costly, requiring expenditures that buttress male power without enhancing productivity, a point we return to below.

We still lack macro-level studies which gather and review available micro evidence on gender inequality and the productivity of investment for a particular country and attempt to synthesise the findings to produce some estimate of the implications of failure to reduce male bias for the country's rate of growth: and to indicate which forms of male bias have greatest quantitative significance for the value of the rate of growth. This is likely to depend on economic structure, with male bias in labour markets being a more significant factor in reducing the return to investment in countries whose production is largely organised through wage employment in private and public sector corporations: and male bias in credit and produce markets being more significant in countries where self-employment and small businesses account for a larger share of output.

Besides the ICOR, the other important parameter in the Harrod–Domar model is the savings propensity. Studies providing direct evidence linking the degree of gender inequality with the value of this parameter are hard to find. Most studies at household level seem to focus more on expenditure patterns than on savings. There is a need for some comparative studies to explore the hypothesis that a greater degree of female control over household budgeting is conducive to a higher rate of saving; and that where women and men have separate income streams, women have a greater propensity to save out of income under their control than do men. The reason for setting up the hypothesis in this form is the intuition that women's responsibilities and obligations in the sphere of social reproduction may lead them to take a longer view, and that women, for cultural reasons, have a greater tendency than men to derive satisfaction and well-being from activities which are less commodity intensive. Some household-level studies which have probed leisure activities have found that women spend their leisure in visiting friends and relatives, going to church, and playing with their children, while men go to football matches and bars and cafes (e.g. Kanji 1993). This is an area where more research is needed. However, there is plenty of evidence suggesting that a more equal gender distribution of income would be conducive to spending patterns that contribute to higher growth rates in the long term in ways that promote human development. To bring this evidence to bear, we need to extend the model to incorporate social reproduction.

Extending the model to incorporate social reproduction

The simple Harrod–Domar model (like most growth models) takes labour for granted and treats it as a non-produced input into production that does not constrain growth (Walters 1995). However, there is now widespread recognition that the productivity of investment depends on the capabilities of the people who use it in production, especially their health and skills.

Mainstream economics recognises this in the concept of 'human capital' and endogenous growth theory gives formal expression to the idea that investment in 'human capital' can overcome the tendency for diminishing returns to investment in physical equipment and infrastructure, and thereby raise the rate of growth (Walters 1995). However, mainstream analysis only recognises investment in the acquisition and acceptance of human capacities through adult individuals investing their own time and money in acquiring additional qualifications and through social investment by governments in education and health facilities. What is left out of account is the process of social reproduction in which women invest time and money in the education and socialisation of children; and in nutrition and healthcare for both children and adults. Feminist analysis emphasises the importance of looking at economies through women's eyes, so that social reproduction is brought into the picture as well as production (Picchio 1992; Sen, G. 1995; Folbre 1994).

Given the prevailing structures of gender relations, household investment in the nutrition, health and education of children tends to be more the responsibility of women than of men. There is a great deal of evidence from all over the world to suggest that there is incomplete pooling of income within households, and that there are significant differences between expenditure from female-controlled income and expenditure from male-controlled income. Women attach a higher priority to expenditure on family nutrition, health and education-related goods (e.g. school uniforms) than do men. Men are much more likely than women to spend part of their income on purely personal consumption of commodities such as alcohol, cigarettes, gambling, higher status consumer durables, and female companionship.

Among the important sociological and anthropological studies to have established this are Kumar (1979), Guyer (1980), Tripp (1981), Pahl (1983) and Dwyer and Bruce (1988). More recently their findings have been corroborated by econometric studies based on a new class of household models which do not assume a single household utility function. For instance, a positive relationship was found between the proportion of cereals produced under women's control and household consumption of calories in Gambian households by von Braun (1988). Similarly, a study in the Philippines found that raising the share of income accruing to wives increased acquisition of calories and proteins (Garcia 1990). Particularly revealing is a study of households in the Cote d'Ivoire which found that doubling women's share of cash income raised the budget share of food and lowered the budget shares of alcohol and cigarettes (Hoddinott & Haddad 1995).

Within the context of an extension of the Harrod–Domar model to include human resources as determinants of growth, this evidence could be interpreted as indicating a greater propensity on the part of women than on the part of men to invest in maintenance and enhancement of human capacities. This gendered difference in expenditure patterns may be partly the result of a greater incidence of maternal than paternal altruism. It may be partly the result of information asymmetries – since men are not so involved in the day to day care of children, they are not so well informed about the needs of children. It is also likely to be determined by efforts to preserve existing sources of power and advantage. One of the few sources of power and advantage to women in many countries is privileged access to their children, especially sons. Women invest in their children to gain and maintain access to this resource. A source of power and advantage to men in many countries is privileged access to an autonomous public sphere life outside the family. Much of their 'leisure' expenditure may be interpreted as expenditure to gain and maintain their access to this sphere, and the alternative to family life that it offers. (Among poor men, this public sphere in which they have 'free time' may also serve to reconcile them to their lack of power in relation to richer men). In both cases an analogy may be made with what economists call rent-seeking behaviour, understood as expenditure to create and retain some position of advantage; but in the case of women's expenditure on their children, much of the expenditure is directly productive; whereas in the case of men's expenditure on leisure commodities, a considerable proportion of it is directly unproductive (e.g. excessive consumption of alcohol, tobacco, gambling), leading to a depletion rather than an enhancement of human capacities, particularly since it is also often associated with violence against women (Elson 1992). It would be interesting to explore the possibilities of estimating the scale of loss of productive output in relation to GDP that arises from the diversion of resources to these forms of activity that serve to buttress male power and at the same time deplete human resources.

The co-ordination of production and social reproduction in the growth process

The simple Harrod–Domar model assumes away any problems of co-ordination between the spheres of production and social reproduction. Il is a full-employment, full-capacity utilisation model. Harrod's original model is more Keynesian in spirit than this and focuses on the issue of what, if any, mechanisms exist to produce a full employment balanced growth path. It results in the conclusion that this will only happen by chance and there is no mechanism which will be sure to bring it about. Subsequent developments in neo-classical growth theory assume away this problem by assuming first that there is a wide array of production technologies, so that labour and machinery can always be substituted for one another; and second that markets will operate so as to price people into jobs (Walters 1995).

The problem with assuming that flexible technology and smoothly functioning markets will serve to co-ordinate production and social reproduction is that social reproduction is not organised along commercial principles. While it would be over-romantic to assume that women work at social reproduction entirely for love, it would be crass to assume that social reproduction can be modelled on the same principle as livestock production. Women and men do not on the whole regard their children as just another crop, to be left to rot with equanimity if the risk of tending them becomes too high. As Humphries and Rubery (1984) put it, social reproduction is relatively autonomous. It has its own norms, procedures, patterns of compulsion and choice which interact with and respond to but are not reducible to those of the market-orientated production of commodities. It is not surprising that if co-ordination is left to the market, the outcomes are likely to be dysfunctional growth patterns identified in the *Human Development Report* (UNDP 1996). The strength of Harrod's growth model is that it recognised this co-ordination problem; but (as Walters 1995 shows), its weakness is that the only method it allows for resolving the problem is via policies which impact on the market demand expectations of investors. That is because Harrod sets up the co-ordination problem as a problem of equating the warranted rate of growth with the natural rate of growth. The warranted rate of growth is that growth rate at which the market demand expectations upon which firms base their investment decisions are confirmed, or warranted, by the spending decisions of consumers. The natural rate of growth is defined as the maximum rate of growth allowed by population, accumulation of capital, technological improvement and work/leisure preference schedule, supposing that there is always full employment (Harrod 1939: 30). The natural rate of growth is treated as exogenously given (which is equivalent to treating social reproduction as fully, not relatively, autonomous). Policy could influence the warranted rate of growth via measures to raise investors' expectations of future market demand – such as the institutionalisation of the state as 'buyer of last resort' through the pursuit of Keynesian macro-economic policies; and industrial planning and information sharing about private sector plans and expectations through corporatist institutions such as business/government/trade union economic councils. Critics of Keynesian approaches have stressed the dangers of inflation inherent in such an approach. But they have ignored the problems posed by the unequal gender division of labour in both production and social reproduction.

Increasing the aggregate demand for labour through planned development is not guaranteed to produce a balanced distribution between men and women of paid work in production and paid work in social reproduction. Instead, depending upon the composition of aggregate demand for goods and services, it may produce overwork for women as they increase their participation in paid work in production, while continuing to do most of the unpaid work of social reproduction; and at the same time leave men in a debilitating idleness or underemployment as they fail to find 'men's jobs' in paid production but are culturally constrained from undertaking 'women's work' in either production or social reproduction. A fully adequate co-ordination of production and social reproduction will require a transformation of the norms about what is 'women's work' and 'men's work' and a transformation of investors' expectations not only about the future rate of growth of consumer demand, but also about the ways in which the sphere of production relates to the sphere of social reproduction. In down to earth terms, this means that firms will need to be transformed so that they do not penalise employees for undertaking domestic responsibilities and there will have to be social investment in providing the infrastructure and services required to reduce the burdens of social reproduction.

Of course, in the late twentieth century, Keynesian policies and development planning have largely been abandoned, and policy makers are urged to rely on deflationary policies and market prices to co-ordinate production and social reproduction. The shortcomings of this approach have been documented in the wealth of research on stabilisation and adjustment policies. In effect, whereas the Harrod-Domar approach to growth assumes that policy makers can manipulate production so as to meet the needs of social reproduction, the World Bank approach to growth assumes that social reproduction will always accommodate itself to the savings and investment decisions made in the productive economy. This is apparent in the formulation of the World Bank's growth model, the Revised Minimum Standard Model, which is used to produce assessments of the aid required to achieve growth targets on the assumption that the level of consumption is residually determined (Tarp 1993). This amounts to assuming that social reproduction can be accomplished with whatever is left over after investment needs have been met. This implies that social reproduction has no autonomy in the growth process, something that can only be taken for granted if people can live on fresh air or women's unpaid labour is available in unlimited supplies (Elson 1991, 1995).

We need more empirical studies of how production and social reproduction interact in mutually determining ways in the growth process, shedding light on the scope and limits of the relative autonomy of social reproduction, and the ways in which gendered norms and institutions are reinforced, decomposed or recomposed. Feminist contemporary economic history (as undertaken by Folbre 1994) has much to contribute here.

Conclusions

The arguments and evidence put forward here point towards the conclusion that measures to restructure gender relations can be a powerful force for producing a growth path which supports human development and balances work in production and social reproduction. We have suggested that gender analysis can deconstruct and reconstruct thinking about savings, investment, productivity, output and employment. Aggregate levels of savings, investment, output and employment can be seen as the outcome of gendered structures. The parameters of simple growth models can be linked to gendered patterns of control over resources. The adequacy of growth models in relation to human development objectives can be linked to the way in which growth models treat the interaction of production and social reproduction. We have been engaged in an exercise in challenging and changing the course of the economic theory of growth. Along the way, we have identified an empirical research agenda for the next few years. We need more comparative empirical case studies of gender equality and productive efficiency; and gender equality and savings, followed by 'scaling up' of microlevel evidence to reveal the macro-level implications; and more contemporary feminist economic history that looks at the interactions of production and social reproduction and the decomposition and recomposition of gender over the last five decades of development.

If this change in discourse and this new empirical research is to make a real difference it will have to be translated into new policies, and that will require public action both to mobilise women outside the policy process and to build coalitions with sympathetic insiders. But that, as they say, is another story, beyond the scope of the present volume.

References

Agarwal, B. (ed.) (1988) *Structures of Patriarchy.* New Delhi: Kali for Women/London: Zed Books.

Aiderman, H., Hoddinott, J., Haddad, L. and Udry, C. (1995) 'Gender Differentials in Farm Productivity: Implications for Household Efficiency and Agricultural Policy', Food Consumption and Nutrition Division Paper 7, Washington, DC: International Food Policy Research Institute.

Birdsall, N. and Sabot, R. (eds) (1991) *Unfair Advantage: Labour Market Discrimination in Developing Countries.* Washington, DC: World Bank.

Bowles, S., Gintis, H. and Gustafsson, B. (eds) (1993) *Markets and Democracy.* Cambridge: Cambridge University Press.

Chenery, H. B. and Strout, A. M. (1966) 'Foreign Assistance and Economic Development', *American Economic Review* 56(4): 679–733.

Collier, P. (1988) 'Women in Development – Defining the Issues', Policy, Planning and Research Working Paper 129. Washington, DC: World Bank.

Collier, P. (1990) 'The Impact of Adjustment on Women', in World Bank, *Analysis Plan for Understanding the Social Dimensions of Adjustment.* Washington, DC: World Bank.

Collier, P. (1994) 'Gender Aspects of Labor Allocation during Structural Adjustment – A Theoretical Framework and the African Experience', in S. Horton, R. Kanbar and D. Mazumdar (eds) *Labor Markets in an Era of Adjustment*, Vol. 1. Washington, DC: World Bank.

Collier, P., Appleton, S., Devon, D. L., Burger, K., Dunning, J. W., Haddad, L. and Hoddinott, G. (1991) 'Public Services and Household Allocation in Africa: Does Gender Matter?', mimeo. Oxford: Centre for Study of African Economies.

Domar, E. (1946) 'Capital Expansion Rate of Growth and Employment', *Econometrica* 14: 137–47.

Dwyer, D. and Bruce, J. (eds.) (1988) *A Home Divided: Women and Income in the Third World.* Stanford, CA: Stanford University Press.

Elson, D. (1991) 'Male Bias in Macro-economics: The Case of Structural Adjustment', in D. Elson (ed.) *Male Bias in the Development Process.* Manchester: Manchester University Press.

Elson, D. (1992) 'From Survival Strategies to Transformation Strategies: Women's Needs and Structural Adjustment', in L. Beneria and S. Feldman (eds.) *Economic Crises, Persistent Poverty and Women's Work.* Boulder, CO: Westview Press.

Elson, D. (1997) 'Gender Awareness in Modelling Structural Adjustment', *World Development* 23(11): 1851–68.

Elson, D., Evers, B. and Gideon, J. (1997) 'Concepts and Sources', Gender Aware Country Economic Reports, Working Paper No. 1., GENECON Unit, Graduate School of Social Sciences, University of Manchester.

Folbre, N. (1994) *Who Pays for the Kids? Gender and the Structures of Constraint.* London: Routledge.

Folbre, N. (1995) 'Engendering Economics: New Perspectives on Woman, Work and Demographic Change'. Paper presented at World Bank Annual Conference on Development Economics. Washington, DC.

Garcia, M. (1990) 'Resource Allocation and Household Welfare: A Study of the Impact of Personal Sources of Income on Food Consumption, Nutrition and Health in the Philippines', PhD thesis, Institute of Social Studies, The Hague.

Gillis, M., Perkins, D., Roemer, M. and Snodgrass, D. (1992) *Economics of Development* 4th Edition. New York: Norton.

Guyer, J. (1980) 'Household Budgets and Women's Incomes', African Studies Centre Working Paper 28. Boston, MA: Boston University.

Harrod, R. F. (1939) 'An Essay in Dynamic Theory', *Economic Journal* 49: 14–33.

Harrod, R. F. (1948) *Towards a Dynamic Economics.* London: Macmillan.

Hoddinott, J. and Haddad, L. (1995) 'Does Female Income Share Influence Household Expenditures? Evidence from Cote d'Ivoire', *Oxford Bulletin of Economics and Statistics* 57: 77–96.

Humphries, J. and Rubery, J. (1984) 'The Reconstitution of the Supply Side of the Labour Market: The Relative Autonomy of Social Reproduction', *Cambridge Journal of Economics* 8(4): 331–46.

Kabeer, N. (1994) *Reversed Realities: Gender Hierarchies in Development Thought.* London: Verso.

Kanji, N. (1993) 'Gender and Structural Adjustment Policies: A Case Study of Harare, Zimbabwe'. PhD thesis, London School of Economics.

Kumar, S. (1979) *Impact of Subsidised Rice on Food Consumption and Nutrition in Kerala.* Research Report 5, Washington, DC: IFPRI.

Ministry of Foreign Affairs, Netherlands (1994) *Guidelines on Programme Aid.* The Hague.

Moock, P. (1976) 'The Efficiency of Women as Farm Managers: Kenya', *American Journal of Agricultural Economics* 58: 831–5.

Ongaro, W. A. (1988) 'Adoption of New Farming Technology: A Case Study of Maize Production in Western Kenya'. PhD thesis, University of Gothenberg.

Pahl, J. (1983) 'The Allocation of Money within Marriage', *Sociological Review* 32: 237–64.

Picchio, A. (1992) *Social Reproduction: The Political Economy of the Labour Market.* Cambridge: Cambridge University Press.

Saito, K., Mekonnen, H. and Spurling, D. (1994) 'Raising the Productivity of Women Farmers in Sub-Saharan Africa', Discussion Paper 230, Washington, DC: World Bank.

Sen, A. K. (1983) 'Development: Which Way Now?', *Economic Journal* 93: 745–62.

Sen, G. (1995) 'Alternative Economics from a Gender Perspective', *Development* 1: 10–13.

Smith, J. B. and Stelcher, M. (1990) 'Modelling Economic Behaviour in Peru's Informal Urban Retail Sector', PHRD Working Paper 469. Washinton, DC: World Bank.

Streeten, P. (1968) 'Economic Models and their Usefulness for Planning in South Asia', Appendix 3 in G. Myrdal, *Asian Drama.* Harmondsworth: Penguin Books.

Tarp, F. (1993) *Stabilization and Structural Adjustment.* London: Routledge.

Tinker, I. (ed.) (1990) *Persistent Inequalities: Women and World Development.* Oxford: Oxford University Press.

Toye, J. (1987) *Dilemmas of Development.* Oxford: Blackwell.

Tripp, R. (1981) 'Farmers and Traders: Some Economic Determinants of Nutritional Status in Northern Ghana', *Journal of Tropical Pediatrics* 27.

Tzannatos, Z. (1992) 'Potential Gains from the Elimination of Labor Market Differentials', in *Women's Employment and Pay in Latin America, Part 1 Overview and Methodology.* Regional Studies Program Report 10. Washington, DC: World Bank.

UNDP (1996) *Human Development Report.* New York: United Nations.

Von Braun, J. (1988) 'Effects of Technological Change in Agriculture on Food Consumption and Nutrition: Rice in a West African Setting', *World Development* 16(9): 1083–98.

Walters, B. (1995) 'Engendering Macroeconomics: A Reconsideration of Growth Theory'. *World Development* 23(11): 1869–80.

Young, K. (1993) *Planning Development with Women.* London: Macmillan.

Zohir, S. (1996) 'Gender Implications of Industrial Reforms in Bangladesh', Draft PhD, University of Manchester.

7

INTERNATIONAL FINANCIAL ARCHITECTURE: A VIEW FROM THE KITCHEN

Following the financial crisis in East and South East Asia in 1997–98, there have been calls for a better integration of social and economic policy; greater transparency and accountability in the governance of finance; and the construction of a new reformed international financial architecture. This paper discusses these issues from a gender perspective, with a particular concern for the implications for poor women living in the South. It proposes a view from the kitchen rather than the boardroom, the dealing room and the counting house.

Decontrol of the dealing room

The Asian financial crisis took place in the context of an international financial architecture in which the building regulations had been substantially changed from those agreed at Bretton Woods in 1944. The post war architecture was built around international flows of public finance from the World Bank and the international Monetary Fund (IMF), both of which had social goals specified in their Articles of Agreement. In the case of the Bank, reference was made to investment in infrastructure 'thereby assisting in raising productivity, the standard of living, and the conditions of labour'. In the case of the IMF, reference was made to the promotion and maintenance of high levels of employment and real income. It was a system with a degree of public ownership, although the voting rights were not democratically distributed. However, there was from the beginning a tension between these goals and the interests of owners of private capital, who were interested in maximizing the returns to their assets, irrespective of social goals. One expression of that tension was the shifting balance between automatic access to the pooled resources of the IMF; and conditional access, with the conditions reflecting ideas about 'sound finance' that required countries with balance of payments deficits to cut public expenditure to reduce these deficits, irrespective of the implications for social goals. From the mid 1970s, conditionality dominated and was increasingly linked to neo-liberal economic policies (Elson 1994; Harris 1988). At the heart of these policies was liberalization of international financial markets, first for 'developed' countries and then for 'developing' countries. It was argued that this would lead to the most efficient distribution of finance, but efficiency was judged only in terms of the use of marketed resources.

The IMF and World Bank as sources of finance became dwarfed by international banks borrowing and lending Eurodollars and petrodollars in offshore financial centres. For instance, Singh and Zammit (2000: 1250) point out that between 1984–89 and 1990–96, net official capital inflows to developing countries fell by nearly 50 per cent, from US$27.2 billions to US$16.8 billions. In the same period, net private capital flows increased by 700 percent, from US$17.8 billions to US$129.4 billions. The most rapid increase in private capital flows to developing countries was in portfolio investment (bonds and equities), which was negligible in the 1970s and 1980s but which was US$51.1 billions in the period 1990–96.The operations of the IMF and World Bank were increasingly geared to maintaining conditions which served the interests of international financial corporations (Harris,1988).

The period of capital market liberalization was also a period of growing inequality, both between and within countries (UNDP 1999). The delinking of social goals and international finance led to deep social divisions in many countries between the rentiers and the rest. A social structure emerged (see Elson & Çağatay 2000) in which the majority of households maintained themselves with a mixture of incomes earned in the public and private sectors, subsistence production, cash transfers authorized by the Ministry of Finance, public services provided by the public sector, and the unpaid care provided by family members; while wealthy households, which constituted a minority, received a large part of their income not from employment but from ownership of financial assets (bonds, shares, stock options, private pensions). These wealthy rentier households became almost as much "offshore" as the international financial corporations. These households made very little use of public services, paid very few taxes, were not recipients of public transfers, derived wage earnings disproportionately from the financial sector, and undertook very little unpaid care for family members, relying instead on paid nannies, nurses, cooks, cleaners, drivers supplied by the other households (or similar households abroad). For women in these households, the kitchen was primarily a place where they gave orders to servants. The most important link from these rentier households to the national economy was through their ownership of financial assets and the return to these assets; but this link was always at risk of being weakened or even severed through capital flight. The majority of households were also linked to financial institutions – but in a different way, as net debtors rather than as creditors. In this, they were similar to the government and to the locally owned part of the private sector.

The position of Transnational Corporations (TNCs) undertaking direct investment in mines, plantations and factories was somewhat different from that of the offshore corporations. Many TNCs were under pressure from financial intermediaries to keep up their share prices or risk takeover bids, creating incentives for short-term time horizons. Unlike the 'offshore' corporations, the TNCs derived some benefits from public expenditure, through contracts, and provision of infrastructure, and from tax breaks (tax expenditures) – the hidden subsidies that corporations get from tax concessions, and which are not nearly as visible as the transfers to households in the shape of food subsidies, or child benefits, or maternity benefits, or pensions. TNCs have bargaining power to extract this 'corporate welfare' because they can threaten to leave – or not to come in the first place.

The non-wealthy majority of households do not have that luxury, the possibilities for permanent migration to become citizens of another country are highly circumscribed, and mainly available to the well-off and highly educated. International financial market liberalization has not been matched by international labour market liberalization. Poor people cannot migrate on the same terms as rich people. Poor and middle income households, local firms, and public sector agencies, are much more 'locked-in' to their country. (Many of the thousands of poor people who try to escape as undocumented migrants or asylum seekers are likely to find the alternative to being locked – in at home is to be 'locked-up' abroad.) Wealthy rentier households (who find they are much more welcome abroad than their poorer compatriots), TNCs, and financial institutions are more footloose (with the latter the most footloose of all).

Decontrol of the dealing room has created a surreal financial architecture. Not only do different inhabitants have different experiences of space, but also of time. The clocks in the dealing rooms run very fast – 5 minutes is a long time during which a lot of money could change hands; whereas in the kitchen the clocks run slow – 5 minutes is a tiny fragment of a human lifetime of cooking and eating. In the dealing room transactions are reversible; but in the kitchen they are not. The time horizons in the dealing room are short, whereas in the kitchen the horizon is that of the nurturing needed over the human life span. The whole building is precariously balanced. A key feature of the Asian financial crisis was massive inflows of short-term capital followed by a sudden reversal: 'Net financial inflows to Indonesia, Korea, Malaysia, the Philippines and Thailand totalled $93 billion in 1996. In 1997, as turmoil hit financial markets, these flows reversed in just weeks to a net outflow of $12billion, a swing of $105 billion, or 11% of the pre-crisis GDPs of the five countries' (UNDP 1999: 40).

The gender implications of financial crises: downloading risks to the kitchen

International markets for money are inherently uncertain and liberalized international financial transactions are fraught with risks for which no objective probability distribution exists –such as currency risk, capital flight risk, fragility risk, contagion risk and sovereignty risk (Grabel 2000). Information is necessarily imperfect and available information is unequally distributed. Such markets are argued by heterodox economists to be intrinsically unstable (eg. Spotton 1997; Singh & Zammit 2000). Periods of economic growth leads to exuberant risk taking and the value of financial assets becomes inflated. But eventually the growing gap between financial values and real returns leads to a subjective reevaluation of risks and holders of financial assets begin to sell them. Herd behaviour magnifies the propensity to sell and further stimulates the perception that risks have increased. The way is paved for crises in which the sudden drop in asset prices sparks panic selling; and the price of assets bought with loans drops below the value of loans outstanding, leading to collapse of credit markets and impending bankruptcy of banks and other private sector financial intermediaries. The crisis may be mitigated by intervention by governments or international public financial institutions to co-ordinate markets, restore confidence and bail out banks and other intermediaries. But such intervention can make things worse if the wrong advice is given and the wrong policies imposed; and bailing out failing firms shifts costs from individual actors in financial markets to other members of society. Moreover the expectation of being bailed out can lead to even greater excess in financial risk-taking when the economy recovers.

It has been estimated that the average costs of government bailouts in banking crashes over the past 20 years amounts to about 9 per cent of GDP in developing countries and 4 per cent of GDP in developed countries (Caprio & Honohan 1999). The most immediately visible costs are to the taxpayers who fund the bailouts, and to the people who lose their jobs. But, as pointed out by Irene van Staveren (2000), the burden of excessive financial risk-taking is also shifted to the people, mainly women, who provide the unpaid care that keeps families and communities going. Particularly in poor and middle income families, women are called upon to spend more time and effort in providing non-market substitutes for marketed goods that their families can no longer afford to buy, and providing substitutes for public services that are no longer available. In addition, women have to seek more paid work in informal employment, where new entrants making 'distress sales' tend to drive down returns. The burdens are thus not fully reflected in the GDP statistics but show up also in the additional stress and tiredness and ill-health experienced by women who are often working longer and harder.

The Asian financial crisis of the late 1990s is a good example of downloading risks to the kitchen. Attempts by the IFIs to manage the Asian financial crisis have been widely regarded as unsuccessful, not only by those outside the IFIs but also by some who were inside them at the time, most notably Joe Stiglitz, then the Chief Economic Adviser at the World Bank (Stiglitz 1998, 2000). The IMF in particular has been widely criticized for giving the wrong advice and imposing the wrong policies during the Asian financial crisis. It imposed cuts in public expenditure though the underlying problem was not a budget deficit; and instead of drawing attention to the strong real economies of most of the afflicted countries, it emphasized the need for much more thorough liberalisation of markets and major changes in corporate governance, doing nothing to restore confidence among panicking investors. In the view of Singh and Zammitt (2000: 1255), 'a relatively tractable liquidity problem was thus turned into a massive solvency crisis, with enormous losses in employment and output.' There was also a substantial increase in poverty, reduced public services and increased social stress (UNDP 1999: 40).

In both Indonesia and the Philippines, the amount of work done by women increased, as women took up the role of provider of last resort. For Indonesia, relevant data is available from the Indonesia Family Life Surveys, which covered more than 30,000 people in 1997 and early 1998 and a follow up survey of a 25 per cent sample in late 1998. Using this source, Frankenberg, Thomas and Beegle (1999) calculate the percentage of the labour force employed in paid work in 1997 and 1998 and show that for men it decreased by 1.3 per cent, while for women it increased by 1 per cent. When unpaid work is also included, there is an increase for both men and women, but for men the increase is only 1.3 per cent, while for women it is 7 per cent. A nationally representative survey conducted by the Indonesian statistical office sixteen months after the onset of the crisis reveals the household coping strategies underlying these figures – especially increasing the labour market participation of older married women with children and producing more goods for home consumption (de la Rocha 2000)

In the case of the Philippines, Lim (2000) using data from the Labor Force Survey shows that both male and female unemployment rates rose between 1997 and 1998: for men from 7.5 per cent to 9.5 per cent and for women from 8.5 per cent to 9.9 per cent. However mean weekly work hours for those employed moved in opposite directions for men and women, with those of men falling while those of women rose. Among the factors that may explain the increase for women is an increase in the hours of work undertaken by home based women working on subcontract (Ofreneo, Lim and Gula 1999). This increase in the average hours that women spend in paid work has occurred in a context in which women typically spend almost 8 hours a day on housekeeping and child care compared about 2 and a half hours for men (UNDP 1997).

In South Korea, it was women who lost jobs more than men. Between 1997 and 1998, data from the National Statistical Office show that employment declined by 3.8 per cent for men and 7.1 per cent for women (Lee & Rhee 1999). In response, the Korean government promoted a national campaign under the slogan 'Get Your Husband Energized', calling on women to provide support for husbands who were depressed due to unemployment or bankruptcy – husbands were not called upon to provide reciprocal support for wives (Tauli-Korpuz 1998).

Social policy, gender equality and financial policy

Singh and Zammit (2000) point out that one influential interpretation of the effects of the Asian financial crisis argued that the social impact was worse because governments in that region had not introduced selective social safety nets and targeted social insurance schemes in the period of rapid growth. If such schemes were in place, then, it was implied, the potential costs of instability and crisis arising from financial liberalization could be absorbed. In this view, a narrowly targeted social policy needs to be 'added on' to pre-existing financial policy, in order to protect vulnerable groups.

Following the Asian financial crisis, the World Bank/IMF Development Committee asked the World Bank to develop, in consultation with other institutions, some general principles to set standards for social policy. The resulting document 'Managing the Social Dimensions of Crisis: Good Practices in Social Policy' (World Bank 1999) exemplifies the 'adding on' approach. Although there is much reference to households and communities, there is no systematic analysis of the way in which the principles of social policy need to take into account the different (and disadvantaged) position of women in comparison to men; and to take into account unpaid care work in households and communities. The principles focus on cutting public expenditure in ways that will not worsen the position of the worst off, but pay little attention to the question of whether cutting public expenditure is the appropriate strategy.

The IMF has also become more concerned with social policy. In explaining to the public its response to the Asian crisis, it states that it is concerned with 'strengthening and expanding the social safety net and encouraging a social dialogue among employers, employees, and governments' (IMF 1999). The IMF has also been paying more attention to the links between social policy and financial policy in the context of debt relief initiatives for the Highly Indebted Poor Countries (HIPC), and has agreed that it will work with the World Bank in preparing explicit ex-ante assessments of the expected effects of its programs on the poor (IMF 1998; IMF/World Bank 1999). However, the IMF and the World Bank take the view that the position of poor people can only be improved through economic growth (IMF/World Bank 1999).

From this point of view, macroeconomic policies need to be designed to 'limit the governments' access to bank credit while ensuring that the private sector receives an adequate share of total credit' (Gupta *et al.* 1998: 2). Public expenditure is seen as competitive rather than complementary to private investment. (This is contested by heterodox economists who point to examples of countries where complementarity has occurred (e.g. Taylor 1991). The IMF line of analysis shows great confidence in the speedy restoration of a sustainable long-run growth path, but we are now in a period of global recession.

The IMF proposes that the national and international financial framework should renewed by strengthening its own surveillance of developing countries (IMF 1999). The latter should be required to restructure their regulatory and financial structures to reduce corruption and promote transparency of their public and private institutions-but the emphasis is mainly on transparency towards international investors, rather than towards their citizens. The IMF will improve the dissemination of information and promote common international standards in financial markets, so as to improve investor confidence. Contingency lending will be created, to be drawn on in times of market instability by countries that follow IMF prescriptions. Financial liberalization is still the ultimate goal, but more attention has to be paid to sequencing, so that it is not introduced until after appropriate financial sector and exchange rate policies are introduced. The view is still that financial liberalization leads to the most efficient distribution of financial resources, with efficiency being judged only in terms of the use of resources that have to be paid for, not of those (such as women's time spent producing good and services for their families) that do not. The idea that financial liberalization can lead, through financial crisis, to irreparable loss of resources is not entertained.

An alternative approach, put forward by heterodox economists, is the creation of new international institutions to regulate global finance. For instance, Eatwell and Taylor (1998) call for the setting up of a World Financial Authority (WFA) to manage systemic risk and pursue *both* financial targets *and* social goals such as high rates of growth and employment. It would develop and impose regulations and co-ordinate national monetary policies. The IMF and World Bank would both have roles to play, under the supervision of the WFA which would have the responsibility of ensuring their transparency and accountability. Eatwell and Taylor are among those economists who are concerned that financial liberalization has imposed macroeconomic policies that keep employment and output below their potential and the WFA is supposed to prevent this from happening. It can be seen as a welcome proposal to re assert social ownership of the building, but it makes no reference to gender equality issues and to ensuring that the kitchen is adequately provisioned.

Likewise, Singh and Zammit (2000) share the concerns about employment and output and argue strongly that limited social safety nets of the kind envisaged by the Bank and the Fund are inadequate and impractical. Full employment is the best safety net, they say. In their view developing countries must be allowed the option of maintaining capital controls. 'The right to control capital flows must be the linchpin of any reform of the international financial system from the perspective of developing countries' (p. 1264). In addition, mechanisms are needed for more equitable sharing of the burden of bad debt between international creditors and debtors in developing countries. They argue that reforming the international economic system so as to promote growth of production and employment on a sustainable basis would benefit both men and women, but that women derive even greater benefits since they bear so many of the costs of instability. They encourage women to formulate and articulate their ideas on what kind of new economic architecture best serves their own interests.

Three biases to avoid in building new economic architecture

One way of responding to the invitation issued by Singh and Zammit (2000) is to identify things that should be avoided in building any new system. In this section three biases are identified that would make the architecture very insecure from the point of view of most women and should thus be guarded against. They are 'deflationary bias'; 'male breadwinner bias'; and 'commodification or privatization bias' (see also Elson & Çağatay 2000).

Deflationary bias in macroeconomic policy is identified as an important issue for women in the recent UN World Survey on the Role of Women in Development (UN 1999). Using similar arguments to Singh and Zammit (2000), the survey defines deflationary bias as macroeconomic policies which keep paid employment and GNP growth below their potential. It is argued that liberalized financial markets pressure governments to keep interest rates high, inflation rates low, and taxation and expenditure low. Evidence is cited to suggest that the negative effects of these policies, which are used to attract private capital inflows, outweigh the benefits of the extra finance, and that these negative effects are disproportionately borne by women. Avoidance of deflationary bias is, however, necessary but not sufficient. As Aslanbeigui and Summerfield (2000) point out, growth of GNP and increased paid employment can have different implications for men and women.

For instance, patterns of employment and the entitlements they bring, can be built around a 'male breadwinner' model, which assumes that women and children will have, and should have, their livelihoods provided by the incomes earned by husbands and fathers. The counterpart to this is the assumption that typical workers will have little or domestic responsibilities. Of course, in reality the majority of households have multiple livelihood strategies, which involve women earning money as well as undertaking unpaid care work. However, women's participation in the labour force is less visible because it is more often informal, home-based, part-time, seasonal, and low paid. So women's 'double day' of unpaid and paid work goes unnoticed. 'Male breadwinner' bias characterises public policies that prioritize decent and remunerative employment for men while ignoring women's rights to decent jobs. 'Male breadwinner' bias relegates women to the status of secondary workers with fewer rights, even when they are playing a large role in maintaining family income. It excludes women from many state-provided social benefits, except as dependents of men. Full employment may reduce the chances of women experiencing material poverty but does not necessarily save women from patriarchal control.

In order to be gender-equitable, full-employment policies must be complemented by policies to ensure an equitable balance between work and family life; and state-based entitlements for the providers of unpaid caring labor as citizens in their own right. This suggests that a target of full employment needs to be supplemented by a target of decent jobs on comparable terms for both men and women, equally family friendly for both.

The third bias to be avoided is privatization bias. This occurs when public provision is judged less efficient than private provision on the basis of incomplete and faulty measures of efficiency, which do not take account of unpaid work and quality of provision. This results in the replacement of public provision by market based, individualized entitlements for those who can afford them– private pensions, private health insurance, private hospitals, private schools, private retirement homes, private paid care for children and old people, privatized utilities charging market rates for energy and transport. Rather than pooling and sharing risks and resources, with scope for the solidarity of cross-subsidy, there is separate insurance for specific contingencies. One point of continuity with 'male breadwinner' bias is that women are still often cast in the position of dependents. The insurable risk against ill health or old age is constructed around male norms of labour market status; and the private system, just like the public system, is accessed by women through their male relatives.

The blueprints for commodification and privatization have been drawn up by the World Bank, and frequently involve sale of assets at knock-down prices; or prolonged subsidies to private corporations. This bias fuels the growth of financial corporations and the corporate welfare state, as is demonstrated in the experience of privatization of social insurance in Latin America (Laurell 2000). The privatisation of pensions in Chile and Mexico will result in the largest transfer of public funds to national and transnational financial groups that has ever taken place in Latin America. It will be paid over a 50 year period and is estimated to cost about 1–2 per cent of GNP in Mexico and 3.5 per cent in Chile. Given the pressure to balance the budget, this is likely to result in cuts in other social programmes (Laurell 2000). The private providers charge the insured workers higher administration costs than the public scheme and risks are shifted to the insured. Their future pensions are uncertain and at the mercy of financial markets. In the case of health, the management of health funds rather than the provision of health services now drives the system, which is increasingly in the hands of health insurance companies, health management organisations and hospital corporations that are based in the US or associated with US firms. There is increasing stratification in quality and access to services. (Laurell 2000).

Thus privatisation bias fuels the growth of financial intermediaries; and the growth of financial intermediaries fuels deflationary bias in macroeconomic policy, and leads to even more pressures to privatize. Rentier households and offshore financial institutions exert pressure for deflation and privatisation threatening to exit if their interests are not given priority. They have an immediate interest in minimizing tax payments, and keeping interest rates high and inflation close to zero, because they are not required to be permanent stakeholders in the country. Under this pressure, social policy becomes a branch of financial policy and can no longer take non-market criteria into account. Rather than the risks of liberalized international financial markets being offset by state-funded services in which risks and resources are pooled, the risks are compounded by funding social provision through financial markets.

To guard against privatisation bias, we need a target of universal entitlement to basic services and benefits for women and men. One possible indicator to consider would be the proportion of women who have access, in their own right, to an adequately functioning primary health care clinic.

Putting social justice first: rebuilding from the bottom up

A new financial architecture needs more than new institutions with new responsibilities. It needs to provide a supportive framework to enable women and men to exercise democratic oversight of how the building is operated. There must be spaces, accessible form the kitchen, for public dialogues on priorities and alternatives. The ability of different interests to exercise 'voice' on how financial policy and social justice should be linked is foreclosed not by the technical requirements of financial policy but by fear of pre-emptive exercise of the 'exit' option by private financial investors. Their ability to exit rather than join in a policy dialogue is, of course, a result of the openness of capital markets.

Ironically the openness of capital markets is conducive to an absence of openness in policy discussion, for fear that the wrong signals will be sent and the volatile 'sentiment' of capital markets will be disturbed. It is difficult to conduct a participatory consultation on how to put financial policy at the service of social goals when some of the key players have no stake in the outcome beyond the next few hours. A neglected argument for some form of capital controls is to ensure that financial institutions have more incentive to engage in discussions with other social interests in the country whose financial instruments they have purchased, and to prevent them from foreclosing discussion by a pre-emptive exit (Elson & Çağatay 2000).

Unfortunately, there is currently no sign of moves towards rebuilding along participatory and gender equitable lines. There have been only a few minor repairs, concerned to improve the comfort of rich investors, not poor citizens. The repairs have been designed by a few rich governments (primarily the G7) though the work of carrying them out falls to the governments of poor countries (Griffiths-Jones 2001). The Financial Stability Forum is a rich man's club not a public meeting place. So we need a twin track strategy. We need to keep alive a vision of what the international financial architecture should be, with the needs of the kitchen, the place of nurture, an important and integral part of the design. We also need to enlarge those small spaces that currently exist for the operation of socially responsible finance.

An example of what might be aspired to at national level is provided by the Canadian Alternative Federal Budget exercise, in which a large number of Canadian civil society groups have joined together to produce an alternative budget and an alternative financial framework that would be free of all three biases identified above (Loxley 1999). This is an example of a growing movement for gender sensitive, democratically organized, public services and social insurance that rebuild confidence in the principles of pooling and sharing through the state. Women are particularly active in gender budget initiatives in more than 20 countries, analysing how government budgets are affecting men and women, and arguing for public finance to be free of the biases identified in section 6 above (see Budlender 2000; Elson (ed) 2000). At the international level there is a growth of ethical investment funds in which middle income people can invest their savings in the knowledge that the money will be lent only to firms that operate in a socially and environmentally responsible way. There is a strong movement for the cancellation of the debt of poor countries and the rebuilding of the kind of development aid that supports human development. There is growing support for an international tax on currency transactions and for controls on short-term capital movements. Little by little, these initiatives, if they are interconnected, may liberate space form the malign flux of the dealing room and enable more of the kitchen to be a place of peaceful enjoyment.

References

Aslanbeigui, N. and Summerfield, G. (2000) 'The Asian Crisis, Gender and the International Financial Architecture', *Feminist Economics* 6(3), 81–104.

Budlender, D.(2000) 'The Political Economy of Women's Budgets in the South', *World Development* 28(7), 1365–78.

Caprio, G. and Honohan, P. (1999) 'Restoring Banking Stability: Beyond Supervised Capital Requirements', *Journal of Economic Perspectives* 13(4), 43–64.

Eatwell, J. and Taylor, L. (1998) 'International Capital Markets and the Future of Economic Policy'. CEPA Working Paper Series 1II. Working Paper No. 9, New School University, New York.

Elson, D. (1994) 'People, Development and International Financial Systems', *Review of African Political Economy* 62, 511–24.

Elson, D. (ed) (2000) *Progress of the Worlds Women 2000.* New York: UNIFEM.

Elson, D. and Çağatay, N. (2000) 'The Social Content of Macroeconomic Polices', *World Development* 28(7), 1347–65.

Frankenberg, E., Thomas, D. and Beegle, K. (1999) 'The Real Costs of Indonesia's Economic Crisis: Preliminary Findings from the Indonesia Family Life Surveys', Labor and Population Program Working Paper Series 99-04, RAND.

Grabel, I. (2000) 'Identifying Risks, Preventing Crisis: Lessons from the Asian Crisis', *Journal of Economic Issues* 34(2), 377–83.

Gupta, S., Clements, B., McDonald, C. and Schiller, C. (1998) *The IMF and the Poor.* Pamphlet Series No. 52, Fiscal Affairs Department, IMF, Washington, DC.

Harris, L. (1988) 'The IMF and Mechanisms of Integration' in Ben Crow and Mary Thorpe (eds) *Survival and Change in the Third World.* Oxford: Polity Press.

IMF (1998) Distilling the Lessons from the ESAF Reviews. http://www.imf.org.

IMF/World Bank (1999) 'Heavily Indebted Poor Countries (HIC) Initiative – Strengthening the link between Debt Relief and Poverty Reduction'. Washington, DC.

IMF (1999) 'The IMF's response to the Asian Crisis'. Washington, DC. www.imf.org/External/np/exr/facts/asia/htm.

Laurell, A. C. (2000) 'Structural Adjustment and the Globalization of Social Policy in Latin America', *International Sociology* 15(2), 306–25.

Lee, J-W. and Rhee, C. (1999) 'Social Impacts of the Asian Crisis; Policy Challenges and Lessons', Human Development Report Office, Occasional Paper 33.

Lim, J. (2000) 'The Effects of the East Asian Crisis on the Employment of Men and Women: The Philippine Case', *World Development* 28(7), 1285–306.

Loxley, J. (1999) 'The Alternative Federal Budget in Canada: A New Approach to Fiscal Democracy'. Paper prepared for Workshop on Pro-Poor Gender- and Environment-Sensitive Budgets, UNDP and UNIFEM, New York, June 28–30.

Ofreno, R., Lim, J. and Gula, L. (1999) 'Subcontracted women workers in the context of the global economy: the Philippine case', paper commissioned by Asia Foundation.

Rocha, M. de la (2000) 'Private Adjustments; Household Responses to the Erosion of Work', Occasional Paper 6, Bureau of Development Policy, UNDP, New York.

Sen, A. (1998) 'Human Development and Financial Conservatism', *World Development* 26(4), 773–42.

Singh, A. and Zammit, A. (2000) 'International Capital flows: Identifying the Gender Dimension', *World Development* 26(7), 1249–68.

Spotton, B. (1997) 'Financial Instability Reconsidered: Orthodox Theories versus Historical Facts', *Journal of Economic Issues* 31(1), 175–95.

Staveren, I. van (2000) 'Global Finance and Gender', Paper presented at IAFFE Conference, Istanbul, August.

Stiglitz, J. (2000) 'What I learned at the World Economic Crisis. The Insider', *The New Republic Online*. http://www.thenewrepublic.com.

Taylor L. (1991) *Varieties of Stabilization Experience: Towards Sensible Macroeconomics in the Third World*. Wider Studies in Development Economics.

Tauli-Korpuz, V. (1998) 'Asia Pacific Women grapple with financial crisis and globalisation', *Third World Resurgence* 94.

UN (1999) World *Survey on the Role of Women in Development*. Division for the Advancement of Women, Department of Economic and Social Affairs, United Nations, New York.

UNDP (1999) *Human Development Report*. New York: Oxford University Press.

World Bank (1999) 'Managing the Social Dimensions of Crises: Good Practices in Social Policy'. Paper prepared for Development Committee of the Bank and the Fund, Washington, DC.

World Bank (2000) *World Development Report 2000*. New York: Oxford University Press.

8

GENDER EQUALITY, PUBLIC FINANCE AND GLOBALIZATION

Introduction

> Global inequalities in the distribution of income, wealth, power and influence are enormous and the spread of rapid and cheap global communications has increased the awareness of hundreds of millions of people of widespread injustice and the unfairness of the global economic and political system. Increasingly it is recognised that equity is a global public good.
>
> (Griffin 2003: 800)

This chapter considers a particular dimension of inequality: the inequality between women and men, and boys and girls. It considers the interrelation between, on the one hand, attempts to make public finance more gender-equitable, and on the other, the fiscal squeeze produced by some aspects of globalization.

The Beijing Platform for Action, agreed at the UN Fourth World Conference for Women in 1995, specifically endorsed measures to 'engender' government budgets, calling in Paragraph 345 for: "the integration of a gender perspective in budgetary decisions on policies and programmes, as well as adequate financing of specific programmes for securing equality between women and men".

Since the mid-1990s, a series of gender budget initiatives (GBIs), in both the South and North, have sought to improve the distribution, adequacy and impact of government budgets at national, regional and local levels, and to secure greater transparency in the use of public money, and greater accountability to women as citizens. The spread of GBIs has itself been an example of globalization, in this case the globalization of action for gender justice, facilitated by email, internet and air travel and supported by international foundations and international development cooperation funds.

But, it may be argued, GBIs have begun to engage with public finance just at the time when governments, especially in the South, have less and less control over public finance decisions, due to other aspects of globalization. Globalization of trade, investment and finance puts pressure on government to reduce tax revenues and reduce public expenditure, even as it creates a need for more investment in public goods to counteract inequality and insecurity.

This chapter considers the weaknesses and strengths of GBIs as they seek to promote gender equality in the diminished national fiscal space, and discusses the changes in global governance that are needed if efforts to make public finance more gender-equitable are to be fruitful.

Gender and public finance: some points of departure

The impetus for advocates for gender equality to focus on government budgets has come from a concern that government budgets have not been designed and implemented in ways that promote gender equality. There has been concern that governments have not been backing their gender equality policies with the funding necessary to implement them, that when they have cut back on expenditure, cuts have fallen disproportionately on programmes of importance to women, and that when they have restructured taxation, they have done so in ways that disproportionately and regressively increase women's tax contribution, through the introduction of sales taxes like value-added tax (VAT).

Feminist analysis of the macroeconomic dimensions of public finance (for instance Elson & Çağatay 2000) suggests that neither the neoliberal nor the Keynesian approach is wholly adequate from the point of view of gender equality. The neoliberal approach tends to result in deflationary bias and commoditization or privatization bias, resulting in outcomes such as: unemployment, 'informalization' of paid work, inadequate public services and low levels of social protection. The Keynesian (and other heterodox approaches) are preferable to the neoliberal approach, but they tend to be marked by implicit or explicit 'male breadwinner bias', in which priority is given to men's employment, as they are assumed to be the breadwinners, and women are treated as dependents of men, their access to public services and social protection conditioned by their relations to men. Neither approach takes into account the unpaid work required to sustain families and communities, work which is disproportionately done by women. Because of this, both approaches are likely to result in underinvestment in the public services that women require in order to achieve a more equal balance between time spent in production and social reproduction, and in underinvestment in forms of social protection that recognize women as autonomous citizens, with claims in their own right.

Feminist macroeconomists consider that the Keynesian approach is however superior, because it incorporates more 'fiscal space': that is, it allows more government discretion about how to manage public finance, both in terms of the general levels of tax and spend, and in terms of how the deficit or surplus is managed. Within that enlarged fiscal space, advocates for gender equality (and for all other types of social equality) have more room for manoeuvre.

Given the current systems of gender relations prevailing in the world today, each method of raising revenue and spending money is likely to have gender-differentiated implications. These can be revealed by additional analysis, bringing further information (such as knowledge of existing patterns of inequality in households, markets and businesses) into play. Banerjee (2003) provides some examples for the case of economies in South Asia. For instance, if a rise in VAT leads to a rise in the price of commercial fuels used for cooking (like kerosene), then there is likely to be a disproportionate effect on women. Poor families are likely to reduce their purchase of commercial fuel and make more use of fuels that they can acquire without money payment from the subsistence economy, such as animal dung and wood. However, gathering and preparing this fuel is disproportionately done by women, who pay an invisible price in terms of additional workload. If the state introduces user fees for primary education, then in a context in which families prioritize educating sons over educating daughters, there will be a disproportionate negative impact on the education of girls.

Various 'tools' have been developed that can be used to conduct various forms of gender budget analysis to reveal more of their gender impacts (see for example Elson 1998; Budlender & Sharp 1998; UNIFEM 2002).

Gender budget initiatives: some examples of practice

The pioneers in taking action were the 'femocrats' in the government of Australia in the mid-1980s. Feminists came into public office in considerable numbers and persuaded the Labour government to launch an annual Women's Budget Statement, issued as part of the federal budget papers for the first time in 1987 (Sawer 2002). This lengthy document (of about 300 pages) attempted to examine the whole budget, tax as well as expenditure, for the likely implications for women in Australia (Sharp & Broomhill 2002).

The gender focus on Australian budgets was promoted by gender equality advocates who had become officials and ministers. They had three goals: to raise awareness within government of the gender impact of the budget and the policies funded; to make governments accountable for their commitments to gender equality; and to bring about changes to budgets and the policies they fund to improve the socio-economic status of women. Sharp and Broomhill (2002) judge that there was some success in achieving each of these goals. They point out that as a result of the Women's Budget, a tax rebate paid primarily to men for dependent spouses was replaced with a cash payment for child care responsibilities to the full-time (usually female) carers of children. However, successes were limited by political factors and by the adverse economic situation of Australia in the early 1990s, which led to the introduction of neoliberal economic policies, including expenditure cutbacks. The Office of Status of Women was not able to persuade the Ministry of Finance to review these policies even if they seemed likely to have an adverse impact on women. The election of a neoliberal government in the mid-1990s led to a suspension of the production of Women's Budget Statements at the federal level, though the practice was continued in some of the states and territories. In 2001 the Australian Labour Party committed itself to the reintroduction of the Women's Budget Statement if it returned to government, but failed to win the elections.

Women in South Africa drew upon the Australian example to develop their own Women's Budget Initiative (WBI), which originated in 1994 through a coalition of civil society activists and parliamentarians (Govender 2002). Debbie Budlender, who coordinates the WBI analysis, notes that the term 'women's budget' may be something of a misnomer (Budlender 2000a). The WBI does not advocate a separate budget for women. It is a form of policy monitoring and audit and is used to inform parliamentarians so that they are able to understand better the gender implications of the government budgets, and to exercise their parliamentary scrutiny function more effectively.

The standard method employed is to take the government's policy framework sector by sector and go through the following steps: (1) review gender issues in the sector; (2) analyse the appropriateness of the policy framework; (3) examine the extent to which the allocation of resources reflects a serious commitment to the policy goals; (4) examine how the resources have actually been utilized (For example how many male and female members of the population have benefited and at what cost); and (5) assess the longer-term impacts on male and female members of the population, identifying to what extent their lives have improved.

As well as producing an annual volume of technical analysis, the South African WBI produces popular handbooks in a number of languages for use in workshops with the women for whom it is advocating. It is engaged in a long-term process of capacity building so that there is a well-informed demand for budgets that deliver the promises of the South African constitution. It has succeeded in influencing the design of particular programmes, such as the reform of child benefit. However, its well-informed analysis and passionate advocacy has not dented the determination of the South African Ministry of Finance to pursue a neoliberal economic policy, in which trade liberalization has resulted in the loss of thousands of women's jobs in the textile and garments industry, and in which a deflationary bias in fiscal and monetary policy has prevented the creation of adequate numbers of new jobs. The Australian and South African examples were among the inspirations for a Commonwealth Secretariat initiative (to which I was an advisor) to promote the use of gender budget analysis by governments as a response to the challenges of economic restructuring. The Commonwealth Secretariat decided to prioritize expenditure, and a set of tools which might be used for gender analysis of government expenditure was put together (Hewitt & Mukhopadyay 2002). Beginning in 1997, the Commonwealth Secretariat supported five Commonwealth governments in undertaking some gender analysis of the expenditure and services of selected ministries. (The governments were those in South Africa, Sri Lanka, Barbados, Fiji Islands, and St Kitts and Nevis.) A notable feature of this initiative was the leadership role of the Ministry of Finance in each government. Some useful analysis was carried out but it proved difficult to get sustained commitment from the Ministries of Finance in the five countries to institutionalize the analysis and to use it to improve their budgets, polices and programmes.

Since 2000, in a growing range of countries, North as well as South, governments have come to see gender budget analysis as a potential tool for mainstreaming gender in their policies and programmes. For instance, in Europe there are government initiatives of varying scope and sustainability: at the national level in France, Belgium, the Nordic countries, Ireland and UK, and at the regional level in Scotland, the Basque country and Emilia Romagna. In Asia, some work has begun in India, Nepal and Malaysia. In Africa, Kenya, Malawi, Rwanda, Mozambique and Mauritius are among the governments that have done some gender analysis of their budgets. In Latin America, Chile has introduced gender analysis into the process by which departments bid for funds from the national budgets, while in Mexico analysis has been done of the budgets of the Ministry of Social Development and of Health. There is a tendency for these initiatives to focus on the narrower questions of distribution by sex of the benefits of particular programmes, rather than on the adequacy of the levels of expenditure, and the appropriateness of the mix and scale of revenues measures.

In some countries, the lead has been taken by gender equality advocates, who have often gone on to develop collaborative relations with governments and parliaments. For example, in 1997 a civil society organization (CSO), the Tanzania Gender Networking Programme (TGNP), began to analyse the Tanzanian budget using the same approach as the South African WBI. The aim was:

> to examine the national budgeting process from a civil society perspective to see how public resources are allocated in national and local budgets and to assess how this allocation impacts women and other groups, such as youth and poor men ... the exercise seeks to lay the foundation of an effective consensus-building campaign to influence the public, policy makers, legislators and government officials on the necessity of increasing resources towards programmes to benefit women and other disadvantaged members of society.   (Rusimbi 2002)

Later the Swedish International Development Agency began funding a parallel exercise in the Ministry of Finance, and subsequently TGNP was brought in as a consultant to the government, to conduct training based on its research, and to develop guidelines for gender mainstreaming. The 2000/2001 Budget Guidelines mandated all ministries to prepare their budget with gender mainstreaming objectives in mind. TGNP has also been invited to contribute to the processes that Tanzania must undergo in order to get debt relief and additional funding from the World Bank, such as the Public Financial Reform Management Programme, the Public Expenditure Review and the production of a Poverty Reduction Strategy Paper. TGNP has expressed dissatisfaction at the limitations of these processes, which leave undisturbed the neoliberal policy framework.

In Mexico, civil society organizations have also been active (Hofbauer 2002). Gender analysis of the allocations for the women's reproductive health services budget was initiated in 1999 by Foro, a network of women's organizations, and one of the network members, Equidad de Género (a CSO working to develop the capacities of women elected to public office), began conducting public finance workshops for women leaders. In 2000 Equidad joined forces with Fundar, a think-tank devoted to applied budget research, in a joint project which began by analysing the gender dimensions of anti-poverty programmes. The election of a new government in 2000 opened up the opportunity for collaborative work with some government departments, especially the Ministry of Health which commissioned the publication of a handbook on gender-sensitive budgeting for the health sector. The Minister of Health expressed a commitment: "to developing a methodology for the gender-sensitive formulation of the sectoral budgets ... in order to progressively achieve their institutionalization toward the end of the current administration" (Hofbauer 2002: 93). However, the implementation of this was hampered by expenditure cutbacks ordered by the Ministry of Finance in 2002.

One important aspect of the GBI in Mexico has been its links, through Fundar. with an international network of civil society budget initiatives focusing on transparency, accountability and the alleviation of poverty. This network is facilitated by the International Budget Project – established by the Center on Budget and Policy Priorities, a watchdog organization in Washington, DC – and financially supported by the Ford Foundation. The first network conference in 1997 was attended by 50 people from 14 countries. The third conference had 100 participants from 24 countries (Krafchik 2002). It has grown up side by side with the spread of GBIs, and reflects a widespread and growing concern with fiscal democracy (see www.intemationalbudget.org). In some parts of Latin America progressive mayors initiated participatory budgeting processes in the 1990s, in which citizens could play a greater role in determining the investment priorities of their town. The best known internationally is Porto Alegre in Brazil, but there are other examples in Brazil (for example San Andre), Peru (Villa El Salvador),

Ecuador (Cuenca), Uruguay (Guyana) and Venezuela (Montevideo). In Peru and Ecuador, women's organizations wanted to strengthen their voice in these processes and in 2001 turned to UNIFEM (United Nations Development Fund for Women) for support in conducting research and training (Vargas-Valente 2002; Pearl 2002). A gender analysis was conducted of the budget of Villa EI Salvador, developing new tools to look at patterns of spending, budget processes and the contribution made by women's unpaid work to the delivery of municipal services. The mayor elected in 2003 has made a commitment to incorporate some of the findings and recommendations into the reform of the participatory budget process. NGOs central to the organization of the participatory process have agreed to include a gender perspective into the training they conduct for the participatory budget committees.

India does not have participatory budgets on the Latin American model (except in the state of Kerala, which has something comparable) but it does have decentralization of funding for some types of economic and social development to local councils, on which 33 per cent of seats are reserved for women. The reservation of seats for women, which was introduced in 1993, brought 1 million women into elected office for the first time. However, they are often excluded from an active role in the preparation and implementation of budgets, which is seen as the province of men. In the state of Karnataka, the Women's Information and Resource Centre is working (with some support from UNIFEM) to enable women elected as representatives on local councils to understand the budget process, decide their priorities and organize to transform budgets to better meet women's needs (Jain 2002; Karnataka Women's Information and Resource Centre 2002). A problem faced by these and other GBIs at the local level in Latin America, Asia and Africa is the devolution of responsibilities to local government, without adequate funding to discharge them.

To summarize the experience of GBIs: by 2002, up to 50 countries in all parts of the world, North as well as South, had hosted some kind of gender budget initiative (Budlender & Hewitt 2002: 8). There is no one template: GBIs have taken place at all levels of government, involving regional and local government budgets as well as national budgets. Moreover, a multiplicity of actors have been involved: government ministers and officials (especially women's ministries, sometimes Ministries of Finance), parliamentarians, policy research NGOs, gender equality CSOs and academics (Budlender *et al.* 2002; Budlender & Hewitt 2002; UNIFEM 2002).

However, some of these GBIs amounted to no more than a sensitization workshop while others are dormant and a few have come to an end. GBIs have often been supported in the South by development cooperation agencies, leading to worries that they are donor-driven rather than the outcome of a demand by women in the South for greater accountability of their governments to them

(Budlender 2000a). The most effective GBIs have produced some institutionalization of gender equality concerns in one or more stages of the budget cycle in one or more ministries, or resulted in an ongoing public scrutiny of the budget from a gender equality perspective. There is an informal global network between GBI activists who email regularly and meet at regional and international workshops. UNIFEM organizes a GBI on-line discussion and a website (www.gender-budgets.org).

Debbie Budlender (2002: 123) summarizes effectiveness in the organization of GBIs by referring to the 'triangle of players': progressive elected politicians, effective government institutions staffed with well-trained officials, and active and well-informed coalitions of NGOs. Effective and sustainable GBIs are generally based on the interaction of all three.

Rhonda Sharp, adviser to the South Australian GBI, points to a different triangle (Sharp 2002: 88), a 'triangle of goals': raise awareness and understanding of gender issues and the impacts of budgets and policies; make governments accountable for their budgetary and policy commitments; and change and refine government budgets and policies to promote gender equality. She also points to a hierarchy between these goals, with the achievement of the first being necessary for the achievement of the second, and the achievement of the first two being necessary for the achievement of the third. In her assessment, there are many examples of success in achieving the first two goals, though fewer in achieving the third.

There are two key obstacles to achieving the third goal. The first is lack of sufficient commitment to gender equality. As Pregs Govender, former chair of the Parliamentary Committee on the Improvement of the Quality of Life and Status of Women in South Africa, points out, a government's budget reflects its priorities. An end to discrimination against women and the promotion of women's empowerment is not necessarily high on the list of priorities, despite lip-service about gender mainstreaming. Creating a budget that is gender-equitable and supports the advancement of women generally means a change in priorities, and there are often strong forces opposed to this. The second obstacle is the constraint on public finance caused by profit-led globalization. This issue is addressed in the rest of the chapter.

Profit-led globalization and public finance

Profit-led globalization entails the reduction of barriers to the mobility of finance and goods and services across national borders. It takes place through reductions of tariffs and quotas on imports; reductions of controls on multinational corporations; and reductions of controls on inflows and outflows of money invested in stocks and shares. As Griffin (2003) points out, it is a profoundly asymmetric globalization, since barriers to the movement of low-skilled labour have been maintained and in some cases strengthened.

New technology facilitates the mobility but it is policy decisions by governments that reduce or abolish controls. Since the mid-1970s, governments all around the world have decided to maintain controls on the mobility of labour and reduce controls over the mobility of capital. Some governments, mainly in the rich countries of the North, have freely chosen to do this (for example the UK government under Mrs Thatcher). Many governments, mainly in the South and East, have done this in order to obtain loans from international financial institutions, both public and private. A highly unequal system of global governance has been created, with three key components: the IMF, the World Bank and the WTO (Khor 2003). Though in formal terms the WTO operates a one-country-one-vote system, in reality this is vitiated by 'green room' deals in which the mercantilism of the rich has tended to triumph.

Neoliberal economic analysis argues that such policies will bring benefits to countries in terms of growth, employment and poverty reduction. For many governments there were short-term benefits in terms of an inflow of capital which financed budget and balance-of-payments deficits, and a growth of exports, often creating more paid work for women. But these short-term benefits had a cost: subsequent unexpected debt burdens when interest rates rose much more than expected in the 1980s; loss of jobs in industries out-competed by imports; volatility, insecurity and financial crisis, when short-term capital left even faster than it had arrived. The result has been stagnation and growing poverty in the weakest economies (especially in Africa), and growing inequality within and between countries. Feminist scholarship has documented how poor women have particularly borne these costs (for a discussion of the literature see Rai 2002).

The capacity of governments to use public expenditure to combat poverty, inequality and insecurity has been weakened by what has become known as the fiscal squeeze (Grunberg 1998). Çağatay (2002) summarizes the key aspects of this. The capacity of governments to raise many forms of revenue has been reduced. Trade liberalization cuts import duties and export taxes, key sources of revenue in many poor countries. Competition to attract multinational corporations and their highly paid executives leads to cuts in corporation and capital gains taxes; tax holidays and other exemptions; and to cuts in top rates of income tax. Development cooperation grants have fallen as trade is supposed to replace aid. Governments have been encouraged or pressured into turning to sales taxes like VAT to raise revenue, but such taxes fall most heavily on poor people and worsen the distribution of income. Revenue has also been raised through the sale of public enterprises and other public assets, but this only gives a one-time boost to revenue, and may result in costs for services, like water, that poor people cannot afford. Charges have also been introduced for public services like education and health, worsening the access of poor people, especially poor women and girls.

With revenue limited and debt burdens rising, the pressure has been on governments to make their budgets sustainable by cutting back on expenditure. This pressure has come from the public international financial institutions like the IMF and the World Bank, and also from private investors, who have seen budget deficits as harbingers of inflation, signals that the value of their assets would be eroded. Initiatives to address the debt problems of poor countries, such as the Highly Indebted Poor Countries (HIPC) initiative, have failed to provide much relief, and access to them is conditional on the continuing implementation of neoliberal economic policies. There is no global 'lender of last resort' and higher-income countries which run into financial crisis are forced by the IMF to cut back sharply on expenditure, thus turning a financial crisis into a recession (Stiglitz 2002). In order to build a reputation for 'sound finance' in financial markets, many governments have enacted legislation (such as balanced budget laws) that severely limit the fiscal space (Bakker 2002). The size of government budgets is now disciplined by financial institutions rather than the votes of citizens (Bakker 2002; Elson & Çağatay 2000). Moreover, the ways that governments can spend the revenues they have raised is becoming more and more constrained by the ever-widening remit of WTO agreements, which stretch beyond trade to encompass government subsidies and procurement policies.

Most GBIs have not yet directly analysed the impacts of profit-led globalization on the fiscal space because they have focused primarily on the expenditure side of the budget, particularly on the social sectors such as health, education and poverty reduction programmes. Most of them have not yet considered the revenue side of the budget or the macroeconomic dimensions of the budget (the issue of the appropriate deficit or surplus and the aggregate levels of revenue and expenditure).

An exception is the South African WBI which has analysed the gender dimensions of taxation in the context of globalization in its budget report in 2000. In this report, Smith documents the dramatic shift in the composition of revenue from direct taxes in the period since 1988-89 away from corporate taxes to personal taxes (mainly income tax). In 1988–89 personal taxes accounted for 30 per cent of total tax revenue, while corporate taxes accounted for 22 per cent. By 1998–99, personal taxes accounted for 42 per cent, while corporate taxes accounted for only 13 per cent of total tax revenue (Smith 2000: 8). The lowering of corporate taxes has been a key element in the South African government's Growth, Employment and Redistribution (GEAR) strategy, which aims to achieve growth and employment creation through exports and private sector investment. It has been complemented by trade liberalization. In the 2002 report of the WBI, it is reported that by 1999–2000 customs duties accounted for only 2.5 per cent of government revenue, whereas in neighbouring Swaziland and Lesotho, they accounted for half of government revenue (Goldman 2000: 11–12). The GEAR strategy was adopted without any pressure from the World Bank or IMF, to which South Africa has few debts. Rather it was a response to the worries of foreign investors following a sharp fall in the value of the rand caused by an outflow of short-term capital. It does not seem to have worked: 'on the whole many more jobs have been lost in the South African economy since 1996 than those created' (Smith 2000: 19). The clothing and textile industry has been particularly hard hit by job losses, predominantly among women, as South Africa lowered tariffs on clothing and textiles faster and to lower levels than required under the WTO (Goldman 2000: 16).

Total revenue in South Africa was projected to fall in relation to gross domestic product from 32.2 per cent in 1997–98 to 30.7 per cent in 2001–2002. The WBI report points to the loss this represents to programmes which would benefit women (Budlender 2000b: 3). The report does not directly challenge the GEAR (perhaps because the government has so far been totally impervious to the widespread criticism of this strategy). But it does call for an end to reductions in corporate taxation, additional efforts to end widespread evasion and avoidance of taxes and import duties, and a system for conducting gender-aware employment impact assessments of trade agreements.

Poor, highly indebted countries have far less room for manoeuvre than South Africa, and are not free to determine their own trade, fiscal and monetary policies but must adopt neoliberal globalization policies required by the IMF and World Bank. The GBIs in some of them have produced critiques of these policies. For instance in Tanzania the TGNP has consistently stressed the need to challenge such policies, arguing that they result in 'limited room for government to support development that is gender-sensitive and owned by the people' (Rusimbi 2002: 125).

In Nepal a gender budget audit produced by the Institute for Integrated Development Studies (IIDS) concluded that: "The impact of the marked shift in budgetary polices since mid-1980s toward a more open economy and a minimalist state has not been gender friendly in general" (IIDS 2002: 74). As in South Africa, the tax system has been restructured to promote private investment, with corporate taxes reduced from 50 per cent to between 20 and 30 per cent, the maximum income tax rate reduced from 45 per cent to 25 per cent, and import duties from an average of 25 per cent to an average of 10 per cent. The ratio of government revenue to GDP has been rising, but in 2001 was still only 12.5 per cent, and the growth of revenue was unable to keep pace with expenditure, which stood at 20.3 per cent of GNP in 2001. There has been some expansion of export-oriented businesses but women have benefited very little from these while they have been hard hit by withdrawal of subsidies (another neoliberal pro-globalization policy) on food and fertilizers. The livelihoods of women farmers have become precarious because of competition from subsidized products from India and other countries. The report argues that there is a lack of measures to reconcile the social needs of the citizens of Nepal, especially those of poor women, and the integration of Nepal into a globalized economy. Nearly 60 per cent of the development expenditure of Nepal is financed by foreign aid, and the report calls for more foreign aid to be oriented to sectors such as income-generating activities for women, and services such as basic education, literacy, primary health care and drinking water. Donors are criticized for focusing on opening up the economy for international capital, and not meeting the promises about levels of aid made in UN forums. The report recognizes that Nepal cannot survive by itself in isolation from the global economy, but criticizes the government of Nepal for not making the process of integration in the global economy 'more gender-sensitive and human'.

Enlarging fiscal space and creating fiscal democracy

To achieve budgets which are more effective in promoting gender equality, there needs to be both more fiscal space, and a more democratic process for determining the use of that space. This requires action at both international and national levels. As a UN report on human development and trade points out: "The international regime cannot and should not be blamed for government failures to design appropriate policies. But it can and should be accountable for restricting government choices and opportunities – or for channelling them in inappropriate directions" (UNDP 2003: 63).

At the international level, we need a system of global governance that does not restrict the ability of governments to raise higher levels of revenue in a more equitable way, and that does not limit their ability to use fiscal policy to cushion their societies against economic shocks.

In the realm of trade, this means a fundamental reshaping of the WTO, so that its rules operate fairly. It requires that poor countries which raise a substantial portion of their revenue from trade taxes should not be pushed into precipitate reduction of tariffs and export taxes, and that WTO agreements should not constrain the way that governments spend public money. As the UN report on trade and human development puts it: "Trade rules must allow for diverse national institutions and standards ... citizens of different countries have different preferences for the role of government regulation or provision of social welfare" (UNDP 2003: 67).

In the realm of international finance, this means cancellation of debts of the Highly Indebted Poor Countries; no pressure from the IMF for countries to liberalize capital markets to permit financial investors to move money freely across borders; no pressure from the IMF for countries hit by financial crises to severely cut back on public expenditure; and the introduction of new systems for dealing with financial crises (Stiglitz 2002; Singh & Zammit 2000).

In the realm of international direct investment, it means no expansion of WTO rules to cover investment, competition and government procurement. Such an expansion would lock countries into a system with gives multinational corporations even greater rights to operate in all countries free from all but minimum regulation. It would severely limit the ability of government to pursue social objectives through their procurement policies (such as affirmative action to give contracts to small businesses owned by disadvantaged groups), since foreign firms and local firms would have to be treated in exactly the same way (Khor 2003: 539).

It means looking at ways of reinvigorating public provision of finance for development through developing global taxation and redistribution schemes. One possibility is to introduce a tax on international currency transactions (the Tobin Tax, originally proposed by Nobel prize-winning American economist, James Tobin) and redistribute the proceeds to finance universal public provisioning of basic social services and gender-equitable social protection schemes (Çağatay 2002: 19). Another is the scheme advocated by Griffin and McKinley (1996) whereby funds would be raised by a compulsory progressive tax on the national income of rich countries and distributed automatically to poor countries, in accordance with their per capita income.

There are many civil society groups, including women's groups, campaigning for all of these kinds of changes in international governance. More links need to be built between them and GBIs:

> ... in the context of globalisation, fiscal policy cannot be rendered gender-equitable or broadly equitable at the national or local levels alone. It is also necessary to address these concerns at the international level and to ensure that there is coherence between the international dimensions of policy and advocacy and the national and local ones ... This can be accomplished through greater dialogue between a) feminists who are involved in national or local budget initiatives and those who do advocacy at the international level; b) between feminists and other groups who focus on democratising macroeconomics polices (such as those who focus on pro-poor budgets or other types of progressive macroeconomic policy-making ... and c) between feminists involved in budget initiatives in the South and the North.   (Çağatay 2002: 19)

An important way to build these links is for GBIs to extend their scrutiny to the Ministries of Finance and Trade and Industry (as the South African WBI has done); and for GBIs in the North to extend their scrutiny to the development cooperation budgets of their countries.

It is however important to remember that within the limited fiscal space left by profit-led globalization, governments can and do make choices; and often these choices are not consistent with gender-equality goals. The IMF and the World Bank do not dictate where the cuts should fall. Governments make these decisions.

For example, in Mexico, cutbacks in public expenditure introduced by both the Zedillo government and the Fox government have tended to fall more heavily on programmes of direct importance to women (Colinas 2003). In 1998–2000 the Zedillo government made cuts in response to a fall in the price of oil (which reduced government revenue from the Mexican oil industry). The Ministry of Finance announced that the cuts would fall on the National Electricity Commission, PEMEX (the state-owned oil company) and the Department of Communications and Transport. In fact, the cuts actually fell on the Ministry of Social Affairs, the Ministry of Health and the Ministry of Education. The Fox government, whose election in 2000 ended a long period of *de facto* one-party rule, also made cuts. In 2002 the Ministry of Finance gave assurances that programmes specifically targeting women would not be cut, but there were cuts in anti-poverty programmes, resulting in fewer resources for nutrition, basic housing, temporary employment programmes and community services. The budgets of the Attorney-General, the Ministry of National Defence, the Ministry of the Navy and the Ministry of Public Security were not cut. The budgets of Ministries of Health and of Education were cut, as was that of the Mexican Social Security Institute.

Mexican women have been fighting back. In September 2002, the Commission on Gender Equality of the federal Chamber of Deputies hosted a public meeting on gender and budgets attended by women from Mexican groups working on gender analysis of budgets, officials from a variety of ministries and some international GBI advocates.

In subsequent negotiations on the 2003 budget, the Commission succeed in getting increases in the amounts proposed by the government: for instance, an increase of 100 million pesos for the reproductive health programme (an increase of 40 per cent on the original proposal). Other programmes for which funding allocations were increased include a programme to reduce maternal mortality (from almost 50 million pesos to 75 million pesos), a programme for women in agriculture (from just over 50 million pesos to 200 million pesos), and a programme for immigrant women (from almost 2 million pesos to 6 million pesos). In addition, it was agreed that all government entities will be required to introduce evaluation mechanisms that incorporate the objective of reducing gender inequality (Colinas 2003). Now the challenge is to ensure that the increased allocations are transformed into activities that have a positive impact on Mexican women. Mexico is not yet anywhere near the point when the whole budget is formulated in a gender-equitable way, but some Mexican women are now using the available fiscal space to struggle to achieve budgetary allocations for public policies that offer prospect of some real gains for Mexican women, especially poor women.

To transform government budget-making so that it is fully consistent with gender equality and the empowerment of women requires the creation of fiscal democracy, a system in which budget processes are transparent, accountable and participatory, and in which every type of citizen has an equal voice (Bakker 2002). In most countries, rich and poor, this is far from being achieved. Even if there is no secrecy about budget allocations and no misappropriation of funds, powerful interest groups connected to the rich elite tend to dominate the setting of priorities, winning tax concessions and expenditure on programmes important *to them*.

Four aspects of fiscal democracy are identified by Norton and Elson (2002: 47–8): governance of budgets by elected representatives; government officials holding consultations with the public; governments sharing decision-making on budget formulation and execution with citizens; citizens holding statutory entitlements to public services, backed up by mechanisms of redress. Goetz and Jenkins (2002) stress the importance of participatory auditing, to ensure that decisions are actually carried out, and that the people who were supposed to benefit, actually do benefit. Both sets of authors stress that for formal structures of fiscal democracy to be democratic in practice, there must be active engagement of well-informed and well-organized citizens. Goetz and Jenkins find that although the state of Kerala in India has introduced an impressive formal structure of fiscal democracy, women have not yet been able to exercise an equal voice within it. They attribute this to the lack of autonomous organizations of women.

Conclusions

Profit-led globalization puts strong limits on what can be achieved by attempts to turn government budgets into instruments for gender equality, but ministers of finance still have important areas of discretion in the way they raise revenue and spend it. GBIs have the potential to be significant actors in the struggle to enlarge the fiscal space and make it more democratic. To achieve this, they will need to make alliances with other initiatives, both those working on transforming globalization, and those working on transforming budgets; and they will need to focus attention not only on the budgets of those ministries that seem most immediately relevant to women, but also on the budgets and policies of the Ministries of Finance, Trade and Industry. They will need to advocate for systems of public finance that redistribute not only internally, but also internationally.

References

Bakker, I. (2002), 'Fiscal policy, accountability and voice: the example of gender responsive budget initiatives', Human Development Report Office occasional paper. New York: UNDP.

Banerjee, N. (2003), 'What is gender budgeting? Public policies from women's perspective in the Indian context'. Follow the Money series, South Asia no. 1. New Delhi: United Nations Development Fund for Women.

Budlender, D. (2000a), 'The political economy of women's budgets in the South', *World Development* 28(7), 1365–78.

Budlender, D. (2000b), 'Introduction', *The Women's Budget Series, 2000 Issue*. Cape Town: IDASA.

Budlender, D. (2002), 'A global assessment of gender responsive budget initiatives', in D. Budlender and G. Hewitt (eds), *Gender Budgets Make More Cents*, 83–164. London: Commonwealth Secretariat.

Budlender, D. and G. Hewitt (eds) (2002), *Gender Budgets Make More Cents*. London: Commonwealth Secretariat.

Budlender, D. and R. Sharp (1998), *How to Do a Gender-Sensitive Budget Analysis: Contemporary Research and Practice*. London: Commonwealth Secretariat.

Budlender, D., D. Elson, G. Hewitt and T. Mukhopadhyay (2002), *Gender Budgets Make Cents*, London: Commonwealth Secretariat.

Çağatay, N. (2002), 'Gender budgets and beyond: feminist fiscal policy in the context of globalisation', paper presented at the conference of the Association for Women's Rights in Development, Guadalajara, Mexico.

Colinas, M. (2003), 'Gender, budgets and development planning in Mexico', MA dissertation, Department of Sociology, University of Essex.

Elson, D. (1998), 'Integrating gender issues into national budgetary polices and procedures: some policy options', *Journal of International Development* 10, 929–41.

Elson, D. (2002), 'Gender responsive budget initiatives', in *Gender Budget Initiatives. Strategies, Concepts, Experiences*. New York: United Nations Development Fund for Women.

Elson, D. and N. Çağatay (2000), 'The social content of macroeconomic policies', *World Development* 28(7), 1347–63.

Goetz, A.-M. and R. Jenkins (2002), 'Accountability to women in development spending-experiments in service delivery audits at the local level'. Brighton: Institute of Development Studies.

Goldman, T. (2000), 'Customs and excise paper', *The Women's Budget Series 2000 Issue*. Cape Town: IDASA.

Govender, P. (2002), 'Lessons from practice: the role of parliament in South Africa's women's budget', in *Gender Budget Initiatives: Strategies, Concepts, Experiences*. New York: United Nations Development Fund for Women.

Griffin, K. (2003), 'Economic globalization and institutions of global governance', *Development and Change* 34(5), 789–807.

Griffin, K. and T. McKinley (1996), 'Development cooperation in the twenty-first century: suggestions for a new framework', *Indian Journal of Applied Economics* 5(4), 161–82.

Grunberg, I. (1998), 'Double jeopardy: globalization, liberalization and the fiscal squeeze', *World Development* 26(4), 591–605.

Hewitt, G. and T. Mukhopadhyay (2002), 'Promoting gender equality through public expenditure', in D. Budlender, D. Elson, G. Hewitt and T. Mukhopadhyay (eds), *Gender Budgets Make More Cents*, 49–81. London: Commonwealth Secretariat.

Hofbauer, H. (2002), 'Mexico: collaborating with a wide range of actors', in D. Budlender and G. Hewitt (eds), *Gender Budgets Make More Cents*, 84–97. London: Commonwealth Secretariat.

Institute for Integrated Development Studies – IIDS (2002), *Gender Budget Audit Nepal*. Kathmandu: IIDS.

Jain, D. (2002), 'Building budgets from below', in *Gender Budget Initiatives. Strategies, Concepts, Experiences*. New York: United Nations Development Fund for Women.

Karnataka Women's Information and Resource Centre (2002), *Building Budgets from Below*. Bangalore: Karnataka Women's Information and Resource Centre.

Khor, M. (2003), 'Globalisation, global governance and the dilemmas of development', in H.-J. Chang (ed.), *Rethinking Development Economics*, 521–44. London: Anthem Press.

Krafchik, W. (2002), 'Can civil society add value to budget decision-making?', in *Gender Budget Initiatives. Strategies, Concepts, Experiences*. New York: United Nations Development Fund for Women.

Norton, A. and D. Elson (2002), *What's Behind the Budget? Politics, Rights and Accountability in the Budget Process*. London: Overseas Development Institute.

Pearl, R. (2002), 'The Andean region: a multi-country programme', in D. Budlender and G. Hewitt (eds), *Gender Budgets Make More Cents*, 23–42. London: Commonwealth Secretariat.

Rai, S. (2002), *Gender and the Political Economy of Development*. Cambridge: Polity Press.

Rusimbi, M. (2002), 'Mainstreaming gender into policy, planning and budgeting in Tanzania', in *Gender Budget Initiatives: Strategies, Concepts, Experiences*. New York: United Nations Development Fund for Women.

Sawer, M. (2002), 'Australia; the mandarin approach to gender budgets', in D. Budlender and G. Hewitt (eds), *Gender Budgets Make More Cents*, 43–64. London: Commonwealth Secretariat.

Sharp, R. (2002), 'Moving forward: multiple strategies and guiding goals', in *Gender Budget Initiatives: Strategies, Concepts, Experiences*. New York: United Nations Development Fund for Women.

Sharp, R. and R. Broomhill (2002), 'Budgeting for equality: the Australian experience', *Feminist Economics* 8(1), 25–47.

Singh, A. and A. Zammitt (2000), 'International capital flows: identifying the gender dimension', *World Development* 28(7), 1249–68.

Smith, T. (2000), 'Women and tax in South Africa', in *The Women's Budget Series 2000 Issue*. Capetown: IDASA.

Stiglitz, J. (2002), *Globalisation and its Discontents*. New York: W. W. Norton.

United Nations Development Programme (UNDP) (2003), *Making Global Trade Work For People*. London: Earthscan.

United Nations Fund for Women (UNIFEM) (2002), *Gender Budget Initiatives: Strategies, Concepts and Experiences*. New York: United Nations Development Fund for Women.

Vargas-Valente, V. (2002), 'Municipal budgets and democratic governance in the Andean region', in *Gender Budget Initiatives: Strategies, Concepts, Experiences*. New York: United Nations Development Fund for Women.

9

GENDER EQUALITY AND INCLUSIVE GROWTH

Introduction

Investment and economic growth are central to development, argued Fred Nixson, who proposed a conceptualisation of development which emphasises its "unevenness, contradictions and costs (human, economic and environmental) but which also recognises its constructive or progressive aspects – the development of knowledge, new institutions, improvements in the position of female children and adult women and higher material living standards, for example" (Nixson 2006: 973). At the same time, Nixson recognised that "Development economics, quite properly, has always concerned itself with economic policy, focused on the achievement of a set of outcomes consistent with some normative definition of 'development'" (Nixson 2006: 977). This chapter engages with these issues through a discussion of gender equality and inclusive growth.

The idea of inclusive growth was introduced as a response to concerns about high levels of inequality in the distribution of income in growing economies (Klasen 2010). It was included in the new development agenda adopted in 2015 by the Member States of the United Nations. The Declaration of the 2030 Agenda for Sustainable Development states: "We resolve also to create conditions for sustainable, inclusive and sustained economic growth, shared prosperity and decent work for all, taking into account different levels of national development and capacities" (UNGA 2015: para 3). This would require reversal of trends of the last forty years, when the extra income created by economic growth has been distributed very unequally. Data on the global distribution of income show that while all income groups experienced positive growth in their real income between 1988 and 2011, the incomes of the poorest 10 per cent of people increased by $65, equivalent to less than $3 extra a year, while the incomes of the richest 1 per cent increased 182 times as much, by $11,800 (Oxfam 2017). Between 1980 and 2020, the top 1 per cent of income earners captured 22 per cent of total world growth, versus 11 per cent for the bottom 50 per cent (Chancel & Piketty 2021).

The increase in inequality between people is related to increasing income inequality between labour and capital in both developed and developing countries. In a group of 16 developed countries, the labour share of national income declined from about 75 per cent in the mid-1970s to 65 per cent in the mid-2000s; and in a group of 16 developing and emerging economies, average labour shares declined from around 62 per cent of gross domestic product in the early 1990s to 58 per cent in the mid-2000s (UNDP 2015: 77). The growing inequality in the functional distribution of income points to inequalities in the system of production that underpin inequality in household or personal income and wealth. These inequalities are founded in the exclusion of workers, except the most highly paid, from ownership and control of the means of production (land, machines and systems). Moreover, class inequality intersects with gender and race/ethnicity since the ownership and control of the means of production is predominantly in the hands of elite men. In recent decades, increases in productivity have not been matched by increases in wages. In 91 of 133 countries between 1995 and 2014, wages did not grow as fast as productivity (Vazquez Pimentel *et al.* 2018). Power in workplaces and in markets underpins the distribution of income and wealth, and the market power of large companies in advanced economies has increased. IMF researchers found that between 1980 and 2015 their mark-ups increased on average by 39 per cent (Diez *et al.* 2018).

When growth was dramatically halted or slowed down by the Covid-19 pandemic in 2020–21, inequality persisted or increased. Global labour income (before taking into account income support measures) in 2020 is estimated to have declined by 8.3 per cent, which amounts to US$3.7 trillion, or 4.4 per cent of global GDP (ILO 2021a). At the same time, Oxfam (2021) notes that while over two million people have died, and hundreds of millions of people were forced into poverty, many of the richest individuals and corporations thrived. The fortunes of the top thousand billionaires, mainly white men, returned to their pre-pandemic highs in just nine months, as after an initial fall, stock markets have been booming, supported by the Quantitative Easing policies of leading central banks.

None of the measures of income distribution cited above explicitly address distribution by gender, but since many women have no income of their own, and when they do earn an income tend to be concentrated in low- and middle-skilled jobs, and moreover own no or only very low assets, the distribution of income by gender is likely to be even more unequal. Unless the gender dimensions of inclusive growth are made explicit, and policies for inclusive growth deliberately aim to improve women's well-being and address gender gaps, it is unlikely that growth will benefit women and men equally. In the 2030 Agenda for Sustainable Development, there is no discussion about whether and how the process of growth needs to be changed to achieve gender equality, though some of the indicators used are disaggregated by gender. Nor is there any recognition that current patterns of growth actually make some people worse off: they not only leave people behind, they push people behind (Elson 2019).

Inclusive economic growth is a focus of the 2030 Agenda's Sustainable Development Goal (SDG) 8, "Promote sustained, inclusive and sustainable economic growth, full and productive work for all", but no definition is offered of these terms, nor of the kind of growth process that is required. Inclusion in income growth is a focus of SDG 10, "Reduce inequality within and among countries". Inclusion is specifically mentioned in Target 10.2: "By 2030, empower and promote the social, economic and political inclusion of all, irrespective of age, sex, disability, race, ethnicity, origin, religion, or economic or other status". SDG 9 calls for the promotion of inclusive and sustainable industrialisation, again without defining these terms, but the focus is on increasing industry's share of employment and GDP. SDG 5, "Achieve gender equality and empower all women and girls", does not mention economic growth, but does call on states to undertake reforms to give women equal rights to economic resources in Target 5.a. The SDG focus on inclusive growth is ambiguous and fragmented.

This chapter uses a gender lens to scrutinise economic growth, and the ways in which it needs to be changed to improve the well-being of women, and to be more inclusive and equitable. The chapter is organised as follows: the first section examines growth as a gendered process, distinguishing the spheres of production, social reproduction and finance. The second section discusses how inclusion in growth can be harmful rather than enhancing, and notes that economic growth frequently has adverse side effects, such as depletion of human and natural resources. Growth of output is not necessarily a route to well-being – much depends on what kinds of outputs are growing, and how they are produced. The third section elaborates what a gender-equitable inclusive growth process would look like, in the spheres of production, social reproduction and finance. The fourth section discusses gender-equitable strategies for recovery from the Covid-19 pandemic. The concluding section highlights the need for new forms of economic growth, focusing on public investment in social as well as physical infrastructure, and for decent work not just participation in the labour force.

Growth as a gendered process

Gender is not only a characteristic of people: economies are gendered structures and economic growth is a gendered process (Elson *et al.* 1997). Analysis of economic growth usually focuses only on the paid economy, where output is counted as contributing to economic growth as measured by GDP. However, there is also an unpaid economy, in which people are reproduced on a daily and intergenerational basis, through unpaid care and domestic work, the majority of which is done by women and girls. Unpaid domestic work, such as collecting firewood and water, and growing vegetables in kitchen gardens, is conceptually included in the system of national accounts as part of GDP, but in practice, the outputs of such work are not measured and not counted as part of national output. Unpaid care work is not conceptually included in the system of national accounts as part of GDP and is not counted as contributing to economic growth (United Nations 2009: 12–13). But it clearly makes an indirect, unmeasured contribution, since without this work, there would be no people to produce economic growth. Economic growth does reduce the amount of time spent on unpaid work, but it does not eliminate it. Even in high income countries a substantial amount of time is spent on unpaid care work.

One way to reveal the economic contribution of unpaid work is for national statistical offices to construct a satellite national account of unpaid household production, in which money values are attributed to unpaid care work and the services it produces. Several developed countries and a few developing countries have already produced such accounts (UNECE 2017). They show that the value of the output of unpaid care work is substantial, ranging from around 20 per cent to around 40 per cent of GDP, based on valuing the unpaid work at replacement cost. For example, the estimate for Australia in 2006 was 41.6 per cent (UNECE 2017: 105); for Mexico the estimate was 23.2 per cent (UNECE 2017: 110). The estimate for Ghana lies between these two at 35 per cent of GDP in 2009 (Ofosu-Baadu 2009).

Both paid work and unpaid work are shaped, directly or indirectly by finance. In the last 30 years, finance has moved to a position of domination over economies and people, with disproportionate power exercised by financial businesses, operating both internationally and within countries (Epstein 2005). Economic growth has been punctuated by financial crises that slow, halt or even reverse economic growth. There were major financial crises in Latin America in the early 1980s and in Asia in 1997, and a crisis, originating in USA, that had global impact in 2008. The policy response to these crises has been marked by deflationary bias: cutting public expenditure to try to reduce budget deficits created by the crisis, limiting access to public services and hampering job creation and economic growth. The financial crises and the policy responses to them have had a particularly detrimental impact on low-income women (Elson 2013; Fukuda-Parr *et al.* 2013).

Analysis of economic growth frequently disaggregates the economy into agriculture, industry and service sectors. However, to understand growth as a gendered process, it is useful to supplement this sectoral disaggregation by distinguishing three spheres: finance, production and social reproduction (Elson 2010: 202). The financial sphere includes profit-oriented banks, insurance companies, hedge funds, etc., and their regulators, comprising central banks and ministries of finance. It also encompasses non-profit businesses such as mutual or cooperative savings and loan funds, subsidised microfinance and state banks, and informal money lending by pawnshops, kerbside dealers, and landlords and merchants. In the sphere of production, goods and non-financial services are produced for sale, through activities such as farming, mining, construction, manufacturing, wholesaling, retailing and supply of leisure services. This sphere includes both formal and informal paid work. The non-market sphere of social reproduction supplies goods and services directly concerned with the daily and intergenerational reproduction of people as human beings, especially through their care, socialisation and education. It includes unpaid domestic and care work in families and communities, organised unpaid volunteer work and paid (but non-market) work in public services such as health and education.

All three spheres are characterised by gender inequalities, such as the division of labour in which the primary responsibility for unpaid care and domestic work is assigned to women, and paid work is marked by gender occupational segregation and gender earnings gaps (UN Women 2015: Chapters 1 and 2 and annexes 1 to 4; 2017: Chapters 4, 5, 6). Large businesses are almost invariably led by men, and households are subject to internal gender inequalities in income, consumption, asset ownership and decision-making (UN Women 2019). The markets that link activities are themselves gendered institutions (Elson 1999). Gender inequalities are supported by social norms that constrain the choices of women and men. Social norms are persistent, but can change in the process of economic growth, such as when it becomes "normal" for women to undertake paid work outside the home. They can also be transformed by deliberate collective action, such as when domestic violence becomes perceived as a crime that governments must address.

Of course, women's lives are shaped by multiple inequalities, not only related to gender but also to class, race/ethnicity and/or location. Gender intersects with different sources of disadvantage, such as a lack of education, place of residence and ethnicity. In many parts of the world, there is a growing gap between women whose economic and personal status has improved, and those who are further disadvantaged as inequalities between rich and the rest widen (ILO 2015; UN Women 2015: 44–8).

Building the picture of a specific economy as a gendered structure, taking account of intersections with other inequalities, calls for collecting and analysing data on several dimensions of all three spheres (see for example UN Women 2016; Fontana 2018). For example, in the sphere of production, it requires sex-disaggregated data, not just on the quantity of employment, but also its quality, such as through measures of gender-based occupational segregation, gender earnings gaps and levels of earnings. Ideally, data should be disaggregated not only by sex but also by other factors such as place of residence, age, educational attainment and migration status of workers, to show how gender intersects with other sources of disadvantage to determine forms of inclusion or exclusion. In the sphere of social reproduction, statistics are required on unequal patterns of time spent on unpaid domestic and care work, as well as usage of services that can reduce unpaid work, such as electricity, water and care services, disaggregated not just by sex but also by household income and place of residence. Data on public spending on social services can help in capturing the extent to which responsibility for care provision is shared between families, the state and other institutions. In the sphere of finance, the degree to which the economy and its people are dominated by financial services needs to be identified, including the role of financial businesses, the regulatory structure and the extent of access to financial services and of indebtedness. Disaggregated data on financial governance and financial inclusion are critical for identifying which groups control the sphere of finance and which groups are most vulnerable to financial predators.

The spheres of production, social reproduction and finance are essential for economic growth, and time trends in the data identified above reveal the ways in which economic growth is gendered. Some types of growth depend on the maintenance of various kinds of gender inequality. For instance, this will be the case if growth depends on keeping wages low and maintaining a gender earnings gap (as is frequently the case in labour-intensive, export-led, foreign-investment-led development), while at the same time keeping taxes and public expenditure low so as to attract foreign investment and relying on women's unpaid work to care for the current and future labour force (Braunstein 2015). In this type of growth benefits go disproportionately to foreign investors, and women's overall working time increases, as paid work is added to unpaid work. Moreover, this growth model holds back the investment in human capacities required to move to higher productivity, higher wage and a more equal economy in the future. When public expenditure on education and health is limited, and household incomes are low, boys tend to get priority over girls. And when women take on paid work without public investment to reduce their unpaid work, older girls frequently have to take on additional unpaid work, to the detriment of their education. The simultaneous pressures on women from paid work and unpaid work can lead to the depletion of their human capacities through physical and mental injuries (Chopra & Zambelli 2017).

Harmful forms of inclusion

Inclusion is typically treated as positive in the SDGs and in much of the literature on inclusive growth. The problem is identified as exclusion, both exclusion from the process of generating GDP growth, and/or from the enjoyment of the benefits produced by it. But inclusion in economic growth can be harmful as well as beneficial (Elson & Fontana 2019). For instance, direct inclusion in growth via employment can entail forcible inclusion (e.g. forced labour, modern slavery); injurious inclusion (e.g. unsafe working conditions, long hours of work); impoverished inclusion (e.g. returns to work not above poverty level); precarious inclusion (e.g. insecure employment); segregated inclusion (e.g. inclusion via low-paying occupations at the bottom of the job hierarchy).

Conditions of indirect inclusion in economic growth via social reproduction can also be harmful. For instance: forcible inclusion (e.g. forced unpaid domestic and care work through forced marriage); and injurious inclusion (e.g. unsafe working conditions and long hours of unpaid care and domestic work, domestic violence).

Financial inclusion can also be harmful. There is a big push on the part of international development agencies and financial businesses to draw as many people as possible into the financial system, and the SDGs include as Target 8.10: "Strengthen the capacity of domestic financial institutions to encourage and extend access to banking, insurance and financial services for all". There is insufficient discussion, however, of the measures required to ensure that financial inclusion is beneficial for well-being and not just a way of enhancing the profits of financial service providers. There is mounting evidence of the ways in which financial inclusion exposes people to the risks of mis-selling financial products, fraud, increasing levels of indebtedness, loss of assets and vulnerability to the depredations of debt collectors (Bateman *et al.* 2018).

Economic growth has many other harmful impacts on human wellbeing, with many millions not just being left behind but being pushed behind, some to lower living standards, some to premature avoidable death (Elson 2019). For instance, many developing countries have recently experienced land enclosure and appropriation in the name of improving productivity and economic growth. Research in Africa, however, found that many land deals were done in secret or without consultation with local communities, and without transparency, accountability and participation (Hall *et al.* 2015). In some cases, new wage employment was created, so people were included in growth, but the number of jobs was far below what had been projected. The jobs involved mainly casual and seasonal work at low pay compared with similar employment in the locality. People who retained some land were often incorporated as out-growers but typically on adverse terms, especially for women whose control of productive resources and cash income was undermined (Hall *et al.* 2015).

Economic growth has increased life-harming pollution overall. While development reduces some forms of pollution, such as from sewage-contaminated water, and indoor cooking stoves using wood, dung or charcoal, new forms, such as outdoor air pollution, are produced by industrialisation and motor transport.

Indoor air pollution from stoves caused an estimated 2.9 million deaths in 2015, but outdoor pollution from vehicles and industry caused 4.5 million deaths. The deaths from outdoor air pollution are set to rise rapidly in many countries unless measures are taken to reduce pollution (Lancet Commission on Pollution and Health 2018). There is no possible compensation that will make good some kinds of damage, such as premature avoidable death due to pollution or the loss of culturally valued ancestral lands. Where compensation would be possible, such as for loss of income and employment, it often does not materialise (Elson 2019).

Rather than simply looking at GDP growth as an indicator of prosperity, it is necessary to look at which kinds of outputs are growing, and which activities are taking place. The references to sustainability in the SDGs (such as Goal 12, "Ensure sustainable consumption and production patterns") do not fully address the risks to human well-being, as they do not link natural resource use to depletion of human capacities and destruction of human life. Thus, as well as a concern with sharing prosperity, there needs to be a concern with avoiding depletion and destruction of human beings and human well-being.

What would gender-equitable inclusive growth look like?

Reduction of gender gaps in employment and income are not enough. Such gaps might be reduced even while harmful forms of inclusion persist or increase. The first principle should be 'do no harm', so measures to reduce gender gaps should also aim to eliminate harmful forms of inclusion and contribute to sustainable development.

A fall in the gender gap in labour force participation rates is often considered an indicator that growth is becoming more gender equitable and inclusive. However, while absence from the labour force tends to exclude women from enjoying an income of their own, presence does not mean equal inclusion in prosperity. Women's employment is more likely than men's to fail to meet ILO standards of decent work (ILO 2016: Chapter 3). Gender-equitable inclusive growth would reduce gender gaps in enjoyment of decent work by increasing the creation of decent work for both women and men in sustainable 'green' jobs that do not harm the environment, with a higher rate of expansion for women than for men, a process that may be described as 'equalizing up'. It is possible to reduce gender gaps by raising the male unemployment rate to that of women and increasing the share of men in non-standard forms of employment to the same rate as women. But this kind of 'equalizing down' would impoverish many women via the impact on men in their households.

Gender-equitable inclusive growth would not just reduce gaps in jobs but also in income. It is tempting to judge how gender-equitable growth is in terms of whether there is a fall in the gender wage gap, but simply looking at the gap conceals whether a fall is an example of 'equalizing up' through rises in women's wages towards those of men; or 'equalising down' through falls in men's wages towards those of women. Moreover, most available data on wages are for employees in the formal sector, a small proportion of the labour force in most developing countries, where many people work in self-employment, family farms and informal businesses. What is needed is data on the gender income gap as well as the gender wage gap.

In 40 countries where data are available on individual incomes by sex, they show that from 2007 to 2013, women were more likely than men to live on less than 50 per cent of median income. Single mothers were much more likely to be in this situation; in 6 countries, at least 40 per cent of single mothers live on less than 50 per cent of median income (UN Women 2018: 114). Gender-equitable inclusive growth would reduce this gender income gap by reducing the proportion of both women and men living at below 50 per cent of median income, but with a faster reduction for women, so as to 'equalise up' rather than 'equalise down'.

Sharing the fruits of growth on a gender-equitable basis would be assisted by reducing wage dispersion between occupations categorised as 'high-skilled' (which are disproportionately occupied by men) and occupations categorised as 'low-skilled' (which are disproportionately occupied by women). It is important to recognise that skill premia are determined by bargaining power and social norms as well as by technical capacities, and do not merely reflect a value-neutral 'productivity differential'. Gender-equitable inclusive growth requires not only more training and opportunities for women to enter 'high-' skilled occupations. It means revaluing the contributions of women in some typically female 'low-skilled occupations such as care work, so that relative wages in these occupations increase. The Covid-19 pandemic showed that much work categorised as 'low skilled' is in fact 'essential' work (UN Women 2021: 10).

As well as employment and income, it is important to look at the composition of output. UNIDO includes some consideration of this in its definition of inclusive industrial development, referring to provision of "new varieties and qualities of goods that become affordable to everyone" (UNIDO 2018). However, the examples provided all relate to privately produced and consumed goods such as frozen food, computers, medicines and household appliances. Much more important for ensuring a gender-equitable composition of output (outputs that equally meet the needs of women and men) is the public provision of affordable housing, clean energy, safe public transport, clean water and sanitation, and health, education and care services, all of which can reduce women's unpaid work and enable them to access decent paid work (Fontana & Elson 2014; ILO 2018). Gender-equitable inclusive growth would ensure that there is adequate public investment to increase such provision so that it is accessible and affordable to all women and delivered through 'green' technologies. This kind of investment reduces the amount of unpaid work that is necessary for social reproduction.

However, as well as investment to reduce unpaid work, gender-equitable inclusive growth also requires redistribution of unpaid work so that it is more equally shared between women and men. Both jobs and social protection need to be redesigned to support this, as is recognised by the ILO Decent Work Agenda (ILO 1999). Measures are required to enable and incentivise men to take on a bigger share of unpaid care work, such as paid parental leave for fathers as well as mothers; changes in business practices with respect to working hours and promotion and collective action to change gender norms. Gender-equitable inclusive growth should not be understood simply in terms of enabling women's lives to become more like those of men, but in terms of transforming the lives of both women and men, so that each is able to participate equally in paid and unpaid work, in production and social reproduction.

This requires profound changes in the sphere of finance, which as currently organised does not support gender-equitable inclusive growth. It is not enough to eliminate gender gaps in access to financial services. Unless financial services are very well-regulated, it is possible for financial businesses to pursue preda-tory inclusion strategies, which incorporate women (and other disadvantaged groups) in ways detrimental to their well-being. Women are often included in the financial system, but in ways that increase their exposure to fraud, mis-selling and indebtedness, putting any assets they own at risk, as well as mak-ing them vulnerable to harassment by debt collectors. An international effort should elaborate a concept of decent finance comparable to the concept of decent work.

At the macrolevel, there is considerable evidence that financial crises and policy responses to them tend to have particularly adverse impacts on women (Elson 2013; Fukuda-Parr et al. 2013), setting back not only the prospects for growth but also for gender equality. Gender-equitable inclusive growth requires measures at the international and national levels to regulate international finan-cial markets and prevent destabilising volatility, and to safeguard countries against pressure for expenditure cuts that will hamper the creation of decent jobs and investment in public services.

Strategies for gender-equitable recovery from the Covid-19 pandemic

The Covid-19 Pandemic of 2019/21 set back the prospects for gender-equitable inclusive growth, both directly through the impact on health, and indirectly through lockdown measures. It is estimated that in 2019 and 2020, women lost more than 54 million jobs globally, a 4.2 per cent loss, compared to 3.0 per cent for men. It was forecast that in 2021, there would still be 13 million fewer women in employment compared to 2019, while men's employment would have recovered to 2019 levels (ILO 2021b).

Cash transfers were introduced in many countries to support people during the lockdowns. However, women were less likely to receive cash relief across 36 out of 45 countries surveyed as part of UN Women's Rapid Gender Assessments (which include all regions of the world), with 17 per cent of women receiving cash relief in response to Covid-19, compared to 27 per cent of men. Single mothers and younger women aged between 18 and 24 years were especially less likely than their male counterparts to report receiving cash or in-kind relief (UN Women 2021: 24).

While hours of paid work fell, hours of unpaid work increased because schools, nurseries and day-care centres shut down during 'lockdown'. UN Women's Rapid Gender Assessments in 45 countries found women were more likely than men to report an increase in childcare responsibilities. With additional hygiene requirements and more people at home, time spent on cleaning and cooking also increased, with women being much more likely than men to report increases. These tasks are particularly arduous in low-income contexts where access to basic services, such as running water and electricity, is lacking (UN Women 2021: 39).

The Covid-19 Global Gender Response Tracker (UNDP & UN Women 2021) found that only 226 out of the total 3099 social protection and labour market measures taken in response to Covid-19 directly address unpaid care, representing only 7.3 per cent of the total. These measures include provisions such as extended family leaves, shorter or flexible work time arrangements, compensations for school and day-care closures, emergency childcare for essential workers and support for longterm care facilities or home-based care services for elderly and disabled people. Europe, North America, Australia and New Zealand accounted for the majority of these measures (139 out of the total of 226) (UNDP & UN Women 2021: Table 1). Globally, only just over 40 per cent of countries took action to support unpaid care (UNDP & UN Women 2021: 13).

UN Women has put forward a post-Covid plan for a sustainable and just economy, with improvements in care services at its centre. It argues that spending on care services should be treated as investment in social infrastructure and placed on a par with investment in physical infrastructure, recognising that both generate benefits that extend beyond the individual recipient to societies at large and into the future (UN Women 2021: 40–41). For instance, spending on high quality early childhood care and education in the short run enables mothers to undertake more paid work and improves the learning and well-being of children. It also creates more 'decent jobs' for women. In the longer run it can improve productivity throughout the economy via channels such as increasing women's labour force experience and attachment and increasing the capabilities of the next generation of workers (Onaren *et al.* 2022).

A study modelling investment in a high quality universal childcare service in three middle-income countries, South Africa, Uruguay and Turkey, using parameters relevant to each country, found that employment rates can be significantly increased, especially for women, as a result of direct, indirect and induced job creation. Although the total annual gross cost of such investment can go up to 3 to 4 per cent of GDP, the net cost can be halved thanks to significant fiscal returns stemming from increased employment and earnings, without changing the tax structure itself (rates and bands) (De Henau *et al.* 2019).

The ILO has published estimates of employment that could be generated by investment in care services using data for 82 countries in all regions of the world, noting that not only would this investment address care needs, it could also provide a powerful economic stimulus to help deal with the aftermath of the Covid-19 pandemic, which saw many jobs and livelihoods destroyed (De Henau 2022). For instance, investment to provide a universal high quality early childhood care and education system (based in centres or community settings and delivered by well-trained staff with 'decent jobs') for all children is estimated to require total annual spending across all regions of the world of around US$2.2 trillion by 2035, with 82 per cent coming from the expansion of services (US$1.9 trillion), a six-fold increase on current spending. This would amount to 1.48 per cent of GDP on average across all regions, ranging from 4.19 per cent in Africa to 1.14 per cent in Europe (De Henau 2022: Table 5). The total of new jobs created by this investment, directly and indirectly, is estimated at 114 million, ranging from 30 million in Africa to 7.9 million in Europe, largely formal employment for women (De Henau 2022: Table 9). The total gender employment gap would be reduced by 7.4 percentage points (from a current gender employment gap of 26 percentage points). The gap would be reduced by half in Africa (from 14 to 6.6 percentage points) and by nearly two-thirds in Europe (from 11 to 4 percentage points).

In addition to generating employment, care provision tends to be more environmentally sustainable. For instance, calculations using Eurostat data suggest that investing in the care sector is 30 per cent less polluting in terms of greenhouse gas emissions than investing the same amount in the construction sector (De Henau & Himmelweit 2020). Moreover, there would also be positive impacts on output and productivity through enabling more women, especially low-income women, to participate in the labour market and in further training; and through improved capabilities of children, when they reach the labour market. Much of the research on returns to investment in early childhood care and education has focused on high income countries and found high returns (Heckman 2008). A recent World Bank report drawing on studies from low- and middle-income countries found benefit-cost ratios ranging between

1.7 and 14.2, suggesting there will also be high returns to investments in early childhood care and education in developing countries (Holla *et al.* 2021).

Public spending on care does need to be complemented by public spending on clean energy, water and sanitation, and transport and communication networks if they are to make a difference for low-income women in low-income countries (Fontana & Elson 2014). However, while public spending on clean energy, water and sanitation and transport and communication networks is already recognised as investment, most public spending on care (with exception of construction of care facilities) is categorised as consumption, not investment. This makes it subject to constraints from fiscal rules and conditionalities that put limits on budget deficits and allow borrowing only for investment (Elson 2016).

The investment required for a gender-equitable recovery from Covid-19 will not be possible without profound changes in the sphere of finance to ensure that developing countries have more fiscal space. These changes include debt restructuring and debt cancellation and more effective action to regulate international financial markets and end tax evasion and avoidance (UN Women 2021: 19).

Conclusion

This chapter has argued for an understanding of gender-equitable inclusive growth as a pattern and process of growth that ensures prosperity is shared between men and women in ways that reduce gender inequality through changes in the three spheres of the economy: production, social reproduction and finance. Gender-equitable inclusive growth means transforming the lives of men and women, so that they share unpaid domestic and care work on an equal basis, and women have an income of their own. These transformations should be achieved through equalising up, not equalising down.

Gender-equitable inclusive growth must be growth that does no irreparable harm to the well-being of women and men. Thus, growth of production using processes that lead to premature avoidable death and permanent ill-health and injury, both within the production process, and through spillover effects that pollute air and water, needs to be halted.

Gender-equitable inclusive growth requires public spending to increase physical and social infrastructure that supports social reproduction so that it is accessible and affordable to all women and men. This means challenging current conventions about what is investment and what is consumption, recognising that spending on social infrastructure, just as on physical infrastructure, is investment in an economic sense. It generates returns over a long period after the initial outlay, returns that accrue widely through the economy, reaching beyond the initial recipients.

Gender-equitable inclusive growth cannot be achieved by focusing only on reducing gender gaps and ignoring the power imbalance between the rich and the rest of society, and between capital and labour. It requires new models of growth that reduce gender gaps while at the same time reducing the gaps between the shares of capital and labour, and the shares of high-, middle- and low-skilled labour. It also requires measures to end the domination of finance over production and social reproduction.

Of course, all this is easier said than done. The work of Fred Nixson reminds us that development is an uneven and contradictory process, but that people have always tried to shape this process to bring about improvements in living standards. He rightly argued that public investment and job creation are critical for this. The argument of this chapter has been that to secure gender-equitable improvements it is important to broaden our understanding of what counts as investment, to include investment in care and other services that reduce unpaid work and to ensure that inclusion in growth is via decent work, that takes into account that no one is just a worker, recognising we all have domestic responsibilities.

References

Bateman, M., S. Blankenburg, and R. Kozul-Wright, eds. (2018). *The Rise and Fall of Global Microcredit: Development, Debt and Disillusion.* London: Routledge.

Braunstein, E. (2015). 'Economic Growth and Social Reproduction: Gender Inequality as Cause and Consequence'. Discussion paper No. 5. New York: UN Women.

Chancel, L., and T. Piketty. (2021). 'Global Income Inequality 1820-2020: The Persistence and Mutation of Extreme Inequality'. Working Paper No. 202119. Paris: World Inequality Lab.

Chopra, D., and E. Zambelli. (2017). *No Time to Rest: Women's Lived Experiences of Balancing Paid Work and Unpaid Care Work.* https://www.ids.ac.uk/publications/no-time-to-rest-womens-lived-experiences-of-balancing-paid-work-and-unpaid-care-work/.

De Henau, J. (2022). 'Costs and Benefits of Investing in Transformative Care Policy Packages: A Macrosimulation Study in 82 Countries'. ILO Working Paper No. 55. https://www.ilo.org/global/publications/working-papers/WCMS_839252/lang--en/index.htm.

De Henau, J., D. Budlender, F. Filgueira, I. Ilkkaraçan, K. Kim, and R. Mantero. (2019). *Investing in Free Universal Childcare in South Africa, Turkey and Uruguay: A Comparative Analysis of Costs, ShortTerm Employment Effects and Fiscal Revenue.* New York: UN Women. http://oro.open.ac.uk/68010/1/Discussion-paper-Investing-in-free-universal-childcare-in-South-Africa-Turkey-and-Uruguay-en.pdf.

De Henau, J., and S. Himmelweit. (2020). *A Care-Led Recovery from Coronavirus.* https://wbg.org.uk/wp-content/uploads/2020/06/Care-led-recovery-final.pdf

Diez, F., D. Leigh, and S. Tambunlertchai. (2018). 'Global Market Power and Its Macroeconomic Implications'. IMF Working Paper 18/3. https://www.imf.org/en/Publications/WP/Issues/2018/06/15/Global-Market-Power-and-its-Macroeconomic-Implications-45975.

Elson, D. (1999). 'Labor Markets as Gendered Institutions: Equality, Efficiency and Empowerment Issues', *World Development* 27(3), 611–27.

Elson, D. (2010). 'Gender and the Global Economic Crisis in Developing Countries: A Framework for Analysis', *Gender and Development* 18(2), 201–12.

Elson, D. (2013). 'Economic Crises from the 1980s to the 2010s: A Gender Analysis'. In *New Frontiers in Feminist Political Economy*, ed. G. Waylen and S. Rai. London: Routledge.

Elson, D. (2016). 'Gender Budgeting and Macroeconomic Policy'. In *Feminist Economics and Public Policy*, ed. J. Campbell and M. Gillespie. London: Routledge.

Elson, D. (2019). 'Push No One Behind'. *Journal of Globalization and Development* 9(2). https://doi.org/10.1515/jgd-2018-0026.

Elson, D., B. Evers, and J. Gideon. (1997). 'Gender Aware Country Economic Reports'. Working Paper No. 1, Concepts and Sources, Department of Economics, University of Manchester.

Elson, D., and M. Fontana. (2019). 'Conceptualizing Gender-Equitable Inclusive Growth'. In *Gender Equality and Inclusive Growth*, ed. D. Elson and A. Seth. New York: UN Women.

Epstein, G., ed. (2005). *Financialization and the World Economy*. Cheltenham: Edward Elgar.

Fontana, M. (2018). *Inclusive and Sustainable Industrial Development: The Gender Dimension*. Vienna: UNIDO.

Fontana, M., and D. Elson. (2014). 'Public Policies on Water Provision and Early Childhood Education and Care (ECEC): Do They Reduce and Redistribute Unpaid Work?' *Gender and Development* 22(3): 459–74.

Fukuda-Parr, S., J. Heintz, and S. Seguino, eds. (2013). Special Issue: 'Critical and Feminist Perspectives on Financial and Economic Crisis', *Feminist Economics* 19(3), 1–288.

Hall, R., I. Scoones, and D. Tsikata. (2015). 'Introduction: The Contexts and Consequences of Africa's Land Rush'. In *Africa's Land Rush: Rural Livelihoods and Agrarian Change*, ed. R. Hall, I. Scoones, and D. Tsikata. Woodbridge: James Currey.

Heckman, J. (2008). 'Schools, Skills, and Synapses'. IZA Discussion Paper No. 3515. Bonn: Institute of Labor Economics – published in *Economic Inquiry* 46(3), 289–324.

Holla, A., M. Bendini, L. Dinarte, and I. Trako. (2021). 'Is Investment in Preprimary Education Too Low? Lessons from (Quasi) Experimental Evidence Across Countries'. Policy Research Working Paper 9723. Washington, DC: World Bank. https://openknowledge.worldbank.org/bitstream/handle/10986/35894/Is-Investment-in-Preprimary-Education-Too-Low-Lessons-from-Quasi-Experimental-Evidence-across-Countries%20%282%29.pdf?sequence=8.

ILO. (1999). 'Decent Work: Report of the Director General'. In International Labour Conference (87th Session). Geneva: ILO.

ILO. (2015). 'Labour Market Institutions and Gender Equality'. In *Labour Markets, Institutions and Inequality: Building Just Societies in the 21st Century*, ed. J. Berg. Geneva: ILO.

ILO. (2016). *Non-Standard Employment Around the World: Understanding Challenges, Shaping Prospects*. Geneva: ILO.

ILO. (2018). *Care Work and Care Jobs for the Future of Decent Work*. Geneva: ILO.

ILO. (2021a). *ILO Monitor: COVID-19 and the World of Work*, 7th edn. https://www.ilo.org/global/topics/coronavirus/impacts-and-responses/WCMS_767028/lang--en/index.htm.

ILO. (2021b). 'Building Forward Fairer: Women's Rights to Work and at Work at the Core of the COVID-19 Recovery'. Policy Brief, July. Geneva: ILO.

Klasen, S. (2010). 'Measuring and Monitoring Inclusive Growth: Multiple Definitions, Open Questions, and Some Constructive Proposals'. Asian Development Bank Sustainable Development Working Paper Series No. 12. Manila: Asian Development Bank.

Lancet Commission on Pollution and Health. (2018). 'Pollution and Health', *The Lancet* 391(10119), 462–515.

Nixson, F. (2006). 'Rethinking the Political Economy of Development: Back to Basics and Beyond'. *Journal of International Development* 18(7), 967–81.

Ofosu-Baadu, B. S. (2009). 'Evaluation of Household Production using Satellite Accounts for Macroeconomic Policies in Ghana'. Accra: Ghana Statistical Service. https://unstats.un.org/unsd/gender/Finland_Oct2016/Documents/Ghana_ppt.pdf.

Onaren, O., C. Oyvat, and E. Fotopoulou. (2022). 'A Macroeconomic Analysis of the Effects of Gender Inequality, Wages and Public Social Infrastructure: The Case of the UK'. *Feminist Economics* 28(2), 152–88.

Oxfam. (2017). 'An Economy for the 11%'. Briefing Paper. Oxford: Oxfam.

Oxfam. (2021). *The Inequality Virus*. Oxford: Oxfam. https://oxfamilibrary.openrepository. com/bitstream/handle/10546/621141/bp-the-inequality-virus-250121-en.pdf.

UNDP. (2015). *Humanity Divided: Confronting Inequality in Developing Countries*. Geneva: UNDP.

UNDP and UN Women. (2021). 'COVID-19 Global Gender Response Tracker: Global Factsheet'. Version 2, 22 March. https://www.undp.org/publications/covid-11-global-gender-response-tracker-fact-sheets#modal-publication-download.

UNGA. (2015). 'Draft Outcome Document of the United Nations Summit for the Adoption of the Post-2015 Development Agenda'. A/69/L.85. New York: United Nations General Assembly.

UNECE. (2017). 'A Guide on Valuing Unpaid Household Service Work'. Geneva: United Nations Economic Commission for Europe. https://unece.org/fileadmin/DAM/stats/ publications/2018/ECECESSTAT20173.pdf.

UNIDO. (2018). *Industrial Development Report: Demand for Manufacturing: Driving Inclusive and Sustainable Industrial Development*. Vienna: United Nations Industrial Development Organisation.

United Nations. (2001). *System of National Accounts 2008*. New York: UN Statistics Division.

UN Women (United Nations Entity for Gender Equality and the Empowerment of Women). (2015). *Progress of the World's Women 2015–16*. New York: UN Women.

UN Women. (2016). *Towards Gender Equality in Vietnam: Making Inclusive Growth Work for Women*. Hanoi: UN Women.

UN Women. (2017). *The UN Women Gender and Economics Training Manual*. New York: UN Women.

UN Women. (2018). *Turning Promises into Action: Gender Equality in the 2020 Agenda for Sustainable Development*. New York: UN Women.

UN Women. (2019). *Progress of the World's Women 2017/18*. New York: UN Women.

UN Women. (2021). *Beyond Covid 19: A Feminist Plan for Sustainability and Social Justice*. New York: UN Women.

Vazquez Pimentel, D. A., I. Macías Aymar, and M. Lawson. (2018). *Reward Work, Not Wealth*. Oxford: Oxfam International. https://www.oxfam.org/en/research/reward-work-not-wealth.

10

ECONOMIC CRISES FROM THE 1980S
TO THE 2010S: A GENDER ANALYSIS

Introduction

In August 1982 Mexico announced a moratorium on repayment of its international debts, and what became known as the Latin American debt crisis began. Latin America suffered a 'lost decade' and did not recover until into the 1990s. Many Asian countries were not affected and grew rapidly, but in 1997 there was an 'Asian' financial crisis, particularly affecting South Korea, Indonesia, Thailand and the Philippines. Growth recovered quite quickly but inequality widened. Just over a decade later, in 2008, there was a global financial crisis, followed in 2010 by a European debt crisis. Three decades after the Mexican moratorium, Greece is the country that cannot repay its debt, with Ireland, Portugal, Spain and Italy also facing repayment difficulties.

This chapter looks at these crises through a gender lens, with particular focus on the financial liberalization that provoked these crises and the austerity policies that were prescribed as the remedy for them, drawing on both my earlier and more recent writings. I reflect on the evolution of my theoretical frames and the challenges of empirical substantiation of hypotheses that involve the unpaid as well as the paid economy.

In relation to the Latin American debt crisis, I was concerned to challenge the account given by neoclassical economic theory of the impact of austerity, which only took account of the market economy and paid work. I developed a theoretical frame that also took account of the impact on the non-market economy and unpaid work, and argued that the policymakers' assumption of a relatively smooth reallocation of resources and resumption of economic growth depended on a hidden implicit assumption that women's supply of labour was perfectly elastic. In relation to the Asian financial crisis, I extended my frame to include the development of the crisis through the liberalization of the financial system, and the creation and distribution of risks, highlighting the way in which women were implicitly called upon to provide the safety net of last resort. In relation to the European debt crisis, I developed a frame that could more fully take into account the gendered character of the spheres of finance, production and reproduction. Throughout the development of these frames, I was concerned to highlight the gender biases in policies that on the surface might appear to be gender neutral and to contextualize the accounts given by neoclassical economics.

I conclude by considering the prospects for creating a gender-equitable, crisis-free global economy, arguing that policy must go well beyond attempts to reduce gender gaps in the sphere of production, to encompass structural changes in production, changes in the operation of the financial sphere to end its domination, and to put finance at the service of production and reproduction, and invest in the sphere of reproduction, especially in care services.

The Latin American debt crisis, early 1980s

As well as Mexico, governments in many other Latin American countries found themselves, in the early 1980s, in difficulties with repaying their debts, as demand for their primary commodity exports fell (due to recession in developed countries) and interest rates soared (due to tight money policies in developed countries). Governments had become highly indebted to commercial banks, having been (mis) sold loans, as petro-dollars were recycled through private rather than public financial institutions. After the four-fold rise in the price of oil in the mid-1970s, oil exporting countries had plenty of dollars, which could have been channelled to other countries through an increase in their contributions to the International Monetary Fund (IMF) and World Bank, and lent at fixed interest with low or no policy conditions. But the dominant powers in the IMF and the World Bank, led by the US government, decided against this. Instead the petro-dollars were channelled through Western commercial banks, facilitated by two innovations in lending: variable interest rate loans and syndication of loans (Harris 1988). Variable interest rate loans meant that the interest rate the banks charged on the loans varied alongside the interest rate the banks had to pay to borrow from each other and from central banks. When monetary policy in the US, the UK and other developed economies tightened, interest rates on existing commercial loans to the governments of developing countries rose. The syndication of loans meant that the risk associated with a loan to a particular country was shared between a large number of banks. These techniques seemed to reduce the risks for each bank of any loan to a developing-country government. But in fact they increased systemic risk; they encouraged banks to lend without considering whether the governments to which they were lending would really be able to earn enough foreign exchange to enable repayment of the loans.

In the early 1980s these systemic risks became evident. US banks were highly exposed to the debt of Latin American governments and they needed to be bailed out, just as much as Latin American governments. The answer was to reschedule the debts, conditional on indebted governments carrying out IMF stabilization programmes and World Bank structural adjustment programmes. These programmes were designed to 'contain the crisis of the early 1980s, prevent debtors defaulting, reduce budgetary and fiscal deficits in developing countries, and keep the commercial banks and the IMF and World Bank solvent' (Elson 1994: 517).

Stabilization programmes gave governments access to loans from the IMF but only in return for cutting public expenditure and devaluing their currency. Structural adjustment programmes gave access to loans from the World Bank but only in return for complying with IMF conditions and liberalization of markets and privatization of public infrastructure and services. These loans meant that governments could continue to service the debts they owed to the Western commercial banks, and constituted an indirect bail-out for the highly exposed Western commercial banks. The loan conditions were based on the view that the cause of the crisis lay in over-extension of the public sector in developing countries. The answer was supposed to lie in reducing the size of the public sector and creating the conditions for the private sector to grow and to export.

Gender, stabilization and structural adjustment

I developed a feminist critique of the theory on which the stabilization and structural policies were based (Elson 1991), arguing that it was characterized by 'male bias', as it failed to consider the gender division of paid work, unpaid domestic work and intra-household divisions in consumption and expenditure. My argument was that the outcome in many countries would be enforced idleness for men and overwork for women, because of gender norms in paid and unpaid work.

With respect to paid work, gender stereotypes about possession of certain attributes (such as 'nimble fingers'[1] and 'muscular arms') create barriers to redeployment of labour across occupations and sectors. Gendered cultural norms about what is 'men's work' and 'women's work' mean that men's labour tends not to be reallocated to 'women's work' where there is a decrease in what is considered to be 'men's work' and an increase in what is considered to be 'women's work'. Men who lose their jobs in the construction industry, as public expenditure is cut, are unlikely to find new jobs in export-oriented garment and electronics

---

1. 'Nimble fingers' was introduced into the development lexicon by Elson and Pearson (1981).

factories. Instead, women are pushed by household poverty into taking any jobs available in these sectors, in which employers typically seek to recruit women.

Subsequent empirical studies using data from labour surveys did find that women's entry into the labour market was accelerated in the 1980s and early 1990s by stabilization and structural adjustment policies (Çağatay & Ozler 1995). But the evidence also suggests that these jobs did not have pay and conditions comparable to those that men had enjoyed (Elson 1996). This acceleration, at least in part, represents 'distress sales', as women were forced to try to make good shortfalls in household income following the loss of male employment. However, as well as entering into export-oriented manufacturing, women also moved in greater numbers into informal services, such as making food at home and selling it on roadside stalls.

I pointed out that the neoclassical economic theory (as epitomized for instance in Lal 1984) that underpins the austerity policies of the 1980s does not recognize that economies are based on unpaid work as well as paid work (Elson 1991). The theory implicitly treats labour as a non-produced means of production, rather than a means of production that is produced on a daily and intergenerational basis by the unpaid work of cooking, cleaning, providing care for children and sick and frail elderly people, and getting water and wood in locations where there is no piped water and electricity. This unpaid work, in practice, is largely 'women's work'. Stabilization and structural adjustment policies are likely to add to this work insofar as they entail cuts in public expenditure that lead to a deterioration of public services. For instance, cuts to the budget for maintenance of the water supply tend to lead to broken pumps and leaks not being repaired, and so women have to travel further to get water. Devaluation of the currency and removal of subsidies tend to lead to increases in prices of food, and women tend to spend more time shopping for bargains and to buy cheaper, less-processed food that takes longer to prepare. Cuts to the budget for hospitals lead to relatives being called upon to provide food and clean bed linen for patients and to provide non-medical care for patients while they are in hospital.

Ignoring these impacts on unpaid domestic work is tantamount to assuming that women's capacity to undertake extra work is infinitely elastic – able to stretch so as to make up for any shortfall in income and resources required for the production and maintenance of labour. However, women's capacity for work is not infinitely elastic and breaking point may be reached. There may simply not be enough female labour time available to maintain the quality and quantity of human resources at its existing level, leading to deterioration in health, nutrition and education.

It might be argued that this could be avoided by changes in patterns of household expenditure; for instance, food expenditure could be maintained without extra shopping and preparation becoming more labour intensive if households cut spending on alcohol, tobacco and leisure. However, I argued that household resource allocation is characterized by gender divisions (Elson 1991). Not all resources are pooled and shared; men in a wide variety of case studies had been found to retain some income to fund consumption of alcohol, tobacco and leisure and were resistant to changing this (see, for instance, Dwyer & Bruce 1988). These gender norms hinder reallocation of expenditure to maintain household nutrition without making extra demands for unpaid work.

It has been argued that lack of data and methodological problems hinder definitive conclusions about whether women did bear a greater share of the costs of stabilization and adjustment measures (Haddad *et al.* 1995). National sample survey data on unpaid work and on the distribution of resources within households were not available, and labour force surveys often left out large amounts of informal paid work. Nevertheless, a number of Latin American case studies provide empirical backing for my argument (e.g. Gonzalez de la Rocha 1988; Moser 1989; Rodriguez 1994; Tanski 1994). These studies suggest that low income women in many places tended to be particularly disadvantaged, primarily because women had to try to provide a safety net of last resort to cushion their families against the negative shocks stemming from the debt crisis and the austerity policies.

As well as harming many low income women, the policies did not succeed in meeting their own objectives (Elliott 2012b). In 1990, the output of Latin America was 8 per cent below the level of 1980. Debt burdens rose rather than fell. Mexico's debt to Gross Domestic Product (GDP) ratio doubled in the five years after 1982 because output collapsed. However, lessons were not learned about systemic risk. Instead financial liberalization accelerated, led by the governments of the US and UK. Furthermore, financial liberalization was increasingly made a condition of loans from the IMF and the World Bank.

Asian financial crisis, late 1990s

The Asian financial crisis of 1996–97 was directly related to financial liberalization. The immediate cause of this crisis was massive inflows of short-term capital into Indonesia, Korea, Malaysia, the Philippines and Thailand, followed by a sudden reversal (UNDP 1999). The systemic risks that underpinned these events were similar to those that underpinned the Latin American debt crisis. In considering the origins of the crisis (Elson 2002), I noted that international markets for money are fraught with risks for which no objective probability distribution exists. Information is necessarily imperfect and available information is unequally distributed. Periods of economic growth lead to exuberant risk-taking and the value of financial assets becomes inflated. But eventually the growing gap between financial values and real returns leads to a subjective re-evaluation of risks and holders of financial assets begin to sell them. Herd behaviour magnifies the propensity to sell and further stimulates the perception that risks have increased. The way is paved for crises in which the sudden drop in assets prices sparks panic selling; and the price of assets bought with loans drops below the value of loans outstanding, leading to the collapse of credit markets and impending bankruptcy of banks and other private sector financial intermediaries.

In contrast to the feminist analysis of the Latin American debt crisis, in the case of the Asian financial crisis, feminists did consider the gender dimensions of the processes leading to the crisis, as well as the response to the crisis (see, for instance, van Staveren 2000). In my analysis I emphasized the ways in which the financial system had developed so that risk was off-loaded from those who took the risks (mainly high-income men) to women, especially low-income women, who had to absorb the risks, because they could not liquidate their responsibility for their children (Elson 2002).

The IMF became, once again, a key player, a source of emergency finance and a gate-keeper to debt re-scheduling. The IMF response was the same as to the Latin American debt crisis of the early 1980s. IMF assistance was conditional on substantial cuts in public expenditure even though the underlying problem was not a budget deficit. In the view of Singh and Zammitt (2000: 1255), 'a relatively tractable liquidity problem was thus turned into a massive solvency crisis, with enormous losses in employment and output'.

I hypothesized (Elson 2002) that these policies were likely to have the same impact as those imposed on Latin America in the 1980s. There is some evidence to suggest that this was the case. For instance, in both Indonesia (Frankenberg *et al.* 1999) and the Philippines (Lim 2000), studies using labour force survey data showed that as men became unemployed, the amount of paid work done by women increased. However, it was still impossible to obtain up-to-date statistics on unpaid work. Although more time-use surveys were available than had been the case for Latin America in the 1980s, they were not conducted at regular, frequent intervals; and household surveys continued to ignore the distribution of resources within households, so the full range of impacts and responses could only be uncovered through new fieldwork, which perforce has smaller sample sizes than household and labour force surveys. A team at the Asian Development Bank (Knowles *et al.* 1999) conducted a fieldwork study of the impact on households in Indonesia, Lao PDR, the Philippines and Thailand. They found that women tried to safeguard their families by increasing their participation in informal paid work, including food vending, laundry and in some cases, commercial sexual services. Women increased their unpaid domestic work in subsistence agriculture, collecting forest products, and growing vegetables in a kitchen garden. Women in the Philippines substituted cheaper, less-processed food in meals, something which tends to mean more time has to be spent on cooking. In Thailand, their health was jeopardized by anaemia, as they reduced their own consumption to try to provide for husbands and children. In Indonesia poor families ate less or went down to two meals a day, as they also did in the Philippines. The study found that while middle and upper income groups could cope with the crisis by using strategies that avoided long-term damage, the same was not true of the poor.

The Asian financial crisis was not followed by a 'lost decade' for Asia, as growth soon recovered, however it was followed by rising inequality in South Korea, Indonesia, and Lao (Asian Development Bank 2012); and there was a growth of precarious employment, particularly for women (Lee 2010).

Biases in macroeconomic policy

It was evident that macroeconomic policy continued to be biased against women. I extended my analysis of these biases in work with Nilufur Çağatay. We argued that conventional policies have inherent in them three biases: 'deflationary bias'; 'male breadwinner bias'; and 'commodification or privatization bias' (Elson & Çağatay 2000). These biases interact in ways that put women at a particular disadvantage.

Deflationary bias refers to macroeconomic policies which keep paid employment and Gross National Product (GNP) growth below their potential. By the end of the twentieth century, full employment had ceased to be a goal of macroeconomic policy in many countries. Instead, the focus was solely on financial variables, such as inflation, the fiscal deficit and debt to GDP ratio. Rates of inflation had been brought down to much lower levels than in the 1980s, but in many regions, this was at a huge sacrifice in public investment, economic growth and decent jobs. Much of the research and policy development on gender equality in employment has been focused on measures to enable women to compete with men on an equal basis. These measures are important, but they are not sufficient in a context of deflationary bias. To the extent that they are successful, they will simply redistribute some jobs from men to women. This will reduce gender gaps, but not in a way that provides full employment and decent work for all. In order for gender equality to be realized in ways that 'equalize up', rather than 'equalize down', there needs to be an expansion of the total number of decent jobs, as well as an improvement of women's access to them.

Women are particularly likely to be disadvantaged by deflationary bias because it interacts with, and reinforces, other policy biases, such as male breadwinner bias – the assumption that men are more deserving of decent jobs because they are assumed to be the principal economic support of families – while women's incomes are wrongly perceived to be merely supplementary and not essential to family wellbeing (Elson & Çağatay 2000: 1354–6). It is difficult for women to undertake employment constructed around male breadwinner norms (fulltime participation in the labour force throughout their adult years, while someone else does most of the necessary unpaid care work at home). *Male breadwinner bias* relegates women to the status of secondary workers with fewer rights, even when they are playing a large role in maintaining family income. It excludes women from many state-provided social benefits, except as dependents of men. There is some evidence of male breadwinner bias in the response in South Korea to the Asian financial crisis in 1997 (Elson 2002). For instance, some South Korean women brought unfair dismissal cases against some corporations that had pressured married women into leaving their jobs, in some cases with threats against their husbands' jobs with the same company (Lee 2010).

Commodification or privatization bias stems from the belief that the private sector is always more effective than the public sector in delivering services, infrastructure and welfare benefits. Elson and Çağatay (2000) pointed to the replacement of welfare benefits and public services by market based, individualized entitlements for those who can afford them – private pensions, private health insurance, private hospitals, private schools, private retirement homes, private paid care for children and old people, privatized utilities charging market rates for energy and transport. This privatization tends to exclude those who cannot afford to pay from access to services and insurance which would cushion them against market risk. Rather than pooling and sharing risks and resources, with scope for the solidarity of cross-subsidy, there is separate insurance for specific contingencies. This bias has been intensified through the out-sourcing provision of services to private sector companies: the service is financed by the public budget but provided by for-profit companies.

These three biases reinforce one another: "If the advice given to the Central Bank and the Ministry of Finance gives priority to maintaining short-run 'credibility' with financial institutions ... deflationary bias and commodification bias will be reinforced ... there will inevitably be pressure on women to act as provisioners of last resort ... male breadwinner bias will also be reinforced (Elson & Çağatay 2000: 1357). This analysis of policy biases was extended by Young *et al.* (2011) to include *risk bias* and *creditor bias*.

Risk bias is present in policies that reduce the extent to which risk is pooled and measures to protect against it are shared, and instead individualize risk. As Schuberth and Young (2011) argue, existing economic institutions, including those within the state, embed gendered assumptions about risk. With few, if any, savings and limited ownership of real wealth, women are affected in a particularly negative way by the individualization of risk. They are often seen as more risky as borrowers than men, and are often integrated into formal credit markets which lend comparatively large sums on terms that are more disadvantageous than the terms open to men. Housing policy in several high-income countries in the last 20 years provides a good example of *risk bias*. The provision of state-supported low-cost social housing to people with low and/or uncertain incomes has been cut back and more and more emphasis placed on people borrowing to buy their own homes. Rules that required women to have a male guarantor for loans have been scrapped and more women have taken loans to buy houses. In the case of the US, Gill and Roberts (2011) point to evidence that women in general, and African American women in particular, pay higher rates of interest on mortgages than men. While there is a progressive aspect to increased numbers of women owning their own homes, it takes many years to pay off a mortgage, and the immediate effect is that women become integrated into financial markets primarily as debtors. Here, women come up against *creditor bias* in financial governance (Young 2010). The increasing power of financial capital on a global scale has meant that the relationship between creditors and debtors has become highly asymmetrical. When women are unable to service their mortgage debts, their homes are taken from them. When important lending institutions, such as big banks, get into difficulty, those institutions are bailed out. All these five biases have been intensified in much of Western Europe by the global financial crisis and the austerity programmes that have followed, as will be argued below.

Global economic crisis, 2008

Despite the Asian financial crisis, financial liberalization continued to intensify. Many new financial products developed by US financial companies were virtually unregulated, including the mortgage-backed securities and credit default swaps that triggered the financial meltdown in autumn 2008, when five of the largest US investment banks failed or nearly collapsed. This was a crisis directly in the heartland of financial capital and it had global reach, because it quickly spread to leading banks in Europe and international credit flows dried up. This had knock-on impacts in developing countries even though there was no crisis in their financial sectors. The main transmission channel was through reduced demand for their exports. The result was a recession in 2009 in most of the high-income western countries and a slowdown in the rest of the world. The form and severity of the financial crisis and its impact has been different in different parts of the world but no country has entirely escaped, demonstrating how quickly adverse economic events are transmitted from one country to another in the context of globalization.

Western banks had been allowed to borrow excessively against too little capital, and to undertake risky innovations without any institution having an overview of how much risk was building up in the financial system as a whole. Many new financial products were not traded in open markets but were traded 'over-the-counter' to specific clients without any transparency. Looked at as a whole, the changes in regulation had further increased systemic risk. When it became clear that the crisis threatened the ability of banks to discharge their obligations to their depositors, and was in danger of leading to a 'run on the banks', the US government stepped in to 'bail out' the large banks. Most of the banks were able to stay under the same leadership that had so mismanaged them. These actions prevented depositors from losing their money, but did not prevent the drying up of credit, with knock-on effects on the labour market and the housing market. Similar measures were introduced in some Western European countries.

Unlike the response to the Latin American debt crisis and the Asian financial crisis, the immediate response to the global financial crisis was not IMF-imposed austerity. The governments of the rich countries initially had much more policy space than governments in Latin America and Asia. Coordinated measures were undertaken by a newly formed G20 group of developed and developing countries[2] to try to offset the credit squeeze with fiscal stimulus and expansionary monetary policy. At the London G20 summit in April 2009, the member governments committed themselves to a US$5 trillion dollar fiscal expansion, an extra US$1.1 trillion of resources for the IMF and other global institutions, and to reform the banks (Elliott 2011). This intervention prevented the crisis being followed by a global depression. Although the economies of many of the developed countries went into recession, the recession was not as deep as it would otherwise have been; and while growth slowed down in the developing country members of the G20, they did not experience a recession. At this stage, it seemed as if 'deflationary bias' no longer prevailed. However, international cooperation to promote recovery was not sustained. In particular, in several Western European countries, the banking crisis turned into a government debt crisis, with some similarities to the Latin American debt crisis, and with austerity policies as the main response, especially in the Mediterranean countries. Deflationary bias was reinstated and reinforced.

Gender analysis of the global financial crisis: finance, production and reproduction

To analyse the generation, the impact and the immediate response to the crisis, in both developed and developing countries, I developed a framework focusing on the gendered global interaction of the spheres of finance, production and

---

2. The members of the G20 are USA, UK, Germany, France, Italy, EU, Japan, Australia, Canada, South Africa, Russia, Saudi Arabia, Turkey, China, S Korea, India, Indonesia, Argentina, Brazil and Mexico.

reproduction (Elson 2010).[3] This framework allows for a more systematic analysis of finance and its interaction with the other two spheres than I had provided for the Latin American debt crisis and the Asian financial crisis. I argued that the crisis was generated by an economic system in which finance had come to dominate over production and reproduction; and in which the safety nets of last resort are provided by unpaid work in the sphere of reproduction.

The sphere of finance includes profit-oriented retail and investment banks, insurance companies, hedge funds, etc. and their regulators, including Central Banks and Ministries of Finance. As well as these 'formal' institutions, there is also 'informal' moneylending by pawnshops, kerb-side dealers, landlords and merchants etc. As well as all these profit-oriented institutions, there are socially useful financial institutions, such as mutual or co-operative savings and loans funds, subsidized micro-finance and state banks.

In the sphere of production, goods and services are produced for sale, through activities such as farming, mining, construction, manufacturing, wholesaling, retailing and supply of leisure services, etc. This sphere includes both formal and informal paid work; and people work as employees, in self-employment and as contributing family labour in small farms and businesses.

The sphere of reproduction is a non-market sphere of social provisioning, supplying services *directly* concerned with the daily and intergenerational reproduction of people as human beings, especially through their care, socialization and education. It includes unpaid work in families and communities, organized unpaid volunteer work and paid (but non-profit) work in public services like health and education. It is in this sphere that the care essential for human well-being is created.

All three spheres are linked internationally through international financial markets, international direct investment, international development assistance, international trade, international migration, international information flows and international networks. The spheres are coordinated through these links. But the coordination is far from perfect and there are frequent ruptures and crises.

All three spheres of economic activity are gendered, both in the ways they are peopled and in the norms that structure their operation. There are gendered divisions of labour and decision making, so that men and women are not randomly distributed throughout these spheres. While men and women work in all three sectors, women's work time is disproportionately concentrated in the sphere of reproduction across all countries. In production, women and men tend to be concentrated in different occupations in different industries. Norms that the primary earners in a household should be men and the primary carers should

---

3. I built upon earlier work in which I had conceptualized economies as multi-sectoral, including unpaid as well as paid work (Elson 1998).

be women tend to be strong in most countries, even if in practice women's earnings are vital to keeping families out of poverty.

Thus the institutions of an economy are bearers of gender. This is often seen as the 'natural' outcome of innate differences between women and men, and the different choices they therefore make. But feminists challenge this, pointing to the ways in which choices are shaped – and differences created. However, gender norms are not set in stone. In a crisis, existing gender norms may be reinforced; or they may decompose, with individual men taking on roles normally associated with women, and vice versa; or they may be transformed through deliberate collective action, by civil society groups or by governments, to overcome gender stereotypes.

Gender in the sphere of finance: a key factor in the 2008 financial crisis?

The gendered characteristics of the financial sphere have been referred to by some commentators as a factor causing the 2008 financial crisis in the US, both in terms of the domination of men in decision making and the prevalence of macho norms of behaviour. For example, Nicolas Kristof, a prominent journalist for the *New York Times*, reported:

> At the recent World Economic Forum in Davos, Switzerland, some of the most interesting discussions revolved around whether we would be in the same mess today if Lehman Brothers had been Lehman Sisters. The consensus (and this is among the dead white men who parade annually at Davos) is that the optimal bank would have been Lehman Brothers and Sisters. Wall Street is one of the most male-dominated bastions in the business world … Aside from issues of fairness, there's evidence that the result is second-rate decision-making.   (Kristof 2009)

There is some merit in this idea, but getting more women into decision-making positions in large banks would not by itself prevent a recurrence of this kind of crisis (as pointed out by Bedford & Rai 2010). It would also be necessary to change the way that banks are regulated, and to change underlying structures of business and society, including the way that finance relates to production and reproduction.

Underlying the financial crisis in the west are global shifts in investment and production, especially to Asia, leading to intensified competition and downward pressure on wages in the west. In the US, for instance, productivity growth over the last 20 or so years has not been matched by growth in wages. In the US, UK, Ireland and other western countries, these factors have led to rising female labour market participation, propelled by rising demand for low-cost labour to meet global competition, and rising supply of female labour as average households need more than one income to be above the poverty line, and to meet the costs of housing. But most women did not get secure 'breadwinner' jobs, with high wages and social benefits. Indeed, fewer men got 'breadwinner' jobs and gender gaps in labour markets fell – but so too did enjoyment of economic and social rights for both women and men. The share of national income going to workers fell and inequality between households rose sharply (Seguino 2011).

In many Western countries, the sphere of reproduction became dependent on the sphere of finance, especially with respect to housing. Women got better access to credit – but often on adverse terms. This was especially the case in the US, where there was 'predatory inclusion' of women in the so-called subprime market for loans, especially mortgage loans related to housing (Balakrishnan *et al.* 2011). Poor quality mortgage loans were aggressively marketed to groups that had previously been excluded from large-scale borrowing. In the US, financial companies targeted new borrowers with interest rates that initially were very low, though after a couple of years the interest rate would rise considerably. Access was easier but terms were more onerous over the life of the mortgage. In 2005, a subprime loan on a median price American home implied US$85,000 more in total payments than a regular loan. Women borrowers in the US were more likely to receive subprime loans than men at every income level (Balakrishnan *et al.* 2011).

In 2007, rises in prices of fuel and food in the US made it harder to pay the mortgage, and the number of people defaulting on their loans began to rise. This rippled out from the housing sector because of the way that changes in financial regulation had facilitated financial innovation. Regular and subprime mortgages were packaged together to produce new assets, which were given the highest ratings, triple A ratings, by the three major ratings agencies in the US: Moody's, Standard and Poor's, and Fitch. These derivative assets were extensively traded and ended up in the hands of banks headquartered in a wide range of other countries (though not in countries like China and India which had more stringent banking regulations). By 2007, the stability of the international financial system depended on the ability of low and middle income holders of subprime mortgages in the US to service their debt. Defaults on these mortgages led to a collapse in the value of assets derived from them. Securitization and funding via global capital markets created channels of contagion in which a crisis originating in one product in one location spread to other products and throughout the world.

Having more women in charge of banks might have led to more careful appraisal of the risks of financial innovation, but it would not have addressed the underlying problem of what some have called the 'financialization of everyday activities'[4] in many developed countries. Credit was presented to people who had hitherto been outside financial markets, especially low and middle income women, as a rational economic way of acquiring a home that would be an asset for their old age. But they were left at the mercy of the financial sphere when market conditions changed. Creditor bias came into play and while banks have been bailed out, low income people unable to service their mortgage have been thrown out of their homes (Young 2010).[5] [6]

Nor would having more women in charge of the international banks by itself have addressed the changing global balance of economic power, brought about by the industrialization of Asia. As I wrote in the late 1980s, 'the more successful Third World countries are in challenging patterns of trade and foreign investment that kept them dependent in the past, the greater the threat of crisis in the international economy' (Elson 1988: 287). The origins of the global financial crisis do not lie solely in the sphere of finance.

The gendered impact of the crisis in the sphere of production

In developed economies considered as whole, the gender gap in the unemployment rate fell, as the unemployment of men rose more rapidly than the unemployment of women: the male unemployment rate rose by 1.1 percentage points from 2007 to 2008, while the female unemployment rate rose by 0.8 percentage points (ILO 2009: 20). In the European Union, the gender gap in unemployment almost vanished (Bettio & Verashchagina 2011). Women were relatively protected by the sectoral impact of the crisis, which fell much more heavily on male-intensive industry and construction than on female intensive services. It is noteworthy that the stimulus packages introduced by many developed countries focused heavily on these male intensive sectors, with a particular emphasis on cars and roads. There were reports in the US and UK press that the recession was really a 'mancession', and speculation about the rise of 'female breadwinners' (see, for instance, Qureshi 2009).

---

4. Financialization of everyday activities refers to how credit and debt mediate getting a living, including acquiring a home, and purchasing consumption goods.
5. Microfinance in developing countries, which has specifically targeted low income women, might be seen as another aspect of the 'financialization of everyday activities' but it is not discussed here as it is not bound up with the origins of the global financial crisis.
6. There has been a reaction against creditor bias in Spain, following two suicides of people due to be evicted from their homes for failing to make mortgage payments. On 12 November 2012, the Spanish banking association announced a two-year freeze on eviction orders following widespread protests (Roberts 2012).

The impact of the financial crisis on production and employment in developing countries came via falling demand for exports, which led to falling output, employment and earnings in the export sectors. This in turn led to falling demand for products intended for the domestic market; and a further loss of employment and earnings. The gendered impact was conditioned by whether the export sector depends heavily on female employment, as it would if garment production is significant, or whether mostly men are employed, as would be the case in mining. In the former case, the loss of jobs, earnings and rights affected women more than men; in the latter case, the loss of jobs, earnings and rights affected men more than women (ILO/ADB 2011; Elson 2010).

The impact of the financial crisis in the sphere of reproduction

Understanding the impact of the financial crisis in the sphere of reproduction continues to be hampered by the lack of regular time-use surveys and the continuing failure of household surveys to reveal the distribution of resources within households. In the US and UK, there were newspaper reports that some men who had lost their jobs were taking on more of the unpaid work of caring for children and elderly parents, especially if their wives had not lost their jobs (Rampell 2009; Wylie 2009). However, it initially seemed valid to assume that the welfare state would act as the main safety net in developed countries.

In developing countries, no such assumption could be made, and a number of rapid fieldwork-based assessments were made. For example, a study of informal workers in 10 cities found that many of them were increasing unpaid home-based production. The study concluded that the crisis had pushed the urban informal workers further into poverty, and was likely to have long-lasting harmful effects on them and their families (Horn 2011).

The European debt and austerity crisis, 2010–

In the period immediately following the financial crisis, the recession caused budget deficits to rise in many European Union (EU) countries,[7] as tax receipts fell and statutory welfare payments, such as unemployment benefits, rose.

---

7. The members of the EU are Austria, Belgium, Bulgaria, Cyprus, Czech Republic, Denmark, Estonia, Finland, France, Germany, Greece, Hungary, Ireland, Italy, Latvia, Lithuania, Luxembourg, Malta, Netherlands, Poland, Portugal, Romania, Slovakia, Slovenia, Spain and Sweden. The United Kingdom left the EU on 31 January 2020.

In addition, in some countries large payments were made to bail out the banks. The stimulus packages further increased the deficits, though they also halted further descent into recession. As a result, the debt to GDP ratios in many EU countries rose, in some cases substantially. Private sector financial institutions responded by charging a higher price to hold the bonds of several EU countries, and the ratings given to these bonds[8] were downgraded. However, the increased costs of government borrowing did not simply reflect the increased government debt to GDP ratios. Consider Germany and Spain. In 2000, the debt to GDP ratio of Germany was 61 per cent and in 2010 it was 77 per cent; the ratio of Spain was 71 per cent in 2000 and 72 per cent in 2010. In 2008, the cost of borrowing was much the same for both countries, at around 4 per cent. Yet while the cost of borrowing fell for Germany, to around 2 per cent in early 2011, for Spain it rose to around 6 per cent in early 2011.[9] It seems that the financial markets were also factoring in the ratio of private debt to GDP, in the expectation that where it was high, governments would have to spend more money in further bailouts for the banks. In Germany, private indebtedness had not increased in relation to GDP, standing at 165 per cent in 2000 and 164 per cent in 2010. But in Spain, private indebtedness had increased from 187 per cent in 2000 to 283 per cent in 2010.[10]

By May 2010, the financial crisis (a private sector financial crisis) had morphed into a Latin American style sovereign debt crisis in several EU countries, including Ireland, Greece and Portugal. In return for loans from the European Central Bank, the European Commission and the IMF, these countries have been pressured into adopting similar policies of structural adjustment and stabilization, as was the case in Latin America, Asia and Africa in the 1980s and 1990s. Doubts have also been cast over the solvency of Spain and Italy, as the rate of interest their governments had to pay to borrow rose, an example of how creditor bias has been at work. Even governments that were not under any immediate pressure from the financial markets switched from fiscal stimulus to fiscal contraction, with more emphasis on expenditure reduction than on revenue increase. Moreover, as well as deflationary bias, there has also been commodification (or privatization) bias, with pressure to privatize any remaining publicly-owned utilities and to out-source many government services to private sector companies.

Some economists (and governments) argued that the austerity policies would be an 'expansionary contraction', as they would restore confidence in

---

8. Government bonds are rated by three US-based privately-owned ratings agencies, Standard and Poor's, Moody's and the much smaller Fitch. The top rating is AAA. The higher the rating the cheaper it is for governments to borrow.

9. For data, see 'What really caused the Eurozone crisis?' www.bbc.co.uk/news/business (accessed 1 December 2012).

10. For data, see 'What really caused the Eurozone crisis?' www.bbc.co.uk/news/business (accessed 1 December 2012).

the financial markets, and stimulate private investment which would lead to a recovery. This has turned out to be completely wrong, and the austerity policies led to a second recession in 2012 in a large number of EU countries, including Austria, Netherlands and the UK, as well as Italy, Spain, Portugal and Greece. Even Germany, the strongest economy, achieved no more than a 0.2 per cent increase in output in the third quarter of 2012 (Elliott & Moulds 2012).

The UK has not experienced a debt crisis of the kind experienced by Mediterranean Europe,[11] but the coalition government[12] that came to power in May 2010 embraced the illusion of 'expansionary contraction' and introduced huge cuts to public expenditure. By the second quarter of 2012, the economy was in recession again, and output was 4.5 per cent below the level of 2008. UK economic performance has been similar to that of Spain and Portugal (Elliott 2012a).

As austerity measures stifled growth, the private sector bond rating agencies discovered a new cause for concern. They down-rated government bonds, on the grounds that falling GDP would lead to falling tax revenues, and governments would thus be unable to service their debts. The ratings agencies do not seem to recognize that they are endogenous to the system: if they down-rate government bonds, costs of borrowing rise for governments, austerity measures are introduced, GDP and tax revenues fall, and if ratings are again reduced, a vicious downward spiral is deepened.[13]

Gender in the sphere of finance: a role in the European debt and austerity crisis?

Most of the key decision makers in the governance of finance in the EU are men. Only 5 per cent of the 22 key decision makers in the European Central Bank are women – and the chair is male. Women are also very much a minority in other EU financial governance institutions (Schuberth & Young 2011: 140). This has persisted even after some reforms were introduced in 2009 (Young 2013: 288). At the IMF, women are also a small minority among the key decision makers, holding only 4.5 per cent of the seats on the Board of Directors (Schuberth & Young 2011: 141), although the managing director is now a woman, Christine Lagarde, the former finance minister of France. Most finance ministers in the EU are men: in 2011, of the 19 finance ministers in the biggest EU countries, only 3 were women (Atkins *et al.* 2011). While there have been moves in the EU to

---

11. The UK was a member of the EU but was not a member of the eurozone.
12. The coalition is led by the Conservative Party, with the Liberal Democratic Party as the junior partner.
13. For more discussion of this point, see Marston (2012).

increase the number of women on boards of public companies, this has not been extended to moves to increase the number of women in the key organizations that decide the evolution of the European sovereign debt crisis.

However, merely increasing the numbers of women would not make a difference in itself. What would make a difference is bringing in a different perspective, one that would consider the impact of decisions not only in the sphere of finance, but also in the spheres of production and reproduction. The only country that has come close to this is Iceland, a European country (but not a member of the EU) that was at the epicentre of the global financial crisis in 2008, but that has escaped the downward spiral into further recession and further austerity that is hitting many EU countries.

The financial crisis led to the fall of the government in Iceland and the election of a new government headed by a woman in early 2009. Women occupied almost 40 per cent of seats in parliament; and a woman was appointed chair of the parliamentary committee on the budget and subsequently became finance minister in 2011. The banks were not bailed out but allowed to fail and taken into public ownership and two women were put in charge of the clean-up, to signal that there would be a change in banking culture (O'Connor 2008). Most importantly, there was more than a change in personnel, with more women in key decision-making positions; there was also a change in policy (Topping 2012). The government introduced capital controls to prevent capital flight; refused to repay foreign creditors of the failed banks; and wrote off any homeowners' debts above 110 per cent of the value of the property. Expenditure cuts were introduced, but so was gender responsive budgeting. According to Topping (2012), education, health and social security were shielded. The financial services industry has shrunk to a fifth of its former size, and creative industries have been promoted. The value of the krona has been allowed to fall and tourism has expanded. The economy grew at 2.7 per cent in 2012; and unemployment has fallen to 4.5 per cent, halved from its peak in the post-crisis recession. Income distribution has become more equal. Even the budget deficit has fallen from 13.5 per cent of GDP in 2009 to 2.3 per cent in 2011 (see Topping 2012 for this data). The women who took charge of Iceland charted a very different course to other European governments severely affected by the crisis; and the people of Iceland seem to have benefited.

The gendered impact of the EU debt and austerity crisis on the sphere of production

As austerity policies began to take effect, women began to lose jobs at a faster rate than before and talk of a 'mancession' stopped. The EU-27 annual average unemployment rates for men were 9.1 per cent in 2009 and 9.7 per cent in

2010, while for women they were 9.0 per cent in 2009 and 9.7 per cent in 2010. However, by 2011, male unemployment had declined somewhat to 9.6 per cent, while female unemployment continued to rise, to 9.8 per cent.[14] This reflects the fact that in many EU countries, public sector employment is relatively female-intensive. Women form on average 69.2 per cent of public sector workers in the EU (EWL 2012: 4).

In the UK, women accounted for all of the increase in unemployment in the period 2010–12. Men's unemployment rate fell from 9.1 per cent in the first quarter of 2010 to 8.6 per cent in the second quarter of 2012, while women's unemployment rate rose from 6.7 per cent in the first quarter of 2010 to 7.5 per cent in the second quarter of 2012 (TUC 2012). The unemployment rates of both men and women would have been higher had it not been for an increase in self-employment and part-time work. Self-employment has risen in the UK since the onset of the financial crisis in 2008, with women accounting for 54 per cent of the increase. Much of this rise represents an informalization of the labour market, with those in self-employment losing rights to benefits, pensions and paid holidays. The median income of self-employed people is below that for employed people. In 2010 to 2011, self-employed working age adults were more likely to be poor than those who were employees (TUC 2012). Women in the UK have always been more likely to work part-time than men, in part related to the lack of affordable child care facilities. What is notable is the increase in the numbers of both men and women who are in part-time employment but who would prefer full-time employment. The TUC report notes that overall there has been a growth of under-employment in the UK, defined as the number of people who want longer hours of paid work than in their current job: in 2012 there were an estimated 1.7 million underemployed women workers, 52 per cent of all underemployed workers.

The EU had a target of increasing the employment rate of women to 60 per cent by 2010 and 75 per cent by 2020. The first target had been met by 2005, but it is most unlikely that the latter target will be met, as women's employment rate has fallen in many EU countries, including Greece, Spain, Ireland and the UK (EWL 2012: 5). The quality of women's employment has also been falling, with more women employed in private sector part-time, precarious jobs that lack social rights.

There are debates about whether austerity is leading to a reversal of progress towards a dual earner/dual carer regime of gender relations, by reinstatement of gender relations based on male breadwinner/female carer model (see for example EWL 2012: 6, 9). Certainly the availability of 'good jobs' for women, of the

---

14. Data from Eurostat, Statistics Explained, http://epp.eurostat.ec.europa.eu/statistics_ explained (accessed 1 December 2012).

kind that would enable women to be co-earners, is falling in many countries; and the public funding of child care, which enabled the growth of dual earner/dual carer families is also falling, as discussed in the next section.

The gendered impact of the EU debt crisis on the sphere of reproduction

It is clear that in many EU countries (though not in Germany, Austria and the Nordic countries) austerity policies are undermining the public services and welfare benefits that have supported the sphere of reproduction in the last 50 years. In 2002, EU member states agreed on increasing the provision of afford-able good quality child care, and this commitment was renewed in 2011. But in fact, austerity policies are reducing access to child care services. Public kinder-gartens have been closed in Greece and Portugal; after-school care at primary schools has been cut in Italy; in the UK, subsidies to help low and middle income families cover the costs of child care have been cut from 80 per cent to 70 per cent (EWL 2012: 8). By 2010, the gap between the employment rates of women with and without small children was already rising, and was expected to rise further (EWL 2012: 9).

There have also been cuts to care services for the elderly and disabled in many EU countries. For instance, in Ireland there have been cuts to publicly-provided home care and to beds in nursing homes (EWL 2012: 8). In the UK, the num-ber of elderly people who get free home care has fallen by 11 per cent between 2009 and 2011 (Ramesh 2012). Cutbacks have reduced access to health care in some countries. For instance, in Greece, many public hospitals have been closed or merged and those that remain open lack staff and supplies. Lack of nurs-ing staff in hospitals has led to female relatives being called upon to help nurse patients (Karamessini 2011). All these cuts to care services are likely to increase the amount of unpaid care work that women have to do, although so far there is not much direct evidence for this. Many EU countries do have time-use data, but are not sufficiently up to date to show this impact.

Services related to violence against women have also been cut (EWL 2012: 10). For instance, in Greece, local government funding for women's centres has been ended. In Spain there are plans in one region to close 85 support centres and 13 women's shelters. In the UK, local government funding for such services has been cut by 31 per cent, from 2010–11 to 2011–12.

The cumulative impact of these cuts is likely to be hardest for the poorest and most vulnerable women. In the UK, the Women's Budget Group estimates that the hardest hit will be lone parents (95 per cent of whom are women) who will lose services worth about 18.5 per cent of their income, and single women pensioners, who will lose services worth about 12 per cent of their income (UK Women's Budget Group 2010).

As well as services, there have been extensive cuts to welfare benefits. For instance, in Ireland, the following welfare benefits have been cut: child benefit, carer's allowance, one parent family payment disability payment, rent subsidy and jobseekers allowance (Barry & Conroy 2011). In the UK, the value of child benefit has been frozen until April 2014, reducing the real value of the benefit by over 10 per cent by that date (EWL 2012: 10). In Spain, the newborn child benefit has been eliminated and the plan to extend paternity leave has been delayed (Gonzalez Gago 2011). Pension entitlements have been cut or frozen in some countries. In Spain, the value of the public pension has been frozen (Gonzalez Gago 2011). Greece has introduced a special tax on pensions, ranging from 3 per cent to 9 per cent (EWL 2012: 11).

Reports are starting to emerge of low-income women having problems feeding their children as incomes fall and prices rise. In Greece, women are cooking more at home, and turning again to the thrifty but labour-intensive recipes that their grandmothers and great grandmothers used in the Second World War (Gatopoulus 2011). Maria, a well-educated but unemployed woman in an agricultural town in northern Greece, explained that supermarket trips happen perhaps once a month, and only to discount stores. Pre-prepared food is out. She makes cheap stews. Her family is dependent on gifts of fruit, vegetables and eggs from her father-in-law, a farmer. Many are less fortunate, and charity food banks in Athens are struggling to keep pace with demand (Chrisafis 2011). In the North East of England, five food banks were operating by April 2012, where previously there were none, and more were on the way to cope with the growing demand from low income families (NEWomen's Network and Women's Resource Centre 2012: 9). The stress of trying to make ends meet is leading to more women having mental health problems, with a big increase in numbers of women seeking help from women's health centres in the North East of England, many of whom attributed their problems to financial pressures and worries about changes in welfare benefits (NEWomen's Network and Women's Resource Centre 2012: 14).

Conclusions: towards crisis-free gender equitable economies

The crises discussed above stem from the dominance of finance over production and reproduction. It is clear that we cannot just focus on gender equality in the sphere of production. Securing a sustainable crisis-free gender-equitable global economy requires a fundamental reorganization of the relations between the three spheres, so that finance and production serve the needs of reproduction, the sphere in which the care essential to human wellbeing is provided. The five policy biases identified above must be removed and economic reasoning must take account of unpaid work and gender norms. Feminists must engage with financial governance, monetary and fiscal policy, and policies for structural change in production and consumption.[15]

Progressive economists have set out proposals for improving the regulation of the financial sphere, including the splitting of High Street banking that serves households and small businesses from more risky activities that serve larger businesses, including financial businesses (Jolly *et al.* 2012: 48–50). Such measures would help to reduce risk bias and creditor bias. But there is also a need to challenge and change the ownership of banks, to create banks that operate to the mutual benefit of depositors and borrowers, and not to make profits for shareholders and executives. Such banks did flourish in some countries before financial liberalization, and in some they continue to exist. More 'mutual' banks should be encouraged, and, of course, they must be operated so as to give women equal access to savings and loans. For long run investment in public infrastructure and to develop new environmentally sustainable production, public investment banks are needed.

In addition, Central Banks should change the way in which they operate to become promoters of employment creation, not simply guardians of very low rates of inflation. To do this Central Banks need to explicitly set goals for employment creation as well as inflation control, and continue to sustain the expansionary monetary policies that many of them adopted immediately after the financial crisis, until their economies are on a path of sustained job-creation (Seguino 2011). This will help to end deflationary bias.

To make socially useful banking feasible, and to create stable conditions for the creation of decent work, it is important to reduce the volatility of financial flows in and out of national economies. Governments can introduce capital controls to stop inflows and outflows of short-term speculative funds. Malaysia did this in the Asian financial crisis of 1997, and as a result was one of the first countries to recover from that crisis (Seguino 2011). Brazil embarked on a similar exercise following the 2007–08 crisis. It is vital that the IMF changes its policy and supports such moves, rather than encouraging countries to keep larger reserves of foreign currency to tide them over during periods of volatility. In addition, the global governance of finance needs reform, as argued by the Stiglitz Commission (UN 2009), including the governance of the IMF and World Bank,

---

15. In doing so feminists may find it fruitful to collaborate with other progressive economists, as Ruth Pearson and I have done in putting forward alternatives for Western Europe. See Jolly *et al.* (2012).

the establishment of methods for orderly default and restructuring of government debt (Jolly *et al.* 2012: 52–60).

To complement changes in financial regulation and ownership in monetary policy, and in global financial governance, we must have fair taxation and equitable public expenditure. Women scholars, activists and elected representatives have done much to try to transform government budgets since the 1995 Beijing Platform for Action called for gender-responsive budgeting. There have been some successes in getting women more voice, and in re-orienting public finance to address women's poverty and gender equality, especially at the local level. However, with a few exceptions, such as the work of the UK Women's Budget Group,[16] gender-responsive budgeting has not as yet fully engaged with the macroeconomics of budgets at national level; with the issues of how tax systems can be equitably reformed to generate more revenue; how high public expenditure should be and how far public services should be out-sourced and privatized; and when fiscal policy should be expansionary and when contractionary.

Taxes need to be fair in terms of gender and class; and also in terms of the relative contributions of households and individuals on the one hand and businesses and banks on the other. All over the world there has been a shift in the balance of contributions, with businesses and banks, especially large ones, paying a smaller and smaller share, and taking advantage of tax havens. Many governments are not raising enough tax revenue, and there is an urgent need to stop tax avoidance and evasion. Rather than campaigning for tax breaks for women's businesses, feminists need to raise their voices in the emerging campaigns for tax justice to raise more revenue at national and international levels, including through currency transactions tax (Seguino 2011: 41).

Many critics of austerity policies are calling for more expansionary fiscal policies, with a focus on restoring and increasing economic growth. But the growth we had in the last 30 years was grossly inequitable, eroded social solidarity and led to environmental degradation. So economic growth in itself is not the answer. It matters what kinds of output grow. In the context of alternative plans for recovery in Western Europe, Ruth Pearson and I have argued for investment in social infrastructure, especially care services (Jolly *et al.* 2012: 29–35). More broadly, we need to rethink what goods and services we want to produce and consume, and what criteria we are going to use to judge economic success. Measures to end crises will not be sustainable if they simply seek to restore growth and greed.

---

16. The UK Women's Budget Group is a network of academic researchers, policy officers in trade unions and women's organizations, and activists. It critically analyses the budgets of the UK government, including both taxation and expenditure. It calls for an alternative macroeconomic policy that would be more gender equitable. I served as Chair of WBG 2010–16. See www.wbg.org.uk.

References

Asian Development Bank (2012). *Asian Development Outlook 2012*. Manila: Asian Development Bank.

Atkins, R., Whiffin, E., Cadman, C., Nevitt, B. (2011). '2011 FT Ranking of European Finance Ministers', *Financial Times*, 22 November.

Balakrishnan, R., Elson, D. and Heintz, J. (2011). 'Financial Regulation, Capabilities and Human Rights in the US Financial Crisis: The Case of Housing', *Journal of Human Development and Capabilities* 12(1), 153–68.

Barry, U. and Conroy, P (2011). 'Ireland. The Untold Story of the Economic Crisis – Gender Equality and New Inequalities', presentation to Conference on Women, Gender Equality and Economic Crisis, Panteion University, Athens, December.

Bedford, K. and Rai, S. M. (2010). 'Feminists Theorize the International Political Economy', *Signs: Journal of Women in Culture and Society* 36(1), 1–18.

Bettio, F. and Verashchagina, A. (2011). 'Crisis and Recovery in Europe: Labour Market Impact on Men and Women', presentation to Conference on Women, Gender Equality and Economic Crisis, Panteion University, Athens, December.

Çağatay, N. and Ozler, S. (1995). 'Feminization of the Labor Force: The Effects of Long-term Development and Structural Adjustment', *World Development* 23(11), 1883–94.

Chrisafis, A. (2011). 'Struggling couples fall back on family ties', *The Guardian*, 3 August.

Dwyer, D. and Bruce, D. (eds), (1988). *A Home Divided: Women and Income in the Third World*. Stanford, CA: Stanford University Press.

Elliott, L. (2011). 'Global financial crisis: five key stages 2007–2011', *The Guardian*, 7 August.

Elliott, L. (2012a). 'Commentary. Disappointing – or downright dire?', *The Guardian*, 26 July.

Elliott, L. (2012b). 'Parallels with Latin crisis painfully clear', *The Guardian*, 28 August.

Elliott, L. and Moulds, J. (2012) 'Eurozone double dip brings ECB warning', *The Guardian*, 16 November.

Elson, D. (1988). 'Dominance and Dependency in the World Economy', in B. Crow and M. Thorpe (eds), *Survival and Change in the Third World*. Cambridge: Polity Press.

Elson, D. (1991). *Male Bias in the Development Process*. Manchester: Manchester University Press.

Elson, D. (1994). 'People, Development and the International Financial Institutions', *Review of African Political Economy* 62, 511–24.

Elson, D. (1996). 'Appraising Recent Developments in the World Market for Nimble Fingers: Accumulation, Regulation, Organisation', in A. Chhachhi, A. and R. Pittin (eds), *Confronting State, Capital, and Patriarchy: Women Organising in the Process of Industrialisation*. London: Macmillan.

Elson, D. (1998). 'The Economic, the Political and the Domestic: Businesses, States and Households in the Organisation of Production', *New Political Economy* 3(2), 189–208.

Elson, D. (2002). 'The International Financial Architecture – A View from the Kitchen', *Femina Politica – Zeitschrift fur feministische Politk-Wissenschaft* 11(1). Reprinted in N. Visanathan, L. Duggan, N. Wiegersma and L. Nisonoff (eds) (2011), *The Women, Gender and Development Reader*. London: Zed Books.

Elson, D. (2010). 'Gender and the Global Economic Crisis in Developing Countries: A Framework for Analysis', *Gender and Development* 18(2), 201–12.

Elson, D. and Çağatay, N. (2000). 'The Social Content of Macroeconomic Policies', *World Development* 28(7), 1347–64.

Elson, D. and Pearson, R. (1981). 'Nimble Fingers Make Cheap Workers: An Analysis of Women's Employment in Third World Export Manufacturing', *Feminist Review*, Spring, 87–107.

European Women's Lobby (EWL) (2012). 'The Price of Austerity – The Impact on Women's Rights and Gender Equality in Europe'. www.womenlobby.org (accessed 1 December 2012).

Frankenberg, E., Thomas, D. and Beegle, K. (1999). 'The Real Costs of Indonesia's Economic Crisis: Preliminary Findings from the Indonesia Family Life Surveys', Labor and Population Program Working Paper Series 99-04, RAND.

Gatopoulus, D. (2011). 'Cookbook offers Greeks a few crumbs of comfort', *The Guardian*, 7 December.

Gill, S. and Roberts, A. (2011). 'Macroeconomic Governance, Gendered Inequality and Global Crises', in B. Young, I. Bakker and D. Elson (eds), *Financial Governance from a Feminist Perspective*. London: Routledge.

Gonzalez de la Rocha, M. (1988). 'Economic Crises, Domestic Reorganization and Women's Work in Guadalajara, Mexico', *Bulletin of Latin American Research* 7(2), 207–23.

Gonzalez Gago, E. (2011). 'Women, Gender Equality and the Economic Crisis in Spain', presentation to Conference on Women, Gender Equality and Economic Crisis, Panteion University, Athens, December.

Haddad, L., Brown, L., Richter, A. and Smith, L. (1995). 'The Gender Dimensions of Economic Adjustment Policies: Potential Interactions and Evidence to Date', *World Development* 23(6), 881–96.

Harris, L. (1988). 'The IMF and Mechanisms of Integration'. in B. Crow and M. Thorpe (eds), *Survival and Change in the Third World*. Cambridge: Polity Press.

Horn, Z. (2011). 'The Effects of the Global Economic Crisis on Women in the Informal Economy: Research Findings from WIEGO and Inclusive Cities Partners', in R. Pearson and C. Sweetman (eds), *Gender and the Economic Crisis*. Rugby: Practical Action Publishing/ Oxford: Oxfam.

ILO and Asian Development Bank (2011). *Women and the Labour Market in Asia: Rebalancing for Gender Equality.* Bangkok: ILO.

International Labour Office (ILO) (2009). *Global Employment Trends for Women.* Geneva: ILO.

Jolly, R., Andrea, G., Elson, D., Fortin, C., Griffith-Jones, S., Helleiner, G., van der Hoeven, R., Kaplinsky, R., Morgan, R., Ortiz, I., Pearson, R. and Stewart, F. (2012). *Be Outraged: There are Alternatives.* http://policy-practice.oxfam.org.uk/publications/be-outraged-there-are-alternatives-224184 (accessed 7 March 2013).

Karamessini, M. (2011). 'Structural Crisis and Adjustment in Greece: Labour Market Effects by Gender and Changes in the Gendered Division of Paid Work', presentation to Conference on Women, Gender Equality and Economic Crisis, Panteion University, Athens, December.

Knowles, J., Pernia, E. and Racelis, M. (1999). 'Social Consequences of the Financial Crisis in Asia', ADB Staff Paper No. 60. Manila: Asian Development Bank.

Kristof, N. (2009). 'Mistresses of the Universe', *New York Times*, 8 February.

Lal, D. (1984). 'The Real Effects of Stabilization and Structural Adjustment Policies', World Bank Staff Working Papers No. 636. Washington, DC: World Bank.

Lee, J-Y (2010). 'Restructuring Women's Employment in South Korea, 1997–2005: The Role of the State and NGOs', unpublished PhD thesis, Department of Sociology, University of Essex.

Lim, J. (2000). 'The Effects of the East Asian Crisis on the Employment of Men and Women: The Philippine Case', *World Development* 28(7), 1285–306.

Marston, R. (2012). 'What is a Ratings Agency?', www.bbc.co.uk/news/10108284 (accessed 10 January 2012).

Moser, C. (1989). 'The Impact of Recession and Adjustment at the Micro Level: Low Income Women and their Households in Guayquil, Ecuador', in UNICEF, *The Invisible Adjustment: Poor Women and the Economic Crisis.* New York: UNICEF.

NEWomen's Network and Women's Resource Centre (2012). 'The Impact of Austerity Measures upon women in the North East of England', NEWomen's Network, Newcastle upon Tyne and Women's Resource Centre, London.

O'Connor, S. (2008). 'Iceland calls in women bankers to clean up "young men's mess"'. *Financial Times*, 14 October.

Qureshi, H. (2009). 'New female breadwinners', *The Guardian*, 24 October.

Ramesh, R. (2012). 'Number of elderly people who get free home care falls by 11%', *The Guardian*, 16 May.

Rampell, C. (2009). 'As layoffs surge, women may pass men in job force', *The New York Times*, 6 February.

Roberts, M. (2012). 'Suicides force Spanish banks to restrict evictions', *The Guardian*, 13 November.

Rodriguez, L. (1994). 'Housing and Household Survival Strategies in Urban Areas: A Case study of the Solanda Settlement: Quito, Ecuador'. In F. Meer (ed), *Poverty in the 1990s: Response of Urban Women*. Paris: UNESCO.

Schuberth, H. and Young, B. (2011). 'The Role of Gender in the Governance of the Financial Sector'. in B. Young, I. Bakker and D. Elson (eds), *Financial Governance from a Feminist Perspective*. London: Routledge.

Seguino, S. (2011). ' "Rebooting" is Not an Option: Toward Equitable Social and Economic Development', in D. Jain and D. Elson (eds), *Harvesting Feminist Knowledge for Public Policy*. New Delhi: SAGE.

Singh, A. and Zammit, A. (2000). 'International Capital Flows: Identifying the Gender Dimension', *World Development* 26(7), 1249–68.

Tanski, J. (1994). 'The Impact of Crisis, Stabilization and Structural Adjustment on Women in Lima, Peru', *World Development* 22(11), 1627–42.

Topping, A. (2012). 'Iceland starts to recover its voice after financial crisis', *The Guardian*, 23 November.

TUC (Trades Union Congress) (2012). *Economic Report No. 7*, September. Congress House, London.

UK Women's Budget Group (2010). 'The Impact on Women of the Coalition Spending Review 2010'. www.wbg.org.uk/RRB_Reports_4_1653541019.pdf (accessed 9 January 2012).

UN (2009). *Report of the Commission of Experts of the President of the United Nations General Assembly on Reforms of the International Monetary and Financial System*. New York: United Nations.

UNDP (1999). *Human Development Report*. New York: Oxford University Press.

Van Staveren, I. (2000). 'Global Finance and Gender', Paper presented at IAFFE Conference, Istanbul, August.

Wylie, I. (2009). 'Redundancy: How to restore balance', *The Guardian*, 26 September.

Young, B. (2010). 'The Gendered Dimension of Money, Finance and the Subprime Crisis', in C. Bauhardt and G. Caglar (eds), *Gender and Economics. Feministische Kritik der Politischen Okonomie*. Wiesbaden: VSVerlag fur Sozialwissenschaft.

Young, B. (2013). 'Structural Power and the Gender Biases of Technocratic Network Governance of Finance', in G. Calgar, E. Prugl and S. Zwingel (eds), *Feminist Strategies in International Governance*. London: Taylor & Francis.

Young, B., Bakker, I. and Elson, D. (2011). 'Introduction', in B. Young, I. Bakker and D. Elson (eds), *Financial Governance from a Feminist Perspective*. London: Routledge.

ACKNOWLEDGEMENTS

This volume is a compilation of academic papers I have authored over the past 45 years. Each chapter represents work previously published in peer-reviewed journals and edited volumes. I am deeply grateful to the respective publishers and editorial boards for granting permission to republish these works in this collected edition. Below is a list of the original publications where these articles first appeared:

Chapter 2   Diane Elson, "Theories of development", in *Elgar Companion to Feminist Economics*, edited by J. Peterson and M. Lewis (Cheltenham: Edward Elgar, 2000). Reproduced with permission from Edward Elgar through PLSclear.

Chapter 3   Diane Elson, "Male bias in the development process: an overview", in *Male Bias in the Development Process*, edited by Diane Elson (Manchester: Mancheser University Press, 1991). Reproduced with permission from Manchester University Press.

Chapter 4   Diane Elson, "Male Bias in macroeconomics: the case of structural adjustment", in *Male Bias in the Development Process*, edited by Diane Elson (Manchester: Manchester University Press, 1991). Reproduced with permission from Manchester University Press.

Chapter 5   Diane Elson, "Micro, meso, macro: gender and economic analysis in the context of policy reform!", in *The Strategic Silence: Gender and Economic Policy*, edited by I. Bakker (London: Zed Books, 1994). Reproduced with permission from Bloomsbury.

Chapter 6   Diane Elson, "Talking to the big boys: gender and economic growth models", in *Feminist Visions of Development*, edited by R. Pearson and C. Jackson (London: Routledge, 1998). Reproduced with permission from Routledge.

Chapter 7   Diane Elson, "The international financial architecture – a view from the kitchen", *Femina Politica: Zeitschrift für feministische Politikwissenschaft* (2002). Reproduced with permission from Verlag Barbara Budrich.

Chapter 8   Diane Elson, "Gender equality, public finance and globalization", in *Human Development in the Era of Globalization*, edited by J. Boyce, S. Cullenberg, P. Pattanaik and R. Pollin (Cheltenham: Edward Elgar, 2006). Reproduced with permission from Edward Elgar through PLSclear.

Chapter 9   Diane Elson, "Gender equality and inclusive growth", in *The Political Economy of Global Manufacturing, Business and Finance*, edited by M. Tribe and G. Kararach (London: Palgrave Macmillan, 2023). Reproduced with permission of Palgrave Macmillan through PLSclear.

Chapter 10   Diane Elson, "Economic crises from the 1980s to the 2010s: a gender analysis" in *New Frontiers in Feminist Political Economy*, edited by G. Waylen and S. Rai (Abingdon: Routledge, 2013). Reproduced with permission from Taylor & Francis through PLSclear.

Permission for republication was granted by the respective copyright holders. Where necessary, the texts have been slightly revised for consistency of style, but no substantial modifications have been made to the original content.

INDEX

Asian financial crisis 14, 105, 107, 109–10, 153, 157–63, 174

Beijing Platform for Action 14, 119, 175
bias 5–6, 14, 160
   commodification 5–6, 14, 160
   creditor 6, 160–1, 166, 168, 174
   deflationary 5, 14, 112, 114, 120, 122, 140, 159–60, 162, 168, 174
   in macroeconomic policy 4–5, 112, 114, 159
   male breadwinner 5, 14, 112–13, 120, 159–60
   risk 6, 160–1, 174
biases in macroeconomic policy 4–5, 112, 114, 159
   commodification bias 5–6, 14, 160
   deflationary bias 5, 14, 112, 114, 120, 122, 140, 159–60, 162, 168, 174
   male breadwinner bias 5, 14, 112–13, 120, 159–60
Boserup, Ester 3, 25–6, 29–30

Canadian Alternative Federal Budget 115
civil society organization (CSO) 123–5
commodification bias 5–6, 14, 160
commodification or privatization bias 14, 112, 159–60, 168
Covid-19 Global Gender Response Tracker 147
Covid-19 pandemic 138–9, 145–9
creditor bias 6, 160–1, 166, 168, 174
critical economists 75, 79–80
critical perspectives 79

Darity, William 33
Das Kapital (Marx) 25
DAWN (Development Alternatives with Women for a New Era) 34–5
De Beauvoir, Simone 1–2

dealing room 14, 105, 107, 115
decontrol of the dealing room 105, 107
deflationary bias 5, 14, 112, 114, 120, 122, 140, 159–60, 162, 168, 174
despotic family 65
development economics 25, 90, 137

economic analysis 22–3, 52, 62–3, 75, 78–81, 94, 127
economic crisis 17, 34, 58, 79, 161
economic crisis gender equality 16
economic growth 3, 8, 12, 17, 27, 29, 31, 89, 137, 139–43, 153, 157, 159, 175
economic growth models 1, 88
economic policy reform 75, 77–85
economic policy reform: micro, macro, and meso 75, 79

female-headed households 41, 44, 66, 94
feminist critical economics 80–1
feminist economics 6, 8, 16, 19, 25, 33, 35
feminist economists 3, 7, 12–14, 17–20, 29, 34
feminist macroeconomics 18–20
financial architecture 114, 107
financial inclusion 142–3
financial liberalization 15–16, 110–11, 153, 157, 161, 174
financial policy 110, 114–15
fiscal democracy 124, 130, 133
Frank, Andre Gunder 28

GBIs *see* gender budget initiatives
GDP growth 142, 144
GDP ratio 157, 159, 168
gender analysis 78, 80, 82, 101, 123–5, 132, 153, 162
gender bias 4, 53, 154
gender budget initiatives (GBIs) 115, 119–21, 124–6, 128–9, 131–3